Shakespeare and the Imprints of Performance

HoTT
HISTORY OF
TEXT TECHNOLOGIES

History of Text Technologies, developed in conjunction with an interdisciplinary research program at Florida State University, is dedicated to new scholarship and theory in the history of books and, more generally, the transformation of sign systems into engineered objects. This exciting new series moves from the analysis of texts as material objects to the analysis of texts as material agents. It is committed to the recognition that texts cannot be separated from the various and changing technologies through which they are created. Included are analytic bibliography, paleography and epigraphy, history of authorship, history of reading, study of manuscript and print culture, and history of media. Rather than being solely a historical overview, this series seeks out scholarship that provides a frame for understanding the consequences of both globalism and technology in the circulation of texts, ideas, and human culture. For more on the series, see the History of Text Technologies website at http://hott.fsu.edu.

Series Editors:

Gary Taylor is George Matthew Edgar Professor of English and the Founding Director of History of Text Technologies program at Florida State University.

Francois Dupuigrenet Desroussilles is Professor of Religion at Florida State University.

Elizabeth Spiller is Professor of English, and a member of the interdisciplinary History and Philosophy of Science program, at Florida State University.

Mapping Ethnography in Early Modern Germany: New Worlds in Print Culture
Stephanie Leitch

Literary Folios and Ideas of the Book in Early Modern England
Francis X. Connor

Shakespeare and the Imprints of Performance
J. Gavin Paul

Shakespeare and the Imprints of Performance

J. Gavin Paul

palgrave
macmillan

A portion of chapter 1 appeared as "Imprinting Performance: Editorial Mediations of Shakespeare's Drama," *Shakespeare: The Journal of the British Shakespeare Association* 4.1 (2008): 24–44 [tandfonline.com]. A portion of chapter 2 appeared as "English Renaissance Drama: The Imprints of Performance," *Literature Compass* 5.3 (2008): 529–540, and was subsequently reprinted in *The Bulletin of the Society for Renaissance Studies* 25.2 (2008): 5–18. A portion of chapter 3, entitled "Performance as 'punctuation': Editing Shakespeare in the Eighteenth Century," appeared in *The Review of English Studies* (June 2010): 390–413. They are reprinted here by kind permission.

First published in 2014 by
PALGRAVE MACMILLAN®
in the United States—a division of St. Martin's Press LLC,
175 Fifth Avenue, New York, NY 10010.

Where this book is distributed in the UK, Europe and the rest of the world, this is by Palgrave Macmillan, a division of Macmillan Publishers Limited, registered in England, company number 785998, of Houndmills, Basingstoke, Hampshire RG21 6XS.

Palgrave Macmillan is the global academic imprint of the above companies and has companies and representatives throughout the world.

Palgrave® and Macmillan® are registered trademarks in the United States, the United Kingdom, Europe and other countries.

ISBN: 978–1–137–43843–0

Library of Congress Cataloging-in-Publication Data

Paul, J. Gavin.
    Shakespeare and the imprints of performance / J. Gavin Paul.
        pages cm
    Includes bibliographical references and index.
    ISBN 978–1–137–43843–0 (hardback : alk. paper)
    1. Shakespeare, William, 1564–1616—Dramatic production.
    2. Theater—Production and direction. 3. Drama—Technique. 4. Books and reading. 5. Theater audiences—Psychology. I. Title.

PR3091.P37 2014
792.9'5—dc23   2014011616

A catalogue record of the book is available from the British Library.

Design by Newgen Knowledge Works (P) Ltd., Chennai, India.

First edition: September 2014

10 9 8 7 6 5 4 3 2 1

For Jeanette, Sebastian, and Imogen
Everything, Always

Contents

Figures

The History of Text Technologies: General Editor's Preface

Texts and images are not just isolated, inert material objects; they are also material agents, made by material agents, catalyzing other material agents. As D. F. McKenzie's phrase "sociology of texts" implies, the relationship of one text to others entails relationships to human makers and human users. Texts cannot be separated from the various, overlapping, and restless human technologies through which those texts are created and then do the cultural work that texts do. To recognize that texts depend upon technologies does not imply any simplistic technological determinism. But that recognition does encourage us to focus on change rather than stability: changes in technology, changes in culture, and the changing relationship between the two.

Text/image technologies have historically been irresistibly invasive and transformative. Unlike most areas of humanities research, the history of text technologies is not limited to a particular nationality, language, or geographical area. "The technologizing of the word," as Walter Ong called it, is best understood as the multi-millennial evolution and dispersal of increasingly complicated, comprehensive, and multisensory artificial memory systems that have driven human cultural evolution. Those memory machines, because they are prosthetic, are proximity engines, recording some part of a culture in a portable form that can then be transmitted and translated into another culture. Travelers like Marco Polo and John Smith could record their own transnational experience in text-packages, which then traveled even more extensively than they had. Texts are travelers, pioneers, immigrants, and founding fathers. The text that has influenced European and American culture more than any other, "The Book," the Bible, migrated from Hebrew and Greek into Latin and then into every European and most native American vernaculars. Texts are time-traveling technologies, too, what Joseph Roach calls "time portals": they can connect two cultures separated by time as well as space. Through texts, Dante could feel a profound personal relationship to Virgil, who had been dead for more than a thousand years, and Montaigne could write one of the most powerful expressions of his own individuality through an essay, "On Some Verses of Virgil." The study of text technologies thus is the ideal engine of interdisciplinary transformation and integration in the humanities, because those technologies for textualizing words and images cross the boundaries that separate nations, ethnicities, and religions. Against the fragmenting of the humanities into ever-smaller identity categories, this series studies the mechanisms by which inherited identities are connected and transformed.

Those mechanisms are not only material, economic, and political but also aesthetic. As they enable, exploit, extend, transform, or resist certain artistic possibilities, text technologies are inevitably also aesthetic technologies. They create media platforms that shape, and are shaped by, evolving and contested generic categories and ideals. The collector's interest in the medieval illuminated manuscript, the Dürer print, or the seventeenth-century French folio as an objet d'art in its own right mirrors the bibliographer's interest in artisanal routines and material products of the book trade. The history of the forms of texts is also a history of human culture in its largest sense, a history that speaks to how we use texts and images to establish ways of thinking, means of knowing, practices of living, assemblings of identity, and definitions of "the beautiful."

Such histories do not simply turn toward the past as an escape from the present. They frame and shape our understanding of possible transnationalisms, possible synesthesias, possible genres of humanness. These histories are explorations of incarnate becomings. And we hope that they will come to be a part of every reader's own becoming.

GARY TAYLOR

Acknowledgments

This book bears the imprints of many generous hearts, hands, and minds. I am grateful for combinations of support, interest, and encouragement offered by Ian McAdam, Goldie Morgentaler, Stephen Guy-Bray, Alex Dick, Dennis Danielson, Elizabeth Hodgson, Mark Vessey, Siân Echard, Jayne Archer, Sarah Knight, Diana Solomon, Tom Grieve, and Betty Schellenberg. I have been extremely fortunate to have received detailed feedback on this project from Stephen Heatley, Miranda Burgess, and Margaret Jane Kidnie—thank you for your time and your insights. The Shakespeare Association of America has offered a range of support and a welcoming atmosphere at all stages of my career. For their assistance, thank you to Stephen Tabor at the Huntington Library; David McKnight at The Horace Howard Furness Memorial Library, University of Pennsylvania; the staff at the Folger Shakespeare Library, and to Sabine Rahmsdorf and Edith Rimmert at Bielefeld University Library.

Thank you to Gary Taylor, for giving me a chance and then knocking on a few doors. I would also like to thank Paul Budra: in addition to helping guide this book from its earliest incarnations, he has always been there when I needed him, and he has been my advocate more times than I can count.

Two individuals deserve special recognition. Patsy Badir took me for coffee on my first day of graduate school, and her generosity has never stopped. I cannot express just how thankful I am for all that she has provided in terms of her time, wisdom, energy, diligence, and creativity. I can never repay Tony Dawson for all that he has given me. His guidance—in all its forms—is one of the greatest gifts I have ever been given, and the spirit with which he bestowed it is another gift entirely.

In the Arts One Interdisciplinary Program at the University of British Columbia I have been inspired on a daily basis by a group of remarkable scholars: Brandon Konoval, Christina Hendricks, John Beatty, Arlene

Sindelar, Deanna Kreisel, and Renisa Mawani. Included in this group is Mike Zeitlin, who has, in a short time, become a mentor and true friend.

At Palgrave, thank you to Chris Chappell and Mike Aperauch for their direction (and their patience); I also wish to express my sincere gratitude to the anonymous reader, who read the manuscript with humbling thoughtfulness and attention.

My dear parents and my wonderful sister have cheered me to the finish line; in truth, they have been cheering for me as long as I can remember, and for that I am forever grateful. Finally, my greatest debt is to my family. Jeanette, the love of my life, thank you, for everything—our story is the one I treasure most. I am endlessly thankful for Sebastian and Imogen—they have, in a very real way, grown up with this project and they echo behind each and every word. They remind me on a daily basis of the genuine pleasures and wonders of reading, which are, the more I think about it, what this book is really about.

Prologue: Prospero's Storm

I will begin at the site of a renowned beginning. That *The Tempest* is the first play to appear in the first Folio (1623) has led to it being charged with a unique valence in examinations of Shakespeare's textual afterlife. Surely, the thinking goes, those involved in collecting, organizing, and printing Shakespeare's works in a systematic fashion must have wanted the Folio to begin with *The Tempest* for a reason. Perhaps the play was understood as Shakespeare's definitive statement about creativity, imagination, and the magical capacity of the theater, and thus it could serve as a useful interpretive lens though which readers could consider the remainder of the volume's works. Perhaps the Folio editors thought it to be most representative of the playwright's talents and artistic affinities. Or perhaps the play was assigned a prominent position because it had not yet appeared in print, and prospective buyers would be enticed by a carefully prepared version that stood as an exemplar of the Folio's craftsmanship. The weight of the conceptual burden placed on *The Tempest* is increased by the fact that the play was written late in Shakespeare's career; clearly those arranging and categorizing the Folio were not bound by matters of chronology, but the conspicuousness of their decision to start with a work so near the end of the playwright's professional life invites speculation. It is probable, however, that the position of *The Tempest* is not laden with meaning at all; the compositors of the Folio had to start somewhere, and a clean transcription of *The Tempest* might have been as good a place as any. Surveying a range of hypotheses, one modern editor of the play suggests that "the evidentiary value of the play's place in the Folio [is] practically nothing" (Orgel, *Tempest* 59).

Despite not knowing for certain what—if anything—*The Tempest*'s placement was meant to represent or portend for readers of the Folio, there is one way in which the Folio text of the play can be read prospectively: it stands as the potential starting point for an encounter with Shakespeare in print. One need not begin a reading of the Folio with *The Tempest*, and many of my arguments in the chapters to come are based on the navigational freedoms possessed by readers of printed drama—reading a play (or collection of plays) is in no way a linear experience. But let us assume that one started with *The Tempest* (See Figure 0.1). What kind of reading experience does the first page of the play initiate? The play begins with the most striking opening stage direction in the Folio: *"A tempestuous noise of Thunder and Lightning heard"* (TLN 2).[1] The majority of plays in the Folio commence with entry directions for those characters who first appear on stage; it is true that a number of plays combine these entrances with dramatically appropriate strains of music—the *"Dead March"* (TLN 2) that begins *1 Henry VI*, for example, or the *"Flourish"* (TLN 2) that opens *Titus Andronicus*, but *The Tempest* and *Macbeth* (with its slightly less descriptive opening direction for *"Thunder and Lightning"* to precede the appearance of the witches), are the only plays in the Folio that begin with a stage direction calling for spectacular effects of the non-musical variety.

Michael Neill writes that what is particularly remarkable about *The Tempest*'s opening direction "is its emphasis upon the aural" ("'Noises'" 37). Building on Neill's observation, I would suggest that *"A tempestuous noise of Thunder and Lightning heard"* serves as a fitting gateway to an encounter with Shakespeare in print in that the direction stands as a captivating, yet impossible, challenge for readers. The direction, that is, invites readers to imaginatively approximate the play in performance and simultaneously tantalizes them with details that can be neither fully recaptured in print nor reproduced by the act of reading. It is not just that the description of the storm introduces an "elaborate sound track" (Neill, "'Noises'" 36) that can only take place in the reader's mind, but that the chaos with which the play is meant to begin serves to emphasize the inherent muteness of *The Tempest* in its textual form. What makes *The Tempest* a meaningful starting point for the Folio is that the play's own beginning succinctly epitomizes both the difficulties and opportunities facing readers of printed drama: the play on the page is inert, demanding that the reader bring it to life.

There are of course many factors determining the contents and shape of this page: scribal tendencies (*The Tempest*'s readerly stage directions, aimed at recollecting or perhaps envisioning details of an actual performance, are understood to be the contribution of the scribe, Ralph Crane); compositorial skill (there is ample white space, and the six entry and five exit directions in the short first scene are all clearly distinguished—tracking the high rate of physical movement on and off the

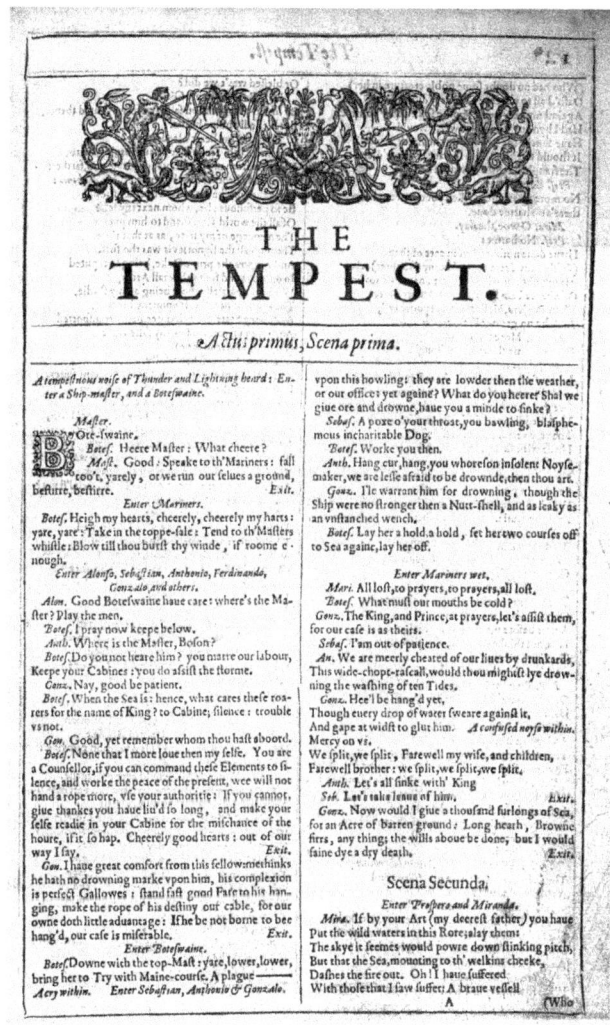

Figure 0.1 The first page of *The Tempest* (F, 1623). By permission of The Horace Howard Furness Memorial Library, Rare Book and Manuscript Library, University of Pennsylvania.

stage is another way readers of the play's opening moments are challenged); the standardized features of the Folio itself, such as its typefaces and double columns.

Moreover, as Shakespeare's works are subjected to greater editorial scrutiny and a page such as this one is modified for a modern readership, the layers of mediation structuring the relations between reader, page, and stage multiply. Tracking the evolution of the opening stage direction in subsequent editions of *The Tempest* reveals a range of strategies for influencing readers' imaginative engagements with the play's performance potential. In the eighteenth century, Alexander Pope specifies that the initial action occurs *"On a Ship at Sea"*; at the end of the century Edward Capell adds further nuances: *"A Ship at Sea. A great Storm, with Thunder and Lightning."* These emendations appear to direct the reader away from what Lukas Erne refers to as "the theatrical representation," and gesture instead toward "the represented fiction" (*Collaborators* 82). Erne's distinction highlights a tension between performed and literary modes of dramatic realization that remains prevalent in current editorial work on Shakespeare. The first commentary note in Stephen Orgel's Oxford edition, for example, addresses the "represented fiction," specifying that "the scene takes place on a ship at sea" (1.1n), while the next note acknowledges the realities of "theatrical representation": "Jacobean theatres had lightning machines, and a *noise of thunder and lightning heard* need not imply that no visual effects accompanied the sound of thunder" (1.1.0.1n).

Perhaps the best indication of the evocativeness of the opening of the play can be seen as early as the frontispiece to the 1709 edition by Nicholas Rowe. This frontispiece—with gigantic waves capsizing an ornate ship that has been set ablaze, Ariel hurling balls of fire, nearly a dozen men desperately clinging to the masts and deck, lightning streaking across a darkened sky populated by winged beasts and serpents, and a rather menacing, shadowy Prospero watching the chaos from the shore with his staff held aloft—forcefully registers the representational complexities of the moment.[2] The details of the illustration greatly exceed both the contents of the Folio's opening direction *and* the possibilities of theatrical production, and thus serve as a reminder that Prospero's storm will always exist for readers somewhere between the page and the stage, relying on a combination of textual codes, editorial mediation, and the reader's own imaginative participation. As Martin Meisel writes (fittingly enough, in reference to memories of past performances of *The Tempest*), "Some aspects of what the play is written to provide are not available in the reading, except as a spectral promise, because so intrinsically bound up with what happens when we are an audience" (222).

Meisel's formulation comes from his study, *How Plays Work*, wherein he describes the unique experience of reading printed playtexts. His thoughts on reading plays, which speak to the issues raised by the opening of *The Tempest*, are worth quoting at length:

> The printed play exists as a manual or a blueprint for performance. It exists as a manual *and* as a representation, in its own right, of that which is to be performed—whether it ever is performed or not, whether it is performed many different times in many different productions, guided and enacted by many different minds, or only once under the eagle eye of the author. Reading plays in the fullest sense, then, means being able to read the dialogue and descriptions as a set of directions encoding, but also in a measure *enacting*, their own realization. It means bringing to bear something of a playwright's or director's understanding of how plays work on an imagined audience in the circumstances of an imagined theatrical representation. (1–2)

Meisel makes clear that engaging with plays in print involves complicated interpretive maneuvers on the part of readers. The challenges arise in large part from the necessity of attending to a play's performance potentialities, to the embodied, active aspects of the theatrical event that resist or refuse textualization. Meisel recognizes that readers' imaginings of performances are facilitated by various forms of code—"a set of agreed on, or at least intelligible, conventions that ideally fade into unobtrusiveness" (2)—marking the distance between the printed play and the play as it has been, or could be, performed. Put differently, the very characteristics that distinguish the printed play as a discrete literary object in need of specialized analytical procedures also gesture beyond the printed play, to the performed modes of realization that it can never contain. Plays in print demarcate the conceptual gaps between text and performance, but simultaneously, they also harbor the capacity to minimize these gaps, without ever completely closing them.

Meisel places text and performance, page and stage, in an inevitable, and inevitably contentious, binary. As he puts it, "Production, as everyone knows, entails making choices, by actors, directors, designers, from the inherent potentialities of the script, thereby putting flesh on the bones" (vii). His metaphor implicitly figures the reading of plays as an act of textual osteology, working closely with skeletal matter (the script) to hypothesize as to what the play's fully formed life on stage might look like. The debate over the proper tools necessary to elucidate the differences between plays in print and plays in performance, however, is a contentious one. Countering Meisel's position are those who would prefer to see the text effectively stay buried, and to see the performance-as-enlivening-the-text analogy discarded altogether. A recent back-and-forth between R. A. Foakes and W. B. Worthen in the pages of the journal, *Shakespeare*, exemplifies the basic theoretical incongruities separating advocates of text and performance from one another. Indeed, the stated principles of the journal itself attest to a desire to alleviate tensions between the poles that the two critics represent: "Its principal aim is to bridge the gap between the disciplines of Shakespeare in Performance Studies and Shakespeare in English Literature and Language. The journal builds on the existing aim of the *British Shakespeare Association*, to exploit the synergies between academics and performers of Shakespeare."[3] Foakes approaches matters from a textual, literary perspective; like Meisel, he figures the text as generative and multivalent, capable of producing a broad horizon of interpretations in performance: "Performance theorists think of the text as 'fixed' and somehow trapping the director or actor when in fact it may encourage them to choose from a spectrum of possible ways of interpreting language, action, and character so as to enhance their way of presenting the play and the connections they may wish to make with their own time" (56). Conversely, Worthen contends that performance does not merely realize the text's instructions but rather absorbs and transforms the text along with various other elements involved in enacting the play; "Performance is an experiment, not an interpretation" ("Texts" 212), he writes, arguing that "the stage doesn't reproduce the text: there may well be first and subsequent performances of a play, but these performances all subject the text to a different, unpredictable order of signification" ("Texts" 210).[4]

The common ground for the two sides is that reading a playtext is a means of dramatic realization that is absolutely unlike live performance; everything else beyond this premise—how much authority to assign to playwrights, the extent to which texts and readings determine performance, the capability of printed plays to communicate the possibilities of performance—is contestable. Without denying that printed plays distort and fragment performance practice, this book negotiates an intractable debate by shifting attention to the ways in which these inevitable distortions can nevertheless enrich a reader's awareness of a play's performance potentialities. I suggest that printed plays possess the capacity to be more meaningfully engaged with the play as performed than they tend to get credit for; to substantiate this claim means examining editorial principles and strategies that constitute, by necessity, a methodological network linking page and stage. My work seeks to establish the facets of the modern edition that are most strongly tied to performance potentialities, as well as locate the various traces of these attributes in the long history of Shakespearean editing. Central to my engagements with the informational structures of the edited page is the term *performancescape*, a textual representation of performance potential that gives relative shape and stability to what is dynamic and multifarious. *Performancescape*, a term that I will deploy in relation to editions ranging from the earliest extant quartos and folios to digital editions powered by hypertext, describes the way in which printed drama allows for readers to move between the material text and the imagined performance, the physical *scape* of the printed page and the virtual *scape* of the absent, performed event.

Chapter 1 defines and models *performancescape*, which I introduce after establishing the overriding inclination of both contemporary editorial theory and performance criticism to stress the undeniably limited ways that texts can account for performance. Chapters 2 and 3 combine to demonstrate that throughout Shakespeare's history in print, formulations of page and stage have been more synergistic than a binary that opposes "literary" and "theatrical" logic will support: chapter 2 will center on representations of performance in early modern printed playtexts, paying particular attention to constructions of a play's performance history and theater audiences in prefatory and ancillary material, while chapter 3 continues to trace a broad historical arc, with the focus shifting to prominent editions of the eighteenth, nineteenth, and early twentieth centuries. Chapter 4 addresses the powerful referential capabilities of performance commentary—a prevalent form of modern editorial mediation that constitutes a major conduit between textual and performed modes of realization. Performance commentary is a memory machine built for the impossible task of describing or returning to the forever-absent play-as-performed; in response to claims that such commentary is an editorial imposition that restricts or precludes interpretive freedom, I assert that performance commentary can be a productive device with which editors are able to acknowledge the limitations and distortions produced by their own subjective, emendatory acts. The final chapter reflects on Shakespeare's printed incarnations through a pragmatic assessment of electronic editions, engaging electronic editions in terms of what they currently make possible for editors and readers, as opposed to discussions that describe these editions predominantly in terms of theoretical potential; ultimately this chapter contends that critical editions shaped and delimited by editorial procedures remain relevant and valuable even in the face of seemingly boundless digital archives.

My approach ranges across different sites in the critical edition, embracing a reader's ability to utilize the stability of the printed page and make tangential moves away from the playtext in order to gain a more nuanced understanding of the play as it has been, or could be, performed. My goals are threefold and interconnected: first, to examine a diverse selection of texts that are particularly rich with printed engagements with performance in order to identify both the strengths and limitations of printed drama's ability to imprint, or encode for, performance. Second, this book stakes a claim for the continued relevance of editorial mediation and decision making amidst calls for "unediting," "open" texts and the tantalizing comprehensiveness of digitization. Third, I mean to highlight the centrality of the reader in the interpretive network formed by editing, printed texts, performance histories, and performance potentialities. Rather than formulating a system in which editors mislead or manipulate readers by promoting their own preferred imagined performances, or one in which readers would be solely responsible for navigating complicated moments of stage business, I offer a way of considering page and stage as functioning symbiotically and facilitating productive interpretive agency on the part of readers.

What follows, then, is a theoretical undertaking, a modeling of a reading process that brings into relief the imprints of performance that inhere in printed playtexts. The ways in which I read drama are not meant to be prescriptive, nor can they account for any and all readers, imagined or actual. I am fully aware that a constructed, idealized "reader" shadows my analysis, but this reader does not eclipse my undertaking, which is to advocate a particular way of conceptualizing and navigating Shakespeare in print. It is no doubt true that readers can utilize editions in different ways than are represented in this book; nevertheless, there is virtue in my deployment of an ideal reader in that it facilitates a sustained consideration of the kinds of readings that drama's text technologies can support. Printed drama requires active participation and analytical labor in order to yield meaning, and this book recognizes that readers do not follow a single path or even end up in the same place; accordingly, the chapters to come articulate a method of reading that is designed to map the vast network of pathways linking printed page and performed event. That other readers can travel in different ways than my admittedly ideal reader is a point that necessitates—rather than invalidates—a study confronting the complex means by which playtexts invite a multitude of readerly navigations.

Before proceeding with this plan, I would like to return to Meisel's notion of the "spectral promise" (222) haunting the reader's movement through the book of the play. Meisel's description is germane because it so effectively evokes the illusory presence of the performed event.

Certain textualized gestures toward performance are made throughout a playtext—in stage directions, speech prefixes, descriptions of dumb shows, illustrations—albeit never in a comprehensive or even satisfactorily detailed way. Attending to these imprints of performance might help a reader to envision a theatrical representation that is likely to be indistinct and lacking precision, a virtual performance that is shaped by textual codes yet never absolutely determined by them. I began with the stimulating opening stage direction of the first play printed in the Folio; to truly begin at the beginning of the play, however, is to recognize that a reader starts not with this direction but with the centered title that looms over the entire page, eclipsing all other textual forms in its size and prominence:

This title is unique amongst Shakespeare's works in that it can be understood not only to assign the play a name but essentially initiate the play's action. By this I mean that the title constitutes and subsequently recalls the play's seminal event, an event that, as I have suggested above, also marks a fissure between textual and performed modes of realization. To read the title is to activate the occurrence that sets the play's textual enactment in motion. To witness the opening scene in performance is to experience one of the countless possible manifestations of "**THE TEMPEST**," whether ultra-realistic, overtly theatrical, or somewhere in between. The ghostly potential of performance can be understood to hover over the initial Folio leaf of *The Tempest* as a permanent signal of the reader's participatory responsibility. In addition, the running title crowning each subsequent page of the play in the Folio serves as a persistent, if subtle, reminder that the entire play is founded on a theatrical spectacle that a reader can only imaginatively approximate in a way that is undeniably incomplete relative to the sensorial complexities produced on stage. All this might seem to figure the reading of plays as a comparatively impoverished activity, though I mean to suggest just the opposite: the initial Folio page of *The Tempest*, with its intermingling of textual codes and the spectre of performance potentialities, is indicative of the representational potency of the play on the page. What makes this page significant is the way it immediately forces readers to confront the incongruities of text and performance, opening up the rich interpretive space between these two modes of dramatic realization. It is into this space that readers conjure the world of the play into existence, their engagement with the text empowered by the fact that, despite its extensive histories in print and on stage, Prospero's storm always begins with the act of reading anew.

CHAPTER 1

Mediating Page and Stage

As an example of the kinds of encounters that lie at the heart of this book, consider Henry's Paris coronation scene (4.1) in Michael Taylor's Oxford edition of *1 Henry VI* (2003). Newly adorned with the French crown, Henry soon finds himself breaking up a potential duel between Vernon and Basset, champions for Richard (Duke of York) and Somerset, respectively. While the large number of bodies on stage at this moment surely complicates a reader's ability to maintain a vivid version of Meisel's "imagined theatrical representation," (2), I mean to address an ostensibly simpler matter of stage business. The dialogue emphasizes the "sanguine colour" (4.1.92) and "paleness" (106) of the roses that Basset and Vernon presumably wear; their division and enmity thus are reinforced visually and linguistically.[1] Here is the central portion of what is Henry's longest speech in the play, as it appears in Taylor's edition:

Let me be umpire in this doubtful strife.
I see no reason, if I wear this rose,
    He takes a red rose
That anyone should therefore be suspicious
I more incline to Somerset than York;
Both are my kinsmen, and I love them both. (4.1.151–5)

The sticking point—for readers, but not playgoers—is how, precisely, does Henry obtain his rose? There is no stage direction in the Folio text; Taylor inserts "*He takes a red rose*" and also includes a note, which is worth reproducing in full:

From where? From whom? [Edward] Burns's [Arden 3] direction specifies from Basset, but Henry might well take it from Somerset himself, from Suffolk even. Better, perhaps, to leave open precisely who and where it comes from, but in the theatre it has to come from someone and from somewhere.

The note reinforces the inherent differences between reading and seeing plays: for an audience in a theater, the matter of the rose poses no interpretive hurdle whatsoever, since actors and directors will have solved the problem in advance. The stage is in a perpetual state of unalterable cause and effect: Henry's rose must come from *someone* and *somewhere*. As we read, however, we have the freedom to imaginatively experiment with different causes and effects, or to not dabble in them at all—it seems entirely plausible that one could read the dialogue and relevant stage direction and be satisfied that Henry's rose comes from *no one* and from *nowhere* but miraculously blooms to life through the necessities and peculiar physics of the imagined environment in which he exists as we read him into being.

Taylor's playful "From where? From whom?" treats the source of Henry's rose as what Meisel terms a "field of possibility" (73), a field that, as Taylor implies, can be reduced to a single interpretation on stage in a number of ways. Taylor's utilization of the marginal space of his edited page to "open" the playtext to the possibilities of performance relies upon the paradoxical properties of the two modes of realization: the necessity of *somewhere* and *someone* in the theater is juxtaposed against the elusiveness and ambiguity of print's relative fixity. If his note works in conjunction with his edited playtext as he intends, users of his edition will be reminded that reading and theater-going are incongruent activities; however, Taylor's note and edited playtext also combine to undo this incongruence. His commentary, that is, challenges readers to envision divergent stagings of a particular moment, a textually entrenched interpretive move that respects and reflects the fluid possibilities of the play in performance. As the ambiguous origins of Henry's rose suggest, and as the remainder of this study will demonstrate, the book of the play is not closed off from the possibilities of performance but is instead a potentially fertile site of cross-pollination that links reading and imagining to performing, page to stage. This chapter has two aims: first, to map the resonant space between textual and performed modes of realization, and second, to offer a conceptual tool for rethinking the complexities and contributions of editorial engagements with performance. Charting the generative capabilities of printed plays is the initial step in building a case for understanding their interpretive networks as a product of both editorial mediation and active readerly participation.

Reading Plays, Reading Bodies

Every printed playtext bears the markings of its own unique performance history. This history tends to be encrypted and fragmentary in comparison to the narrative history that can be written about a play's ongoing manifestations on stage, but it nevertheless constitutes an essential signifying property of a play in print form. The imprints of performance take heterogeneous forms and appear with unsystematic and inconsistent frequency from play to play, text to text. In terms of the extant texts of Shakespeare and his contemporaries, some traces seem indicative of performance practices in the early modern theater, as theatrical data that offer brief glimpses of how certain moments were to be staged have somehow entered the complicated transmission process from manuscript to print: one thinks, for example, of stage directions rich with details clearly intended to guide performance—recall the Folio's direction that Coriolanus "*Holds her* [Volumnia] *by the hand silent*" (TLN 3539). Other traces anticipate performance potential rather than reflect performance practice: here one might consider signs of textual revision or unstable speech prefixes, both of which seem in certain instances to gesture at conceptions of a play's fictional characters and the real-world actors bringing them to life (think of "Lady Capulet" shifting between *Wife*, *Capulet's Wife*, *Mother*, and *Lady*). And still other traces—such as scenes that lack the requisite entrances or exits for certain characters or those haunted by the (non) involvement of silent ghost characters like "Innogen," identified as the wife of Leonatus in the opening stage direction of *Much Ado About Nothing*—are less remnants to be gleaned than lacunae to be filled, interpretive gaps that necessitate a consideration of the realities of performance. When texts undergo the interpolative work of editors as they are prepared for modern readers, certain traces of performance can be made explicit, some can be muted or even effaced, and new links to the play in performance can be forged. Broadly speaking, my concern is with the editorial mediation of these imprints: the necessity editors face of having to decode (and usually recode) the markers of performance they find in the extant playtexts they are working from, as well as their ability to encode for performance wherever they deem useful to do so (in introductions, commentary notes, interpolated stage directions). My work is governed throughout by the belief that to read a printed play is to confront both the page and the possibilities of the stage, to engage with what Worthen calls "the interface of performance and writing" (*Print* 162).

That a printed play gestures toward, yet forever remains separate from, its existence on stage means that the continued production and close study of edited playtexts occur at the crossroads of a number of often disparate forms of inquiry: textual theory, bibliography, theater history, as well as various forms of performance criticism, all have a considerable interest in editorial practice.[2] The reciprocal relationship between editorial practice and other modes of inquiry is a relatively recent phenomenon that came into being in the wake of the New Bibliography. Until the latter half of the twentieth century, the production of authoritative critical editions and the scholarly labors subsequently performed on these editions were seen as more or less discrete activities; editing and literary criticism were understood to speak fundamentally inharmonious dialects, with the former developing detailed systems of notation as well as sophisticated hypotheses to account for things like lost authorial manuscripts and memorial reconstructions, while the latter concerned itself with the pursuit of a different kind of truth—definitive readings rather than definitive editions. Under the New Bibliographers, editing rose to prominence as it became more nuanced in its historical attentiveness and theoretical sophistication; significantly, the ongoing refinement of editorial activity was countered by a burgeoning critical awareness of editing itself as a powerful interpretive act. Attentiveness to the effects of editorial labor (which began in earnest in the 1970s and was energized by the ascendancy of poststructuralism and New Historicism—both of which tend to destabilize texts and multiply authority) has become an indispensible facet of literary criticism. Calls for an approach to texts that "would keep in play not only multiple readings and versions but also the multiple and dispersed agencies that could have produced variants" (Werstine, "Narratives" 86), and of "rethink[ing] Shakespeare in relation to our new knowledge of collaborative writing, collaborative printing, and the historical contingencies of textual production" (de Grazia and Stallybrass 279) remain pervasive, and the desire for readers to be cognizant of editorial influence is now commonplace. In the words of one scholar, "the more aware we are of the processes of mediation to which a given edition has been subject, the less likely we are to be caught up in a constricting hermeneutic knot by which the shaping hand of the editor is mistaken for the intent of the author, or for some lost, 'perfect' version of the author's creation" (Marcus, *Unediting* 3).

To compress a rather convoluted story then, the decline of the New Bibliography toward the end of the twentieth century was precipitated by a scrutiny of critical editions and editorial customs that focused on the ways in which editorial practices inherently distort, and unrealistically stabilize, the production and transmission of texts.³ For those studying the Shakespearean canon and other early modern dramatic texts, the ramifications have been significant: in addition to expanding the scope of inquiry to include the numerous nonauthorial agents and factors that influence textual production, editors and textual theorists have endeavored to develop a more detailed understanding of the interconnectedness of a play's textual and theatrical manifestations. In short, engaging a play's history in print is now largely inseparable from considerations of its performance potentialities.⁴

While the means by which editors grapple with issues of performance has become a popular subject for critical examination, the bulk of commentary on this issue tends to stress the fundamental differences between page and stage, and emphasizes the inability of texts to adequately represent the realities of performance. David Scott Kastan, for instance, writes that "performance operates according to a theatrical logic of its own rather than one derived from the text; the printed play operates according to a textual logic that is not derived from performance" (*Book* 9); similarly, Worthen states that "a stage performance is not determined by the internal 'meanings' of the text, but is a site where the text is put into production, gains meaning in a different mode of production through the labor of its agents and the regimes of performance they use to refashion it as performance material" (*Force* 23), and Lukas Erne claims that English Renaissance plays have a "double existence, one on stage and one on the printed page" and calls for "a reception that takes into account the respective specificities of the two media. To sim plify matters, performance tends to speak to the senses, while a printed text activates the intellect" (*Literary Dramatist* 23). So entrenched is this line of thinking that critical editions of the late twentieth and early twenty-first centuries, although more alert to matters of performance than ever before, frequently concede the incongruity of text and performance as a matter of protocol. The general introduction to the Oxford Shakespeare, to provide a well-known example, stresses that more often than not an editor faces an inescapable choice: "Should he offer his readers a text which is as close as possible to what Shakespeare originally wrote, or should he aim to formulate a text presenting the play as it appeared when performed by the company of which Shakespeare was a principal shareholder...?" (xxxv). Striking a similar chord, editors of a collected edition of the works of John Webster claim that

the Poem is editable, and available for discussion, while the Play is certainly not [...]. We cannot edit the Play since too much of the necessary

> data has been lost in the dark backward and abysm of time; we must
> therefore edit the Poem, which is what everybody has been doing all
> along, though not always in as explicit an awareness as could have been
> desired that this was indeed what they were doing. (Gunby et al. 37)

A heightened awareness of the thorny interconnections of text and
performance—Poem and Play—in editorial circles is inseparable from
developments in Shakespeare studies generally. Just as editors have seen
fit to give more prominence to performance within their editions (sometimes, as we see in the quotation from the Webster editors, by conceding
their inability to account for it as meaningfully as they might like), so
too have text and performance been continually reprioritized in other
streams of critical practice. One major consequence of the widespread
resistance to locating meaning "in" the text is the belief that plays
should not be read and interpreted as literary texts at all but are instead
dramatic scripts intended solely for performance that should be interrogated by critics using specialized analytical procedures. An emphasis
on dramatic scripts has, to various degrees, underwritten performance
criticism for the past 30 years or so, an eclectic movement that Erne has
called "perhaps the most important development in Shakespeare studies
in the last century" (*Literary Dramatist* 21).[5]

The ascendancy of performance criticism was accompanied by the
falling fortunes of explicitly literary close readings of Shakespeare,
which were increasingly perceived as theoretically unsophisticated
and historically short-sighted. As Worthen has demonstrated at great
length, however, there remains a certain mode of Shakespearean performance criticism that "tends to regard performance...as a way of realizing the text's authentic commands" (*Authority* 160).[6] What is at stake
in marking habits of critical reasoning and writing that are implicitly
dependent on notions of textuality? For Worthen, to imply that performance is the result of merely realizing textual commands is to ignore
the dynamic meanings and responses that are *produced* in performance,
"to tame the unruly ways of the stage" (*Authority* 3). Worthen's metaphor is indicative of the ongoing struggle at the core of critical engagements with performance: the desire to allow the nontextual elements of
performance to remain undistorted and "untamed" while also managing to somehow bracket performance and subject it to critical analysis.
Writing about performance is a task not unlike the one faced by the
Third Gentleman from *The Winter's Tale* who reports on the apparently spectacular reunion of Leontes, Perdita, and company; despite a
presumably accurate and detailed account deeply colored by his own

interpretations and responses (Perdita "did ... bleed tears; for I am sure my heart wept blood" [5.2.88–9]), he concedes to his rapt listeners that the event in question was "a sight which was to be seen, cannot be spoken of," an "encounter ... which lames report to follow it, and undoes description to do it" (5.2.42–3, 57–8).[7] As the Third Gentleman suggests, it is the physical immediacy of certain encounters that provide them with much of their signifying and affective power (and here I am extending his claim to include theatrical encounters between actors and between actors and audiences), and a certain undeniable measure of both immediacy and affect is lost almost as soon as they are produced, never to be recaptured in any account, no matter how detailed. The Third Gentleman's interpretation of the reunion can be voiced to his interlocutors in the world of the play, to the audience of the play in the world, and assume a typographical form in the play as printed text, but all of these versions of his report to some degree resist such textualization, the experience in question rendered "lame" (his words) or "tame(d)" (Worthen's).

The primacy given to texts and textual meanings is something that performance criticism has become alert and responsive to; a consideration of a recent essay can help to reveal the extent to which its practitioners have endeavored to theorize performance in ways that do not reflexively defer to the text but rather embrace what James C. Bulman calls "the radical contingency of performance—the unpredictable, often playful intersection of history, material conditions, social contexts, and reception" (1). The title of Ric Knowles's "Encoding/Decoding Shakespeare: *Richard III* at the 2002 Stratford Festival" announces his focus on one such point of intersection. Noting that most performance criticism "has concentrated its attention primarily on ... the performance text" (302), Knowles offers instead an expanded tripartite model of performance analysis that considers not just the performance text but also the conditions of production (including actors, directors, the rehearsal process, and the neighborhood in which the play is staged), and the conditions of reception (the historical/cultural moment in which the play is received). If (adapting Worthen's formulation) performance is inevitably "tamed" when subjected to critical scrutiny, then what we find in Knowles's essay is that the interpretive arena in which performance must be enclosed is made as expansive as possible. Thus, his attempt to answer how the opening night of a particular staging of *Richard III* generated "radically different readings of the same production" (297) means that Knowles takes into consideration everything from the play's central (and nostalgic) position in the Festival's advertising campaign, to its *mise en scène*, to ticket prices, to the makeup of the Stratford Festival's board of governors. Utilizing his theory of "materialist semiotics," Knowles seeks not the meanings that Shakespeare might have originally intended when writing *Richard III*, nor meanings that are otherwise frozen within the text. In fact, Knowles stresses that no production (textual or theatrical) *contains* meaning; instead, "they *produce* meaning through the discursive work of an interpretive community and through the lived, everyday relationships of people with texts and performances" (300).[8] Consequently, Knowles's project is "designed to undertake precise ideological analyses of the conditions, conscious and unconscious, both of production, within and through which performance texts come into being and make themselves available to be 'read,' and of reception, spatial and discursive, within and through which audiences perform those readings and negotiate what the works mean for them" (302). It is clear that in Knowles's essay any recourse to the notion of stable, authorially intended texts and textual meanings has become secondary to broader historical, cultural, and ideological lines of inquiry.

Part of this broadening is accomplished by Knowles's use of "performance text," which is a deliberate move away from "playtext," one that reinforces the notion of printed plays as scripts intended for performance rather than texts available for more literary forms of analysis. The attractiveness of "performance text" for its proponents is that the term identifies performance as a *source* of meanings rather than a means through which the play's immutable textual meanings are revealed and/ or interpreted; performance is not assumed to be derivative, a play's existence in print is not assigned any prior or preferential status. In the words of Barbara Hodgdon (who has done much to define and explore performance as a distinct, nonderivative form of textuality that can be read in meaningful ways), "performance text" is meant to invert (or at least undo) the traditional hierarchy by challenging "the notion that the written word represents the only form in which a play can possess or participate in textuality" (*End Crowns All* 18). The understanding that performance *participates* in textuality, rather than being dictated by it, has been instrumental in the continued prominence and relevance of performance criticism, allowing critics to free themselves from the rigidity of formulations that propose a deterministic relation between text and performance. Hodgdon's work consciously shifts its focus away from the authority of the text to consider instead "how performers and readers activate that authority in relation to other cultural contexts and discourses" (*Shakespeare Trade* xiii)—Knowles's essay, it seems to me, is very much in this spirit.

My intention is not to offer a systematic critique of Knowles's piece, but to use it to provide an example of how certain forms of performance criticism have now expanded the discussion well beyond the text/ performance polarity. It is important to recognize, however, that this polarity is not removed from the equation in essays such as Knowles's, only reprioritized, since any effort to write about performance involves textualizing it, to one degree or another. As Worthen admits, despite the concomitant distortions, textualizing a performance in order to engage with it (via description, recollection, critical inquiry, etc.) is not only inevitable, but useful as well: "A theatrical performance is not a text, but considering performance as though it participated in textuality helps us to see some of the work, the theoretical work, it performs" (*Authority* 183).[9] The conclusion of Knowles's essay crystallizes this point: Knowles zeroes in on Tom McCamus's delivery of Richard's lines from 5.3 (the morning of Bosworth), claiming that the actor's reading "resonated as the surfacing of tensions among the various encoded discourses that I have been analyzing" (316). Knowles's insistence that McCamus's "was the most clearly schizophrenic reading I have seen of Richard's speech on the morning of Bosworth" (316) implicitly begins to demarcate Knowles's prior interpretation of the text that he brings with him to the theater as a Shakespearean scholar and playgoer. The antecedence of his own understanding of the play is what allows him to identify and measure the choices made by those involved in the production—his baseline reading establishes a kind of interpretive mean for *Richard III*, which in turn enables him to recognize deviations from that mean that occur during performance. In this case, "most schizophrenic" suggests "more schizophrenic than any other actor I have seen playing Richard" but also "more schizophrenic than I understood Richard to be in my previous reading(s) of the text"; this latter point is evidenced when Knowles cites a portion of the speech in question, providing "different typefaces for the different vocal registers used by the actor" (316)—if the extreme schizophrenic reading that Knowles is attempting to recapture was readily available to a reader, presumably these alterations to the text would be unnecessary. In short, while I do not dispute that Knowles is "reading" performance here, underlying this is the text and his (prior) reading(s) of it; indeed, the fundamental conflation of textual and performed modes of realization is evidenced in his description of "the most clearly schizophrenic *reading* I have *seen* of Richard's speech on the morning of Bosworth" (emphasis added). The essay ends by returning to a specific moment and ostensibly entrenching various lines of argument *in* the performance, with the strength of Knowles's conclusions resting on the claim that the institutional and cultural fissures that he has highlighted throughout his study can be understood to be "housed in [the actor's] body" (316) at this particular moment of the play. Whether this is true or not is beside the point; in the end, what is significant is that Knowles's essay does and does not return to performance, or rather, it does not return to performance so much as to a textualized recollection and representation of it: an isolated portion of a prominent speech that is relineated and bolded in accordance with Knowles's understanding of the performance that he is trying to read.

The remarkable scope of Knowles's essay is representative of a new orthodoxy in performance criticism, one very much invested in recognizing and limiting the influence that printed playtexts might maintain over interpretive procedures. It goes without saying, however, that there remains a school of thought that would prefer to see printed playtexts retain the central position that they have long enjoyed in Shakespeare studies. That being said, the stability of texts has been so thoroughly undermined that those defending textual analysis can no longer remain a meaningful part of the debate by merely invoking scholarly tradition or claiming proximity to authorial intentions. To advocate the validity of reading dramatic texts closely entails defending such practices in increasingly sophisticated ways. One of the most theoretically informed counterattacks to the ascendancy of performance-oriented criticism remains Harry Berger Jr.'s *Imaginary Audition: Shakespeare on Stage and Page*. Since Berger's stated goal of explicating the validity of "imagined performance, of stage-centered reading that submits to literary rather than to theatrical controls" (28) speaks directly to my own interests, I would like to consider his work at some length. Berger would no doubt be untroubled by Worthen's conclusions that much Shakespearean performance criticism "tends to regard performance . . . as a way of realizing the text's authentic demands" (*Authority* 160); that performance criticism must be vigilant not to reinscribe certain textual biases only confirms Berger's conviction that texts and the activity of reading texts are always prior to any performance. Berger's belief in the primacy of the text is never really in question, and he positions his book in direct opposition to a performance criticism that is either largely uninterested in reading printed plays or believes that "performance should provide the model and criteria that govern reading" (xi). Shrewdly though, despite its textual biases—Berger identifies himself as a "confirmed armchair interpreter" (xiv)—the opening pages of *Imaginary Audition* seem to indicate that Berger is not intending to reaffirm a deterministic relationship between text and performance. The main thrust of Berger's argument is that one can be an armchair interpreter and simultaneously remain cognizant of the stage, reading with an eye (or more accurately, an ear) attuned to the play as performed. Early on, Berger gives the impression of wanting to bridge the gap between page and stage, to refine what he perceives as the caricatured dichotomy of the "Slit-eyed Analyst and the Wide-eyed Playgoer" (xiv) perpetuated by "New Histrionicism [otherwise known as performance, or stage-centred, criticism]" (xiv). What his book purportedly models is a method of reading that corrects both "the reductive practice New Histrionicists advocate" *and* the "excesses of armchair interpretation which...they properly criticize" (xii); this practice of "stage-centred reading" is what he terms "imaginary audition." What the book ultimately details, however, is something quite different.

But before explaining what I mean by that, I want to examine Berger's deployment of "imaginary audition," and in particular, question the extent to which it actually encompasses a "stage-centred" method of reading. The practice is first articulated as follows:

> ...it involves an attempt to reconstruct text-centred reading in a way that incorporates the perspective of imaginary audition and playgoing; an attempt to put into play an approach that remains text-centred but focuses on the interlocutionary politics and theatrical features of performed drama so as to make them impinge at every point on the most suspicious and antitheatrical of readings. (xiv)

A certain air of rapprochement pervades this brief outline: Berger has no desire to leave the confines of his armchair, but from his position of interpretive solitude, he seems willing to entertain some of the signifying elements unique to the play as performed and bring these elements to bear on the literary forms of analysis that he favors; moreover, he suggests that this imaginative engagement with the stage will *strengthen* a text-centered reading. What soon becomes apparent, however, is that the aspects of playgoing and the "theatrical features of performed drama" that he will incorporate into his mode of reading are narrowly defined—it is the "audition" of "imaginary audition" that is absolutely central to Berger's claims. If Berger's readings are indeed "stage-centered," then the imagined stage that is synthesized with the text is almost exclusively an auditory one—the mind's ear(s) are called into service, but the mind's eye can effectively stay closed. Imaginary audition is first and foremost the readerly activity of imagined overhearing, what Berger refers to as "auditory voyeurism" (141). Premised on the belief that Shakespeare's major speakers—even in their most formal and public utterances—"seem often to be listening to and acting on themselves" (75), Berger performs an extended demonstration of imaginary audition via a close reading of 3.2 in *Richard II*; Richard's dialogue, argues Berger, throughout the play, but particularly in this scene, assumes a unique valence "when we read it with imaginary audition attuned to its theatrical as well as its dramatic dimensions—when, that is, we distinguish between its character as performance before a theater audience and its character as utterance to fictional interlocutors" (77). To read with the aim of attending to the "theatrical circumstances" (xiii) of *Richard II* is to "listen" to Richard listening to himself.

But to refer to a practice that focuses so intently on overhearing locutionary acts without attempting to account for other physical aspects of playgoing (particularly the visual) as "stage-centered" seems misleading. Berger can attempt to equate ears and eyes synesthetically—"Like the eyes of tennis watchers, readers must follow with their 'ears' the movement and meaning back and forth from speaker to auditor, from one auditor to another, from auditor to speaker, and—most important— from speaker to himself" (75)—but the fact remains that the performed version of *Richard II* that Berger imagines as he reads is for all intents and purposes static, if not completely invisible. His program does not require him to imagine (or remember) other variables that might conceivably enhance a reader's sensitivity to the "theatrical features of performed drama" (xiv), such as a particular *mise-en-scène*, or any specific movements by, or physical interactions between, actors. In essence, a reader practicing imaginary audition could envision a vigorous dramatic reading of a play rather than an actual performance, and the end result of the interpretation would be seemingly unchanged.

Despite some conciliatory gestures towards performance, Berger never actually modifies his default assumptions in which the text's position relative to performance is one of absolute primacy; reading a text is the principal way in which a play's "meaning" can be determined, and any and all "alternate and potentially stageable interpretations [are] *inscribed in the playtext*" (14, emphasis added). Theater audiences, in Berger's estimation, are extremely limited (relative to readers) in terms of both the amount of information they can take in during a live performance and the speed at which they can process that information. By continually stressing the nuances that can only be gleaned through close reading as well as readers' unique ability to "decelerate" and "reaccelerate" the tempo of their engagement with the text, Berger is determined to remind his readers of "how much is withheld from an audience that can only hear and see, how much is occulted in the text they cannot read" (149). Berger's reminder, however, is only half of an important equation: it can also be said that dramatic texts—particularly critically edited dramatic texts—remind us that despite the likelihood that reading a play allows one to process information in arguably more detailed and efficient ways, there remain myriad forms of information relayed in a performance that refuse textualization. This point leads me to the portion of Berger's study that I find especially revealing. Berger cites Gary Taylor's *Moment by Moment by Shakespeare* as an exemplar of the New Histrionicism that ignominiously disregards the "generosity or generativity of the text" (31). Berger takes Taylor to task for his treatment of *Henry V,* believing that Taylor's performance-oriented readings are posited on distorted and oversimplified constructions of both the literary critic and the "innocent playgoer" (32). In his critique of Taylor's approach, however, there comes a point at which Berger playfully and ironically asserts that the very elements of performance that Taylor argues a reader is unable to imagine via "imaginary audition or visualization" (28) paradoxically brings those elements to the mind of Berger himself:

> . . . Taylor's own readings of the language lesson and several other scenes are finely imagined. They help at least one reader to a vivid apprehension of some of the ways performance can interpret the complexities of text. His account of the language lesson reduces my inability to "hear" or respond to the jokes as if delivered. I suspect that Taylor's ideal deprived reader is as inexperienced in theater as I am. Yet when he mentions the army and the empty space and great volume of the theater that do not exist for that reader, they begin to exist for this reader. Taylor helps me imagine the effect of Alan Howard's passionate Henry aiming his Harfleur aria at me, and the effect of the resonance of the French king's voice giving life to the list of nobles. Even as Taylor belittles the reader's ability, he increases it by his forceful literary portrait of a production. (28)

What is intriguing about Berger's digression is that it assigns qualities to Taylor's interpretive program that are also applicable to the interpretive work often done by editors in their own efforts to mediate text and performance for readers of critical editions. Considering the primacy that Berger is committed to assigning to the text, it is curious that *Imaginary Audition* makes no real mention of editorial activities, especially since information provided by editors has the potential to create the kind of "forceful literary portrait of a production" that Berger evidently finds so influential. The most obvious illustration here would be Taylor's own Oxford edition of *Henry V*; a glimpse at Taylor's edition reveals that it includes options as to how the Harfleur scene (to take just one item from Berger's list) might have originally been staged in its commentary notes to 3.1, and the introduction to the play mentions different interpretations of the siege by actors such as Charles Kean, F. R. Benson, and Lewis Waller. Why cannot the work of editors—whose fingerprints, one must assume, are all over the texts that Berger wants to read closely—be utilized to enhance "stage-centered" readings? This is a question that Berger, uninterested in "the psychological constraints that playgoing imposes on interpretation" (xiii), does not entertain, but it is to this question and its implications that the remainder of this chapter now turns. How might the textual mechanisms of the edition help to power the engines of imaginative engagement? In my mind, a richer version of what Berger terms "stage-centered" reading can be realized by including in one's scope the various forms of performance data that editors seek to explain, highlight, and in some instances, supply. To only imagine moments of audition leaves large gaps in the virtual playgoing experience, and filling these gaps facilitates a more complete assessment of how one can read drama and remain attuned to the possibilities of performance.

Texts and Paratexts

In assessing the state of late twentieth-century editorial practice, Marvin Spevack writes that "when all is said and done," editions of Shakespeare since the early twentieth century "are, in their core substance interchangeable" (79), adding that "as far as substantial verbal changes are concerned the text of Shakespeare is for all intents and purposes fixed" (80). Spevack is erring on the side of hyperbole here, but if we accept his basic point—that from a macroscopic perspective there is little variation in the "core substance," or dialogue, of critical editions of the same play—then it follows that substantial distinctions between critical editions exist primarily in the interstitial matter of the playtext, in the editor's manipulations of acts and scenes, speech prefixes, and stage directions. In many ways, these interstitial markers—what R. B. McKerrow refers to as a dramatic text's "accessories" (19)—are where the line between the authorial and the social begins to blur, where the playwright's authority is willingly dissipated amongst those involved in utilizing the text in performance, where Poem and Play shade into one another.

Scholars have situated a text's "core substance" and its "accessories" in a number of ultimately analogous binaries. Gary Taylor writes of Shakespeare's dramatic works as having a "written text... depend[ent] upon an unwritten para-text which always accompanied it"; he also notes that this paratext—"an invisible life support system of stage directions"—tends to be missing from the earliest editions of a play, while "modern editions, more or less comprehensively, attempt to rectify the deficiency, by conjecturally writing for him the stage directions which Shakespeare himself assumed or spoke but never wrote" (*Companion* 2). Similarly, in *The Literary Work of Art*, Roman Ingarden makes a firm distinction between dialogue and stage directions in his discussion of dramatic works; Ingarden differentiates between "the 'side text' [*nebentext*] or stage directions—i.e., information with regard to where, at what time, etc., the given represented story takes place, who exactly is speaking, and perhaps also what he is doing at a given moment, etc.—and the main text [*haupttext*] itself" (208). Ingarden's *nebentext* appears more inclusive than Taylor's paratext, expanding as it does to include scene designations and speech prefixes; Taylor and Ingarden also diverge in that Ingarden's basis of differentiation is not what is left unwritten or incomplete by the playwright, but what is potentially spoken and unspoken in performance: "The main text of a stage play consists of the words spoken by represented persons, while the stage directions consist of information given by the author for the production of the work. When the work is performed on stage, the latter are totally eliminated; they perform their representing function and are really read only during the reading of the play" (377). Despite these differences, Taylor and Ingarden are essentially making the same distinction between a "core substance" and "accessories"; that Taylor moves forward from what the playwright did or did not supply for readers while Ingarden moves backward from what is and is not vocalized in a performance is a reminder that any such demarcation testifies to the often permeable and unfixed boundaries between page and stage.[10]

Taylor's text/paratext and Ingarden's *haupttext/nebentext* distinctions thus help to define an editor's mediatory position at a threshold of two types of textual information. Formulating a distinction between dialogue and ancillary, yet indispensable, directions for performance differentiates the editing of dramatic works from other forms of printed literature in that editors of drama engage—by necessity—with two arenas of signification: the literary and the theatrical. Theoretical discussions of editorial practice tend to gravitate to one extreme or the other (literary/textual/authorial or theatrical/performative/social); the act of editing, however, is a more pragmatic affair since editors must negotiate *both* modes of production. In a series of essays, Margaret Jane Kidnie has thoughtfully explored the ramifications of this bifold authority for both editors of critical editions and their readers. Kidnie points out that unlike the "ultimately ephemeral" staging choices made by directors, editorial decisions have a material resonance, since "the editor's staging choices, embedded in the script *as* text, impact on all subsequent literary interpretations and potentially even on those offered in performance" ("Text" 468). The materiality of editorial interpretations and emendations, while motivated by the desire to assist readers, can nevertheless be understood to cut in the opposite direction; adopting Ingarden's terminology, Kidnie explains what "embedded" interpretations can mean for the appearance of the text:

> ...any alteration an editor may choose to make to the staging of a script will inevitably embed critical interpretation in the dramatic text. In a modernized edition the dramatic text no longer consists of the unity of *haupttext* and *nebentext* but that of *haupttext*, *nebentext*, and editorial interpretation of the staging, with the last two elements frequently presented to the reader as the same thing. ("Text" 467)

Here then is one crucial point at which understandings of editorial practice diverge: to what extent are an editor's attempts to bridge "undeniable...gaps in the *nebentext* of an early modern script" understood to be productive, and to what extent are such interventions viewed as restricting a reader's own interpretation by, as Kidnie puts it, "subjectively imposing staging on a dramatic text" ("Text" 465, 468)? Kidnie believes that editors have become too complacent in their belief that "interventionist editing of staging [is] a means by which the reader gains a richer understanding of the play in performance"; she argues that because of the inertia of the status quo, modern critical editions "impos[e] on the script editorial staging premised either explicitly or implicitly on modern theater practice," and that rather than altering the text and subsequently misleading readers (especially "unspecialized" ones), editors of Shakespearean drama should instead seek a way to "acknowledge or embrace radical uncertainty, offering readers historicized understandings of both theatrical conventions and vagaries of performance with which to develop independent, even idiosyncratic interpretations of staging" ("Text" 465–6, 470).

Kidnie's interrogations of the issues at hand are extremely insightful, but here she treads a slippery slope. If an editor's ultimate goal should be the acknowledgement and perpetuation of "radical uncertainty," then one must wonder whether the production of a critical edition is the best way to promote such an understanding of early modern dramatic texts. Seeking to historicize and destabilize the text to such an extent verges into a grey area in which a socialized orientation implicitly begins to undermine editorial activity itself. It is telling that "asking readers to interact with the dramatic text as necessarily unfixed and unstable" means for Kidnie that "editors might resist modifying or supplementing extant stage directions altogether" (470). Indeed, it goes without saying that editing with an eye towards perpetuating an "indeterminate textual condition" (470) often means not editing at all (or at least not making the kinds of decisions traditionally associated with critical editions). The intractability of Kidnie's position (would not extant or facsimile editions be more accurate representations of a text's "radical uncertainty"?) is representative of the knife's edge on which editorial work must often balance: while working to bridge unavoidable "gaps in the *nebentext*," an editor simultaneously invites the reader to "interact" with the very ambiguities and instabilities that the bulk of editorial decisions are designed to smooth over. Or put another way, an editor inevitably constructs an interpreted version of a text, but this version should ideally be constructed in such a way that it does not preclude other, different interpretations.

Finding the means to address both the gaps that readers require to be filled for them and the gaps that they should fill (or at least confront) on their own in order to appreciate a playtext's ambiguity is no easy task—the very gaps that are identified as substantive and the ways in which they are subsequently dealt with will vary from play to play, and from editor to editor. To her credit, in a subsequent essay, "Staging Shakespeare's Drama in Print Editions," Kidnie has explored what an edition that more fully acknowledges or "embrace[s] radical uncertainty" might look like. She proposes an edited page that arranges its information in a much different way than what is typically found in modern critical editions (a primary network of dialogue and stage directions taking up most of the page, with sections of collation and commentary beneath it). Influenced by Umberto Eco's idea of the "open work," where the "blank space surrounding a word, typographical adjustments, and spatial composition in the page setting of the poetic text—all contribute to create a halo of indefiniteness and to make the text pregnant with infinite suggestive possibilities" (qtd. in "Staging" 158–9), Kidnie experiments with small sections of *Troilus and Cressida* and *Romeo and Juliet*, seeking a means to "transfer the interpretive activity from the editor to the reader" (165). She attempts to do so primarily through the use of *marginal* stage directions, a strategy conditioned by her belief that "scripts are not comparable to performance, nor can they encode it" (158). Rather than a continuous interlacing of dialogue and stage directions within her edited text, all stage directions in Kidnie's experimental pages are moved to a separate "box" running down the left-hand side of the dialogue—a move that Kidnie justifies by referring to a similar positioning in some surviving early modern manuscript plays and playbooks; the stage directions thus remain a conspicuous (perhaps *more* conspicuous) part of the printed page but are now apart from the bulk of the edited text.[11] Certain directions (especially entry or exit cues, to which Kidnie attaches arrows so as to highlight their fluidity) take on an indefinite, floating quality—this is deliberate on Kidnie's part, reflecting the fact that many directions are variable in performance, and might even take place over a span of spoken dialogue rather than *at* a specific moment (as they might appear to do when "fixed" in traditional critical editions).[12] The increased demands put on the reader to skip between the two boxes is likewise intentional: according to Kidnie, the reader is implicitly given "permission" to decide when to "dip into" or even ignore the stage directions, with any disruptions to the "smooth flow of the reading experience" intended to reflect the text's inherent instabilities (169). All in all, Kidnie believes that modifying the appearance of the edited page simultaneously recognizes textual uncertainties and allows for readers' interpretations to proliferate: "Instead of trying to fix (in both senses of the word) an unstable print document, this strategy builds into the spatial presentation of the page the textual indeterminacy typical of directions found in early modern printed and manuscript drama" (165).

Indeterminacy, indefiniteness, suggestive possibilities, ambiguity: these terms need not be understood as mutually exclusive from editorial labors that intervene in the playtext. Indeed, there is a paradoxical splinter nagging at Kidnie's efforts to transfer interpretive activity from editors to readers by way of conspicuous and influential forms of editorial mediation. It must be said of her compelling proposal that although Kidnie understands most critical editions to severely circumscribe readerly interpretations, designing a text to promote notions of instability and indeterminacy is just the flip side of the same coin: Kidnie's format might "demystif[y] the editorial function" (169), but her particular interpretation (of early modern dramatic texts, if not of the plays in question) is still encoded into the text itself—if Kidnie's text works as she intends, readers will understand playtexts to be indefinite, unstable objects (a revealing way to think about them, though only to a point). Kidnie's experimental pages remain a highly mediated way of encountering a play, they just emerge from the mediatory process looking different than the pages of standard critical editions. And while Kidnie is adamant that text and performance are fundamentally incongruous, that "performance is never contained within the script" ("Text" 458), her rethinking of the editorial treatment of stage directions is intended to bring the two modes of production into the closest proximity that the printed page will allow. She suggests, for example, that the left-hand box of stage directions can, at certain points, create "an impression of activity in the margin of the page" ("Staging" 169), and even more provocatively, that freeing stage directions from being "graphically fixed to a certain moment in the dialogue... creates as an effect in the print medium the sense one has when watching a theatrical performance of action occurring in space and time" (172). Live theater cannot be captured on the page (of this there can be no dispute), but the nature of Kidnie's proposed revisions to editorial practice speaks to editors' capacity (be it tapped or untapped) for keeping text and performance in meaningful contact with one another within the bounds of the printed page.

For my purposes, more important than debating the potential benefits of Kidnie's experimental pages is engaging with the issues and questions that her work brings to the fore. Kidnie's hypothesis and the reasons why we can even begin to entertain its usefulness are founded on certain assumptions about how editors' mediations of text and performance are largely determined by the ways they choose to select, organize, and transmit certain kinds of information to readers. Following Jerome McGann, Kidnie notes that "the visual design of a page encodes information in a manner quite apart from the linguistic meaning of the words printed on that page, or to put that yet a different way, readers construct meaning, not just by *reading* a page, but by *looking at* a page" (169). That Kidnie's manipulation of "the spatial presentation of the page" (165) might have major ramifications for a reader's interpretation of both text and performance—producing what she terms "*textual performance[s]*" (172, emphasis in original)—suggests that the scheme that editors follow for constructing the space of their page (and I would add, the space of their edition) is an integral factor in any inquiry into the treatment of text and performance in editorial practice. What merits consideration is not just the design and appearance of the edited page but also the basic elements selected to put it together, the information an editor deems necessary to provide. Editorial interpretations and interventions do not necessarily preclude or limit the interpretive possibilities of readers—Kidnie's proposal is itself implicitly founded on this assumption. As an alternative to figuring the relationship of editors and readers in terms of the "transferring" of interpretative authority (which connotes exclusivity and polarization), it is possible (and perhaps more accurate) to recognize an ongoing negotiation between editors and readers. A commentary note introducing or dismissing certain staging possibilities can, I would argue, produce or encourage a specific kind of textual performance, as might a collation that includes notable decisions made in other editions, or a marginal invitation to consider prefatory material related to a play's performance history. These are just some of the ways, in addition to Kidnie's suggestions, that a critical edition is able to facilitate a reader's ability to span the gap between the printed text and its transformations in, and by, the theater. In the final portion of this chapter, I will introduce a concept intended to help fill this gap as it exists in the critical vocabulary used to discuss text and performance in studies of editorial practice. That concept is *performancescape*.

Performancescape: Navigating Pages, Imagining Stages

My goal in implementing *performancescape* is to shift the discussion away from the incongruities of text and performance to focus instead on the symbiotic exchange between the two modes, as well as the ways this exchange can be structured in print. My development of the term is indebted to Kidnie's description of how readers can process the heterogeneity of text and performance:

> ...in a dramatic text (the play as literature) the stage directions interact with the dialogue to create not the image of a real or potential performance but a sort of *virtual* performance, a theater of the mind. What the dramatic text can therefore provide us with is an ideal performance as imagined by the author and shaped by the dominant theatrical conventions of the historical and cultural moment of the play's creation as literature. ("Text" 464–5)

I want to modify this claim by utilizing *performancescape* to consider the critical edition more broadly. While Kidnie's understanding of "*virtual* performance" or "theater of the mind" is restricted to the interactions of dialogue and stage directions (as is Berger's "stage-centered reading"), to base such terminology on only the edited copy-text portion of critical editions reflects a somewhat narrow view of what these editions actually encompass. With new editions of Shakespeare's plays growing in size, the edited text in question usually occupies only a fraction of an edition's total page count (and often only fractions of *those* pages, given that more detailed collations and notes are perpetually expanding from the margins). What Kidnie calls a "*virtual* performance" can potentially be shaped by more than just the interaction of dialogue and stage directions: an edition's prefatory material, commentary notes, appendices, illustrations or photographs—all of the performance-related information that is collected and organized in fashioning the book of the play—are meaningful sites of interaction between text and performance. Ancillary information provided to readers is not a part of the playtext, but is often bound to it so firmly as to imply that a reader's navigation of the playtext is dependent on it.

Performancescape can best be defined as a property of dramatic texts that is activated as a reader negotiates between the text proper and various forms of textual mediation: as dialogue, stage directions, and supplementary information intermingle, a virtual performance (or a variety of potential virtual performances) begins to take shape. I must stress that the term is not a solution to a particular problem—it does not simplify or solve the intractable challenges of reading printed drama; rather, the term is meant as a conceptual tool for articulating and thinking through the interpretive demands—and opportunities— that printed plays pose to readers. A *specific* performance cannot be extracted from the raw material of the text (just as a representation of a cityscape cannot reproduce or recapture in full the multiple layers of detail and information that exist when one actually experiences a city by moving through it), but *performancescape* focalizes the ways that a text can begin to represent performance *potentialities*, to give relative shape and stability to what is dynamic and multifarious. *Performancescape* is meant to point in two directions at once: it refers to an imagined performance of a textual moment or moments (the virtual "scape" of the imagined scene), as well as the attempts to represent and communicate that virtual performance via the strategic arrangement of information within the edition itself (the "scape" of the page); once embedded in a text, a *performancescape* functions as an invitation for readers to share (and perhaps subsequently modify or discount) an interpretation of the moment as it has been, or might be, performed. The term's value is that it offers a flexible model for discussing the interactions between editors, dramatic texts, and readers; that is, *performancescape* can be deployed to recognize the ongoing negotiation between *mise en scène* and *mise en page*, a recognition that does not come as readily from phrases such as "virtual performance" or "imagined performance."

On the surface my interest in how information is arranged on a page, and distributed amongst pages, appears materialist in nature, but I would stress here that printed editions and how they are constructed and interpreted must be understood to be more than just derivations of the materiality of the page. Hardline materialist approaches to bibliography that claim to move "outside metaphysics" by proposing that texts can be conceived of as having a purely material existence—"in the materials of the physical book itself: in *paper*" (de Grazia and Stallybrass 280)—often fail to attend to *how texts get used*, that is, to the activity of reading, which, as David Schalkwyk reminds us, is "a fundamentally *meta*physical problem, one that cannot be confined to physics" (221). Or, as Zachary Lesser puts it, "part of what makes a history of reading so difficult to write is that reading occurs at the intersection of the material and the immaterial, the physical and the psychical, the letter and the spirit" ("Typographic" 99). Issues of materiality will be salient to a thoughtful consideration of the history of the Shakespearean text, but what must also be taken into account are the uses to which the text can be put, the intentions and interpretations of those individuals shaping critical editions and the inevitability of their confrontation with the intentions of an originary author. Part of the appeal of *performancescape* is that in gesturing toward both the *scape* of the printed page and the *scape* of the imagined scene, the term registers the usefulness and the limitations of materialist analysis—keeping both kinds of *scapes* in play recognizes that editorial activity engages the material and the ideal, the tangible document and the intangible work. To focus exclusively on literary works as they exist "in their concrete embodiments" (Marcus 33) is the privilege of the textual theorist, but not of the editor producing a critical edition; acts of imagination are inherent to the editing of literary works and by extension, to the construction of edited texts. It is difficult to theorize away the fact that when it comes to emending an ambiguous or even a clearly corrupted textual moment, an editor must often *imagine* a version of the text that is uncorrupted and unambiguous, and it is quite possible that this imagined, corrected version never had a material existence at all. As Anthony Dawson makes clear in a discussion of New Bibliographical practices, "disciplined form[s] of imaginative reconstruction" are not incompatible with an "extremely careful analysis of material facts," and further, such imaginative reconstructions represent "*historical* endeavour[s]" that must not be dismissed out of hand as "fanciful or irrational" ("Imaginary" 141, emphasis in original).

Performancescape is thus a concept that attempts to engage with the immaterial via the material text, with the aims of reconstruction shifting from authorial intentions and lost manuscripts to what for readers is the absent play-as-performed. Recourse to the imagination is hardly the height of critical fashion (a point that teases at the early modern currency of "scape" as a thoughtless transgression, [*OED n¹ 2*]), but embracing the role that this faculty plays in editorial activity helps to avoid succumbing to the impulses that might formulate page and stage as mutually exclusive. Any conceptualization of the links between the two modes of production, it seems to me, must allow for an imaginative element. The longstanding "zombie-theory of drama" (Worthen, *Print* 8) in which performance is understood to be absolutely derivative of the text, a mere realization of the text's instructions, implicitly involves some sort of animating, interpretive force to awaken that which lays dormant on the page. More recent, nuanced treatments of the two modes of production that have rightly supplanted this "zombie-theory" must likewise account for the interpretive activity that facilitates the transition from text to performance: Worthen writes, for example, of "the theatre necessarily subject[ing] print to use, to labor, in ways that render it not the container of meaning, but raw material for new meanings" (*Force* 56)—" labor" (which is understood to entail "interpretive and behavioral practices" (55)) becomes the term utilized by Worthen to fill the conceptual and rhetorical gaps between text and performance. A sharper sense of what Worthen might mean by "labor" appears in a recent essay in which he describes "theatrical practice [as] consist[ing] of using writing to make an event that reframes verbal signification in the embodied, kinesthetic means of nonverbal action" ("Intoxicating" 313). If the dynamics of the stage are not contained within the text but are a product of nontextual labors, it does not necessarily follow that an edition's *performancescapes* lack validity or usefulness, even though these approximations of performance will always be fragmentary, incomplete, and heavily reliant on the imagination. To edit is, at a fundamental level, to recognize that readers require certain levels of mediation. Ideally, when it comes to giving readers a sense of how a play might function on stage, editors will not abandon readers in the face of obscurity, but provide the means to help bridge interpretive gaps by giving them a sense of the variability of performance. This is not to say that readers are free from analytical responsibility or that they must slavishly adhere to, or agree with, every emendation or piece of supplemental information that an editor supplies. I am advocating an approach to reading drama in which readers are attentive to the ways in which theatrical events can be linked to, and yet are not determined by, the printed playtext. Decisions made by editors frequently transform the shape of the playtext, but these editorial interventions are an important means for stabilizing and stimulating readerly participation; as Worthen makes clear with persuasive force, the relationship of text and performance is far from simple, far from deterministic, and the shared participatory inputs of editors and readers can be a means by which the complexity of the relationship comes into focus.

The reader's position in the mediatory processes that *performancescape* is meant to explicate is rooted in the term itself, which can be read *performance-scape* or *performance-escape* (with the central *"e"* doing double-duty, ending one word and beginning the next).[13] Emphasizing the *"scape"* invokes the material and virtual aspects detailed above. Alternatively, emphasizing the embedded *"escape"* functions in two ways: first, as an imaginative effort to "escape" the page and imaginatively approximate performance. Such an escape is always partial and temporary, just as an awareness of the *"escape"* in the term itself cannot permanently break from the fixity of print, the *"performanc(e)"* that precedes it. Second, the embedded *"escape"* is meant to imply that an edition's *performancescape* is something that some readers will be able to resist or "escape" from. Even *performancescapes* that appear prescriptive are not necessarily so, since a reader might very well be able to imagine an alternative virtual performance that runs counter to an edition's *performancescape*; moreover, a reader can simply (or perhaps not so simply) ignore the supplementary matter provided by an editor. The potential to read the term two ways nicely encapsulates certain tensions between orality and literacy that contribute to the fundamental rift between performance and text. Walter Ong explains: "Sound . . . exists only when it is going out of existence. I cannot have all of a word present at once: when I say 'existence', by the time I get to the '-tence', the 'exis-' is gone. The alphabet implies that matters are otherwise, that a word is a thing, not an event, that it is present all at once, and that it can be cut up into little pieces . . ." (91). Similarly, to give voice to *performancescape* is to recognize the ephemerality of dialogue uttered on stage and of performance in general—I must pronounce *"performance-scape"* or *"performance-escape,"* but cannot pronounce both terms at once; however, to print and read the term is to recognize the paradoxical fixity that print assigns—paradoxical in the sense that this ostensible fixity carries with it an awareness of how a printed word (and by extension, text) can be altered or "cut up." Ong argues that writing can produce "exquisite structures and references [that] far surpass the potentials of oral utterance" (85), a point that has major ramifications for those attempting to measure the text/performance divide. How to treat the multiplicity of meanings inherent in printed texts is a function of one's critical orientation: Berger, for example, incorporates "the range of alternate and potentially stageable interpretations inscribed in the playtext" (14) into an argument that ultimately champions the primacy of the printed play over the play as performed; conversely, for Philip McGuire, performance becomes the primary mode of realizing a play since at key moments performance limits a playtext's pervasive ambiguity: "only during a performance of the play," writes McGuire, do "sets of meanings and effects... take on specific shape and coherence" (122).

Regardless of whether it is fashioned as an interpretive limitation or benefit, the inevitability of a performance's foreclosure of certain textual ambiguities speaks to a crucial distinction between a reader's and an audience member's reception of a play. Relative to a playgoer, a reader assumes a greater interpretive responsibility but also faces a lack of interpretive urgency, and, as Taylor points out, unlike those seeing a play performed, a reader "can govern the speed and direction of his reading, as an auditor cannot; he has time to puzzle out the lines, time to attempt to relate them" (*Moment* 202).[14] A reader's freedom to set some of the basic terms of engagement with a play (tempo of reading, length of time spent reading, direction of movement within the playtext) is another reminder of just how dissimilar the activities of reading and seeing a play can be. Berger emphasizes this incongruity in his description of "decelerated microanalysis," an interpretive tool exclusive to readers that "enlarges and emblematically fixes features not discernible in the normal rhythm of communication" (148). Put more simply, Berger places special emphasis on a reader's ability to "decelerate" and "reaccelerate" his or her reading of a text, temporarily "holding it still in order to tease out its meanings" (143). That a reader must continually decelerate and reaccelerate a reading in order to fully explore and appreciate a text's potential meanings is, for Berger, suggestive of both the richness of literary engagements with a play and the interpretive limitations facing playgoers: on the one hand, Berger argues that playgoers receive more information than they can process efficiently or sufficiently, while readers, on the other hand, possess the luxury of processing information at a rate they find suitable, slowing down over passages they find particularly difficult or significant, likely even rereading them. I believe this observation can be extended: what Berger does not explore is a reader's ability to determine the *amount* and *type* of ancillary information brought to bear on an engagement with a critically edited play. Readers can slow down, speed up, pause, stop, and restart, but they can also read in a variety of nonlinear directions (as Berger's frequent juxtapositions of passages from *Richard II* attest). I would put forth that readers of critical editions are often decelerating, pausing, or stopping their reading of a playtext in order to look up information located elsewhere on the page or within the edition—notes, appendices, glossaries, dictionaries, illustrations, photographs, references to other plays and works of criticism are all forms of interpreted data that hold the potential to help one "tease out" a text's meanings. The imposing bulk of modern critical editions of Shakespeare is due, at least in part, to the assumption that readers might find it helpful to stop reading the playtext, gain information from elsewhere, and start reading again.

In *The Textual Condition*, McGann refers to this process as "radial reading" (119), and he cites the critical edition as the most striking example of a text that encourages constant participation on the part of readers: "one moves around the edition, jumping from the reading text to the apparatus, perhaps from one of these to the notes or to an appendix, perhaps then back to some part of the front matter which may be relevant, and so forth" (120). McGann argues that by continually directing readers to other acts of reading within and external to itself, the edition accrues a complexity that "allows one to imagine many possible states of the text" (121); I would add that in the case of critical editions of dramatic texts, one such altered state that is imaginatively available is the text as utilized in, and for, performance. Rather than considering a reader's decelerations, reaccelerations, and changes of direction as qualities that make the reception of texts and performances fundamentally incongruous, I propose that these interpretive tools— which are always available—afford readers the opportunity to imaginatively approximate performance to the fullest extent that printed texts can allow. My proposal involves an underlying irony: it seems likely that the harder editions work to address the potential significations of the play in performance, the more explicitly one will be reminded of just how *unlike* the act of reading and the experience in a theater are. Digressing through other portions of a critical edition essentially highlights the static nature of the play in print-form, since for as long as it takes a reader to navigate a tangential move away from the playtext, the printed play is paused, patiently waiting for reengagement in a way that the play in performance never will. But, while the printed play is temporarily paused, reduced to mere marks on a page—while, in other words, it is at its most inert, *most textual*—a reader's negotiation of tangential information can result in a more nuanced understanding of the play as performed. The materiality of the *scape* of the page allows for a richer vision of the *scape* of the imagined scene. Since *performancescape* deals with a reader's movement from the immediacy of the text to abstract conceptualizations of performance, there is a danger of falling into the familiar trap of placing text and performance into a deterministic relationship; in light of this, I stress that the term is intended to complicate such a hierarchy. *Performancescape* describes a textual experience, but it is not meant to assert the primacy of textual meanings over those produced in the theater, an assertion that would only perpetuate the intractability of the text/performance divide. In fact, applying *performancescape* to the study of critical editions allows one to see that in negotiating an edition, readers can come to recognize that all of a play's performance potentialities are *not* located exclusively in the text, that meanings are produced in performance, and that these meanings and interpretations are constantly shifting. Editors of *Henry V*, for instance, can inform readers of productions that have glorified the English triumph as well as productions that have emphasized the horrors of war, just as editors of *Measure for Measure* can make clear that the treatment of Isabella's silence at the end of the fifth act can have a significant impact on understandings of her character and the play as a whole. No extant text of *Henry V* provides a macroscopic blueprint detailing how directors and actors should handle the issue of warfare, and on a smaller scale, the same can be said for *Measure for Measure* and how a production decides to treat Isabella's response to the Duke's proposal. In Worthen's words, "theatrical choices arise at the intersection between the text and the formal strategies of its meaningful production as theater" (*Authority* 175); my intention with *performancescape* is to enhance awareness of such "intersections" and to foster alertness to the fact that editions, past and present, direct readers toward performance options—some of which are relatively obvious and grounded in the text, some decidedly less so. A production of *A Midsummer Night's Dream*, for instance, might involve Hippolyta responding to Theseus's "Now, fair Hippolyta, our nuptial hour / Draws on apace..." (1.1.1–2) speech with genuine affection, or with acerbity and derision, or maybe even boredom. In his Oxford edition of the play, Peter Holland's first commentary note on this speech references a production for the San Francisco Actors' Workshop in 1966 where Hippolyta was "brought on as a captive animal wearing black body makeup and a leopard-skin bikini in a bamboo cage, her lines snarled with biting sarcasm"; Holland goes on to note that "in the Reinhardt-Dieterle film (1935), which opened with a grand triumphal procession for Theseus and his army, Hippolyta was later seen isolated and moody, turning their dialogue into a private scene, rather than the public, court occasion that QF suggest" (131). This confluence of playtext and mediation—this *performancescape*—can spark a reader's awareness of potential fluidity in the significations of Theseus and Hippolyta's exchange, and thus demonstrate the ways in which page and stage intersect—in the full sense of the word as both meet *and* diverge.

I realize that I am setting up *performancescape* to bear a sizable interpretive weight, but I am confident this burden is preferable to the void posed by the lack of alternative terminology able to straddle textual and theatrical modes of production. While the term's adaptability will be fully conveyed in the chapters that follow, for now, I will provide a brief example of the manner in which it can be deployed in relation to a recent edition of *Othello*, a play that poses a multitude of textual problems for any editor. Specifically, I would like to look at the opening stage direction of the play's final scene in Michael Neill's Oxford edition (2006). The initial stage direction of 5.2 is just one of a legion of differences between the 1622 Quarto (Q) and the 1623 Folio (F) versions of the play: Q prints the direction, "*Enter* Othello *with a light*," while F prints "*Enter Othello, and Desdemona in her bed.*" Understandably, Neill conflates the two, yielding a direction that reads "*Enter Othello with a light, and Desdemona in her bed asleep.*"[15] The variant stage directions can be reconstructed by way of reference to Neill's collation, which prints both readings in full at an interstitial position on the page, beneath the edited playtext and above twin columns of commentary. Neill's commentary note on the stage direction shuttles readers to opposite ends of his edition "for a discussion of the staging": forwards, to an appendix of Longer Notes, and backwards to a small portion of his introduction. Flipping to the Longer Note reveals three hypotheses as to the handling of the bed in the play's original staging: either the bed was "discovered" by way of drawing a curtain to the discovery space of the tiring-house, or it was placed within a curtained structure that was brought on stage, or it was "'put forth' on to the stage through one of the tiring-house doors" (467). Neill does not completely discount any of these possibilities, although he has reservations about the feasibility of bringing a special structure onstage, believing that this would "interfer[e] with the sightlines of a significant portion of the audience in the galleries" (467). The section from the introduction discusses the immense signifying power the bed would have had as a theatrical property; in early modern culture, writes Neill, the bed was "almost oppressively over-determined in its public and private meanings," "the site of both the beginning and end of life," and central to "nuptial consummation and perpetuation of the lineage" (173). Neill stresses that within the world of the play, "the final spectacle of three corpses lying side by side on the same bed" is an "atrocious parody" that capitalizes "on the intimate association of sexuality and death" (173); he goes on to discuss the fatal irony of Desdemona's attempts at "a symbolic reaffirmation of their marriage bond" (173) by providing Emilia with the two-pronged instruction to "Lay on my bed my wedding sheets" (4.2.105) and "If I do die before thee, prithee shroud me / In one of these same sheets" (4.3.22–3). It is possible, then, that a reader moves from the opening stage direction of 5.2 to the collation (where it can be discerned that Neill is conflating what is found in Q and F), to the commentary notes (where he or she is invited to read elsewhere), to the Longer Notes, and back to the introduction, all before the scene itself "starts." During this tangential escape from the playtext, the reader negotiates three different kinds of information on a single page before delving into other sections of the edition distinct from the edited play itself, all the while gaining snippets of data that can potentially flesh out an imagined performance. Should the bed be an elaborate property (Neill draws comparisons to "ornate tester tombs, canopied beds of gilded marble") that recognizes the "almost totemic significance accorded to the marriage bed" (173) in its original context, or might a simplified version that in no way distracts from the interactions of Othello and Desdemona be preferable? Where should the bed be located on the stage? How might Desdemona—and later, the three corpses—be positioned on it? Should the bed realistically sit flat on the stage, or should it be angled in some way so that the audience can better view the bodies that end up there?

I am describing a complex network of textual circuitry—there is no guarantee that readers will make the same series of connections that I have outlined (or that they would be spurred to ask the same questions), and it is certainly true that a reader can navigate the edition in less complicated ways. But the point is that Neill's edition is hardwired to "fire" in this way if the reader makes certain connections; the edition, that is, carries with it enough information to enable readers to meaningfully consider the relationship between the printed play and the play as performed, and further, to contemplate the sort of interpretive work that needs to be done to fill the space between where the *mise en page* of the text leaves off and the *mise en scène* of performance begins.

If Neill's textual note goes unread and a reader thus does not pause his or her reading of the playtext, there are other kinds of recorded intersections between text and performance that are much harder to ignore. About halfway through Othello's "It is the cause" speech in the same scene, he speaks of having "plucked thy rose" and then says, "I'll smell thee on the tree" (13, 15). As Neill points out in his textual note, "smell thee" is "an implicit stage direction" that strongly implies Othello pauses to smell, and likely kiss, Desdemona (his next line begins, "O balmy breath...")... Even if a reader skims stage directions and ignores editorial commentary, textual moments that embed stage business in the primary text (and *Othello* is rife with "implicit" directions of this sort) reveal particularly permeable boundaries between page and stage. In the same note, Neill briefly locates the gesture in the play's performance history: "[John Philip] Kemble insisted that Othello must bend over Desdemona at this point...and, in a detail later imitated by Patrick Stewart, Olivier deliberately anticipated the gesture when he made his first entry inhaling the fragrance of a red rose" (373). The note provides the most fragmentary of glimpses as to how the moment might be performed, raising more questions than it answers—as the actor playing Othello leans over Desdemona, how long does he linger? In what manner does he smell her? And if he does kiss her at this point, what is the nature of that kiss? No edition could possibly answer all of these questions and the countless others that one can think of, but what is worth pointing out is that the playtext and editorial note combine to encode certain performance potentialities—the act of leaning, of smelling, and (perhaps) kissing. Especially keen or curious readers might push even further, choosing to take advantage of the stasis that the printed play will so readily assume by decelerating their reading and changing direction to return to Neill's extensive discussion of Olivier's performance in the edition's introduction. There they will find a photograph of Olivier's lithe, angular Moor—a "combination of aristocratic swagger and savage otherness," (88) writes Neill—as well as an extensive examination of the controversy raised by Olivier's "stereotypical exaggeration" of "blackness" (59). The nature of tangential moves away from the playtext on the part of a reader is what *performancescape* is meant to account for: to recognize that a critical edition contains a breadth of interpretive resources devoted to the play as performed and that these resources can come to inform a textual engagement with the play. Text and performance represent distinct modes of realizing a play—I am not disputing this—but the overall incommensurability of the two modes must not obscure instances of symbiotic exchange. Moreover, Neill's interpretive hand dictates and shapes the pathways available for readers to explore, and yet the reader's willingness to actively negotiate these pathways can result in the proliferation of possibilities and meanings;

to trace the *performancescapes* in his edition is to encounter a subjective imposition as well as indeterminacy, indefiniteness, suggestive possibilities, ambiguity.

Neill's edition of *Othello* is a decidedly modern example of a printed Shakespearean play that has the weight of hundreds of years of editorial practice and performance history behind it; accordingly, Neill has recourse to an assortment of apparatuses that those originally printing Shakespeare's plays did not: a critical introduction, photographs, commentary notes, appendices, etc. Nevertheless, early modern playtexts also grappled with what was the burgeoning dual existence of plays on the page and on the stage—albeit for different reasons, and by resorting to different kinds of printed codes. The next chapter returns to these early texts and the admittedly more difficult task of locating their intersections with performance.

CHAPTER 2

Text and Performance on the Early Modern Page

Having offered some preliminary suggestions as to the potential usefulness of *performancescape*, I must now confront its interpretive limitations, which become apparent when the term is applied to plays as they were printed in the early modern period. Given that *performancescape* is meant to help triangulate the dynamic relationship between editors, printed texts, and readers, early modern methods of textual production, printing practices, and modes of reception introduce a number of complicating factors that restrict the term's scope and limit its utility. Editing—as we think of the task today—can only be applied anachronistically to the early modern publishing trade; this is not to say that texts printed during this time went unmediated, only that the types of mediation that took place were not discrete activities systematically aimed at emendation, organization, or elucidation. That mediation took place is undeniable; indeed, the understanding that mediation *always* takes place—that *all* texts are mediated texts, or as Alan Farmer writes, "those who participate in the production and transmission of a text inevitably affect its final form" (164)—is beyond dispute. In the case of drama, the forces brought to bear on the transformation of written manuscripts into printed books are well documented. Scribal and compositor studies initiated by the New Bibliographers have demonstrated the ways in which a range of individuals could modify—perhaps emend, perhaps corrupt—texts in various ways, though it is only in rare instances that these modifications can be considered to have been executed with the same rigor or motivated by the same concerns that we now associate with editorial activity.[1]

Recent studies have expanded this sphere of influence, establishing that the efforts of publishers, printers, and certain playwrights to identify, construct, and market to specific readerships had a significant impact on the material shape of printed plays.[2] Extant claims of mediation are not uncommon; the difficulty lies in establishing what pseudo-editorial methodologies—if any—might underlie these claims. John Heminge and Henry Condell refer to themselves as "Presenters" in the Folio's dedication, but beyond matters of manuscript collection and perhaps the organization of the Folio itself, their influence over the final form of the texts printed in 1623 is unknown. Although it seems fair to think of Heminge and Condell as Shakespeare's first "editors," this designation stems from their administrative, rather than emendatory, efforts: in their words, their task was to "gather his workes, and giue them [to] you."[3] Some have recently put forth that Heminge and Condell were not the first to systematically prepare Shakespeare's texts for printing but that the distinction belongs to the playwright himself; citing the 1598 quarto of *Love's Labour's Lost* that advertises a play "Newly corrected and augmented / By W. Shakespeare," Farmer suggests that "though he was not the first author to be identified on the title page of a play from the early modern professional theater, Shakespeare was the first editor to be named on one" (158). The line break between the claim and the attribution to Shakespeare, however, makes matters more ambiguous than Farmer's proposal allows, and as Sonia Massai has argued, "privileging authorial over non-authorial corrections, even though they cannot easily, if at all, be told apart, may misleadingly suggest that authors were the only agents responsible for, and willing to invest in, the perfection of dramatic copy for the press" ("Editorial Pledges" 105). Even titular assertions that ostensibly deny any mediating agent between the play as performed and the play newly printed—like the title page of Q1 *Richard II* (1597), which offers a text "*As it hath beene publikely acted by the right honourable the Lorde Chamberlaine his seruants*" (variations of this formulation abound on title pages from the period)—must nevertheless be understood to frame printed plays in meaningful ways for potential readers.

As for those readers, they are (in any historical period) notoriously difficult to identify; for this reason, their habits and expectations must be reconstructed in largely hypothetical, generalized ways. Reading, as Heidi Brayman Hackel reminds us, is a "historically invisible skill" that "survives in the historical record only when it is accompanied by writing" (" 'Great Variety' " 141). With Hackel's observation in mind, this chapter approaches early modern drama via its most conspicuous sites of interaction between those who produced printed plays and those buying and reading them: the various forms of preliminary and paratextual matter that adorned printed playtexts. These apparatuses can be probed for insights into topics ranging from stemmatics to the early modern book trade; I will consider them in a very specific light: rather than connecting prefatory material and other textual apparatuses like title pages and marginalia to issues of authorship, manuscript circulation, collaboration, or the complicated transmission processes from playhouse to printing house, I will examine instead their ability to construct, and engage with, the play as performed. Paratexts are, in this regard, especially rich in that they look both backward and forward along a spectrum of readership: they can be understood as material evidence of individual readings (a form of reading-captured-in-writing that Hackel refers to), and they can also be analyzed as efforts to promote and subsequently guide other future readings. Adopting Hackel's terminology, the question "What did readers do with their books?" is less my focus than is "What did books tell readers to do?" (*Reading* 9).

To be sure, in discussing things like title pages, epistles to readers, or dedications, I cannot claim that all readers would have understood them in the same way or prove that they would have worked on readers with as much of the efficaciousness that I might retrospectively assign to them; instead, what I will argue is that particular kinds of readings and imaginings were encouraged (with varying amounts of zeal) by the ancillaries that accompanied printed plays, often rooted in the laudatory language of advertisement. As Lesser astutely argues, for example, the well-known preface to the second issue of Q1 *Troilus and Cressida* (1609) from "A neuer writer, to an euer reader" is primarily thought of as a somewhat cryptic marketing campaign, but it is also "a *reading* of the play," a reading that "attempted to determine [how] customers would read it as well" (*Renaissance Drama* 2, 3, emphasis in original).[4] Lesser's impressive study reads paratexts in the context of publishing practice and the book trade. Reading paratextuals with an eye toward the play as performed brings different issues to the fore: if publishers of plays endeavored to "successfully predict and creat[e] the desires of early modern book-buyers" (Lesser, *Renaissance Drama* 35), what role did a play's performance history have in creating interest amongst potential consumers? More specifically, how was the absent play as performed meant to inform the reading experience? And how did printed plays ask readers to imagine the relationship between the page and the stage?

Shifting attention to paratextuals also necessitates a shift away from Shakespeare's extant texts to the texts of other prominent playwrights from the early modern period. Save for direct addresses in the *Troilus and Cressida* quarto, Q1 *Othello* (1622), and the Folio (1623), printed plays attributed to Shakespeare in the period have very little to say to their potential readers. The *Troilus* epistle is worth pausing over, however, since it can be understood to epitomize the complicated, even intractable, relation between text and performance in the period. As mentioned, the epistle only appears in the second issue of Q1, helping to tighten the Gordian knot of the play's printing history. The first, epistle-less issue of the quarto had boasted on its title page of being *"acted by the Kings Maiesties / seruants at the Globe,"* a claim removed from the revised issue. In place of acknowledging the play in performance, the second issue provides the briefest of plot summaries: *"Excellently expressing the beginning / of their loues, with the conceited wooing / of Pandarus Prince of Licia."* If this change to the title page is a subtle means of shifting authority away from the play as performed, the epistle—in which "the playtext is radically reauthorized, even isolated as precisely a *text*" (Weimann 69, emphasis in original)—makes the printed play's association with the theater devastatingly clear. *"Eternall reader,"* begins the epistle, *"you have heere a new play, neuer stal'd with the Stage, neuer clapper-clawed with the palmes of the vulger, and yet passing full of the palme comicall"* (¶2r). Accurately or not, the epistle denies that staged performances have left any residue on the book of the play—this is a newly printed play that has not been tainted by the stage, but instead passes directly (with the assistance of the publishers) from the playwright's creative parentage into the custody of discerning readers: *"it is a birth of your* [Shakespeare's] *braine, that neuer vndertooke anything comicall, vainely"* (¶2r).[5] In disavowing a performance history for *Troilus* and formulating print as the sole medium for experiencing the play, the epistle presents Q1 *Troilus* to potential buyers as a specialized commodity, one that they might have to *"scramble for"* later should they pass it up now, *"at the perrill of your pleasures loss"* (¶2v). Despite initially minimizing the relevance of performance, however, the epistle does gesture toward theatrical modes of realization. Through some extended punning, the writer of the epistle envisions a situation in which *"those grand censors"* that denigrate plays and theaters would

> *flock to them for the maine grace of their grauities: especially this authors Commedies that are so fram'd to the life that they serue for the most common Commentaries of all the actions of our liues, showing such a dexteritie*

and power of witte that the most displeased with Playes are pleasd with his Commedies. (¶2r)

That Shakespeare's *"dexteritie and power of witte"* are apprehensible in print is the epistle's larger point, but the reference to groups of people flocking together to take pleasure in actors portraying *"the actions of our liues"* serves as a reminder that playtexts hold the potential to be utilized and transformed by the various collaborative forces participating in the theatrical event—neither mode of producing the play exists in a complete vacuum, despite the epistle's explicit claims to the contrary. Indeed, that the epistle's writer has performance in mind when discussing Shakespeare's greatness is evidenced in the next paragraph with a nod to *"his representations"* (¶2r). The epistle does not suggest that the playtext is an encoded or memorialized record of an exchange system between "author's pen" and "actor's voice" (Weimann 9), but the affective possibilities of staged performance do nevertheless seem to bubble just below its surface.[6]

In the latter portion of the epistle, text and performance are again figured as mutually exclusive, this time as the ignorance of playgoers is conflated with the cloying sensorial experience of the theater: readers are asked to "[not] *like this the lesse, for not being sullied with the smoaky breath of the multitude; but thanke fortune for the scape it hath made amongst you"* (¶2v). I will seize on the deployment of *"scape"* here, which in the context of the epistle refers to an *"*(e)scape*"* into the relatively unpolluted medium of print, where readers can engage with Shakespeare's play in a purified form. The manner in which I am incorporating the term throughout this study allows *"scape"* to reverberate more extensively, in ways no doubt unintended by the epistle's writer, but that speak to the equivocal juxtapositioning of text and performance that permeates the epistle itself. The *"scape"* that the play makes, away from performance, into print and the hands of readers is made possible by the relative fixity of the printed page. The epistle insinuates that this escape into print—into the realms of typography, bibliography, and the entrepreneurial rhetoric of publication—marks the printed play as fundamentally different than the play as performed, and this is certainly true; for one thing, the play in print can be surrounded by discourses and narratives that have no direct counterpart in performance. The very existence of the epistle attests to the ability of paratexts to frame playtexts in particular ways, a point that the epistle's writer is cognizant of, since he hints that the preface could have contained *more* ancillary material than it already does: *"And had I time I would comment vpon* *it, though I know it needs not*" (¶2r). That the materiality of the page allows for the play to be reconfigured and interpreted in unique ways is also demonstrated in modern incarnations of the work, where editors of *Troilus* often produce a text that includes the epistle found only in the second issue of Q1, begin the play with the Prologue found only in the Folio, and mix Q and F readings throughout. But it is also true that the attempt to describe the two modes of realizing a play as mutually exclusive is undermined by the fact that the epistle, in importing references to the effects of performance in its efforts to promote the printed play, cannot completely deny the interconnectedness of page and stage. To push even further, "*the scape it hath made amongst you*" might also be read as a general affirmation of a reader's ability to synthesize playtexts and their paratexts and imaginatively engage with the absent play as performed. That is, the epistle (despite its claims to the contrary) relies on a reader's understanding that performance can powerfully represent "*the actions of our liues*"; the epistle does not involve a *performancescape* in the sense of inviting its readers to produce a virtual rendition of a particular moment from *Troilus*, but its use of "*scape*" highlights the text's connection to both printed and performed modes of representation. A broader conception of "*scape*" emphasizes the readerly navigation between the material and the immaterial, the printed text and the imagined realization of the potentialities encoded therein.

The *Troilus* epistle is thus representative of the issues at the heart of this chapter: the ways in which printed plays do and do not engage with their performance history, how they construct both reading and theater audiences, and their traces (or lack thereof) of encoded performance potentialities; it is especially tantalizing because no other Shakespearean text printed in his lifetime asks its readers to face such matters so directly. Works by playwrights such as Marlowe, Jonson, Webster, and those ascribed to the tandem of Beaumont and Fletcher are much more explicit in their paratextual attempts to fashion the reading of plays as an imaginative experience distinct from, yet somehow still related to, what could be apprehended in a theater; accordingly, these other playwrights and their printed playtexts will receive the bulk of my attention. As will become apparent, the disparate plays and paratextual materials that I survey transmit different and often contradictory messages to their readers. Such discordant transmissions can be attributed to an understanding that "author's pen" and "actor's voice," while indelibly linked, are nevertheless distinct—opinions diverge (then, as now) as to what precisely the two modes share, as well as what, exactly, one mode can offer that the other cannot. The arc that I trace in what follows, then, confirms that printed playtexts of the early modern period are perhaps best understood as a burgeoning site of exchange between two incongruent modes of dramatic production in the midst of learning to identify and understand their relation to each other. The argument in this chapter thus builds on Robert Weimann's and Douglas Bruster's description of "the joint transaction, the joint appeal of the two different media," and their cautioning that "it is helpful neither to overemphasize divisions and contestations of authority in the relations of these two media nor to postulate any given pattern of concurrence and complementarity between them" (1–2, 15). The imprints of performance on the early modern page are sometimes sharp, sometimes muddy, sometimes effaced, but cumulatively, these imprints mark printed plays as interpretive fields requiring multidirectional traversals on the part of readers who are explicitly and implicitly invited to imaginatively partake in both the printed text and the absent performance in order to produce knowledge and make meaning.

Printed Narratives of Performance

Henry Turner argues that due to certain bibliographic conventions—such as speech-prefixes, pagination, lineation, act and scene divisions, and distinctions between verse and prose—"the book makes the play thinkable in formal terms that are quite distinct from theatrical performance, where a different set of conventions, meaningful units, and interpretive responses are required" (18). Turner's point is an important one: to print a play is to allow that play to absorb certain bibliographic and typographic properties from print culture, and these properties can be construed as misrepresentative of the play's existence in the theater. To produce a book of a play is to implicitly and explicitly encode that play's identity in the language of print production and the literary;[7] for better or for worse, the printed play lends itself to considerations of authorial origins and intentions, to considerations of the work's stability and reproducibility. Furthermore, as discussed in chapter 1, it is the reader who sets crucial terms of engagement with the printed play, starting and stopping the reading process, proceeding in any number of directions, and juxtaposing otherwise disparate passages. As vital as Turner's point is, however, it is imperative that the inevitable distortions of the printed page are counterbalanced by another, equally important, observation: fundamentally, conventions of printed plays are reliant on readers' familiarity with how plays function on stage. In other words, while different interpretive responses are produced and required by printed and staged modes of production, these responses, while distinct, are not mutually exclusive; typographic representations or indicators of performance established themselves in the second half of the sixteenth century as theaters were institutionalized and writers and printers experimented with how printed drama could meaningfully distinguish itself from other genres. The typographic markers that ultimately proved most useful in conferring this distinction—speech-prefixes and stage directions clearly distinguished from spoken dialogue, act and scene divisions, unique prefatory or other ancillary matter that often utilized images and metaphors from the theater, and less frequently, lists of *dramatis personae*—were effective largely because they provided readers with the means to conceptualize the play as a performance. If the printed play inevitably directs the reader's gaze away from the stage, away from the nuances of a live, performed event, it does so in a Janus-faced manner, glancing back toward the stage at the same time.

The doubled gesture intrinsic to printed plays equipped with what we now think of as standardized conventions is brought into relief when one considers the material appearance of dramatic texts before the establishment of professional theaters. As Julie Stone Peters explains,

> throughout Europe in the first half of the sixteenth century, dramatic *mise en page* looked much like the *mise en page* of other kinds of works; only in the later sixteenth century did it develop conventions that reflected the drama's generic particularity. The majority of fifteenth- and early sixteenth-century dramatic texts (cheaply printed saints' plays, farces,...various kinds of dialogues...) long continued to be nearly identical to other kinds of works...with no *dramatis personae*, no distinctive generic identification, no mention of performance, and (most telling) narrative description rather than stage directions or conventionalized speech-prefixes. (23)

Generally speaking, the narrative descriptions that muddle printed drama's generic status and normalize its appearance become unnecessary as writers, printers, and readers slowly work out a system of encoding the relevant narrative and theatrical information in abbreviated forms.

For instance, the lack of an established method of encoding and a concomitant reliance on narrative conventions are evident throughout the 1528 printing of *Everyman*; the title page of the book of this play roughly outlines the events to follow, presenting itself as "a treatyse...in maner / of a morall playe." The prose description on the title page is funnel-shaped, seemingly aimed at directing the reader's eye toward the emblematic figures of Everyman and Death that dominate the lower two-thirds of the page; further, judging by the manner in which words on the title page are broken—"heuen sendeth dethe to so- / mon euery creature"—it appears that the integrity of the funnel shape was of greater importance than the clarity of the message.[8] A much longer, more detailed narrative summary, provided by a Messenger, begins the play in earnest: it ends, "Here shall you se how Felawshyp and Jolyte / Both Strengthe, Pleasure, and Beaute / Wyll fade from the as floure in Maye / For ye shall here how our heuen kynge / Calleth Everyman to a generall rekyenynge / Gyue audyence and here what he doth saye" (A2r). The emphasis on "giving audience" and on seeing and hearing—imperatives originally aimed at an audience present at a performance—are made conspicuous as soon as they are translated to print, becoming an implicit reminder to readers of the relative deficiency of sensory stimulation that will mark their engagement with the drama. One might be tempted to conjecture that the translation of the Messenger's speech to print implies a spurring of imagined approximations of performance on the part of readers—they should read with the aim of "giving audience" in their mind's eye; this is certainly possible, but the remainder of the printed version of the play, because it is so rooted in narrative and scribal customs, does little to enable the ability of readers to attempt such approximations to any great effect. Where the title page of *Everyman* utilizes the white space of the page for stylistic purposes, the printed text itself rarely uses white space to distinguish the drama as a unique printed genre inviting specialized interpretive procedures on the part of readers. Changes in speakers are indicated by paragraph markers that function in unison with marginal speech prefixes running down the right-hand side of recto pages and the left-hand side of verso pages; such a strategy becomes rather awkward on recto pages, as a reader's eyes must either read the dialogue from left to right and then associate the speech with a particular speaker, or the eyes must move to the right margin of the page to learn who is speaking before they move to the left margin to begin reading the speech in question. Following the Messenger's narrative summary, there immediately follows a centered direction, "God speketh," as well as a marginal speech prefix, "God." Although this "speketh" direction is not used consistently throughout *Everyman*, the redundancy it creates supports Peters's claim that "creators of the earliest printed playtexts felt required to explain that a character was about to speak . . . rather than (as in texts to which we are accustomed) simply offering an abbreviated version of the name of the character, typographically differentiated from the actual speech" (23). Early in the printed text there are centered directions that identify Death and Everyman and essentially mark their entrances, but after "Felawshyp speketh" (B1r), neither centered directions nor the "speketh" direction are used again—the other emblematic figures that pervade the drama simply appear unannounced on the printed page and start talking. The book's colophon asserts the work as being a "morall playe," but cumulatively, the typographic features of the book do not make the same insistence in material terms. With little white space and marginally differentiated speeches providing the illusion of one long, interrupted narrative, the book of *Everyman* looks unlike many popular plays printed later in the century.

I am using *Everyman* to sketch the pertinent background in broad strokes, though highlighting what appears to modern eyes as its inconsistent or incomplete representation of itself as a printed version of a work intended for performance is not the same as arguing that the interpretive responses produced by page and stage must be understood to function antagonistically or parasitically. It is more appropriate to think in terms of printed and performed modes of realization informing one another in dynamic ways, or, in Douglas Brooks's words, to consider that "various networks of engagement...both enabled and inhibited the materialization of plays as they passed from the stage to the page" (2). The first printed octavo edition of *Gorboduc* (O1, 1565) serves as a revealing example of the complexity of these "networks of engagement" as they existed in the middle of the sixteenth century.[9] The title page of the "Tragedie" crams information above and below the printer's centered emblem: the portion above the emblem establishes the relationship of the printed version of the play to the play as performed, while the details below the emblem pertain to the play's publishing history—its journey through the print shop and subsequent emergence into the book trade. Brooks comments on the significance of this presentation: "the '*dis*junction' of printers and playwrights is represented here spatially as a kind of balance of power by the emblem that separates the two activities that have converged to make the printed dramatic text possible. Nearly all extant dramas printed subsequently would follow this format on their title pages" (27). The title page thus spatially distinguishes between print and performance but suggests that the printed book of the play serves to bridge the gap between the two modes—a point reinforced by the mediating position of the printer's emblem. Both methods of realizing the play are acknowledged in some detail: the play occurred at a specific time and place—"in her hignes / court of Whitehall, the xviij day of January, / *Anno Domini*. 1561. By the Gentlemen / of Thynner Temple in London"—and now, since being

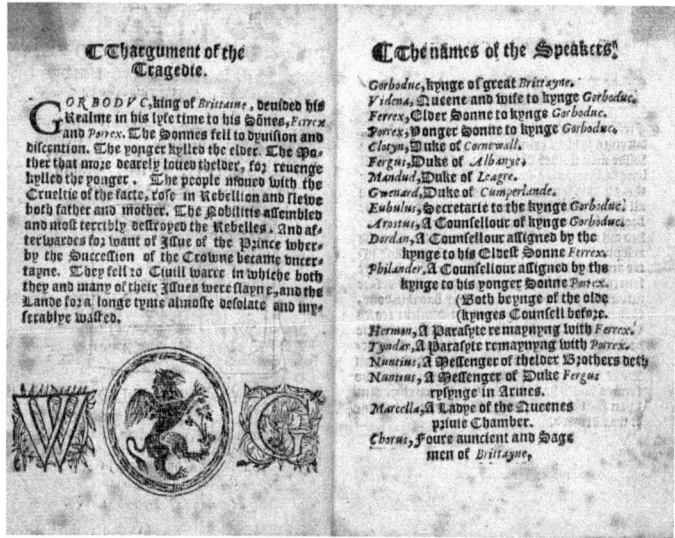

Figure 2.1 "Th[e] argument of the Tragedie" and "The names of the Speakers." Facing pages of O1 *Gorboduc* (1565). By permission of The Huntington Library, San Marino, California.]

"IMPRYNTED AT LONDON / in Fletestrete, at the Signe of the / Faucon by *William Griffith*," it exists in a more widely disseminated form. Significantly, however, the printed version locates its authority in its fidelity to the original performance: "Sett forthe as the same was shewed before the / QVENES most excellent Maiestie." Print and performance are linked, with the former implicitly figured as somehow able to record or recapture the latter.

The remainder of the *Gorboduc* octavo displays several salient features that enable us to measure the play's distance from earlier printed works like *Everyman*. Following the title page is a summary of the "argument of the Tragedie" situated opposite a comprehensive list of "The names of the Speakers" (see Figure 2.1). These para(llel)-texts look both backward and forward along the developmental lineage of printed plays: the detailed argument signals a lingering reliance on narrative traditions, while the list of speakers foreshadows the ways in which emergent printing conventions will eventually come to make narrative foregrounding and summary unnecessary. That is, the information abbreviated in the list of speakers renders the narrative substance of the "argument of the Tragedie" somewhat redundant: "The names of the Speakers," in addition to informing readers of key familial and political connections in the play, also hints at developments in the play's action. For example, Dordan and Philander—counsellors to Ferrex and Porrex, respectively—are parenthetically identified as "Both beynge of the olde kynges Counsell before"; Nuntius is described as "A Messenger of the [e]lder Brothers deth"; and a second envoy (also named Nuntius) is "A Messenger of Duke *Fergus* rysynge in Armes." Certain emblematic characterizations are also communicated: Hermon is "A Parasyte remaynyng with *Ferrex*," and Tyndar is likewise "A Parasyte" clinging to Porrex. Readers proceeding to the playtext from this list of speakers thus carry with them a proleptic awareness that informs and shapes their engagement with the play; crucially, this awareness of things to come marks the potential interpretive responses to the printed play as distinct from the play in performance, while at the same time infuses the act of reading with information intimately connected to the play as originally performed. For readers, the knowledge that Ferrex will eventually be killed might color some of his lines—such as his early boast that "My brothers pride shall hurt him selfe, not mee" (A4)—with shades of irony that were perhaps unavailable to an audience who presumably had no access to a printed *dramatis personae*; further, a reader's understanding of the parasitical natures of Hermon and Tyndar allows for a richer understanding of how these characters might have been played—information explicitly communicated through the actors' bodies and intonations, while not available to readers in the same way as it is for an audience, is nevertheless transformed and retransmitted, encouraging users of the book of the play to imagine characters in ways that will approximate their representations in performance.[10]

When it comes to the printed playtext of O1 *Gorboduc*, distinctions between speeches and speakers have become clearer, relative to what is exemplified in *Everyman*. There are no paragraph markers in the playtext (although the markers do linger in other places, preceding the opening argument as well as in the summaries of the dumb shows), and there are no marginal speech prefixes; instead, speech prefixes are centered, resulting in a more generous allotment of white space on the page. Even so, because *Gorboduc*, devoid of stage action, contains so many lengthy, moralistic speeches, some pages look very similar to *Everyman*—white space that is so conspicuous during exchanges of dialogue vanishes when characters wax moralistic and politic for pages at a time. In addition to the varying amounts of white space that by turns differentiates the printed drama as a distinct genre and confuses it with other narrative forms, there is another element that further complicates the intersections of text and performance in the first printed version of *Gorboduc*. Emblematic dumb shows introducing the play's thematic concerns precede each act, which the printed version of the play, true to its claim to "Sett forthe" the play as it "was shewed," describes in no small detail. The possibilities for typographically representing the performance of these dumb shows, however, are limited, since with no dialogue to record, the printed text is essentially rendered mute; the text's primary compensatory means of representing the dumb shows in print is to describe them, and these descriptions—indeed, the inevitability of them—paradoxically assert the very differences between page and stage that are ostensibly being minimized. As the printed play attempts to represent the figures and actions involved in the dumb shows, its only recourse is to deploy more detailed forms of narrative; here, for example, is its treatment of the first dumb show:

> Firste the Musicke of Violenze began to playe, durynge whiche came in upon the Stage sixe wilde men cloathed in leaues. Of whom the first bare in his necke a fogot of smal stickes, which thei all both seuerallie and togither assaied with all their strengthes to breake, but it could not be broken by them. At the length one of them plucked out one of the stickes and brake it: And the rest pluckinge oute all the other stickes one after an other did easelie breake, the same beynge seuered: which beyng conjoyned they had before attempted in vayne. After they had this done, they departed the Stage, and the Musicke ceased.[11]

In its ekphrastic digression, in trying to make readers "see" and understand the action of the dumb show, the book of the play must amplify the conspicuousness of its own textuality. Crucially, though, this heightening of the fundamental split between text and performance does not necessarily undermine the reader's ability to imaginatively negotiate the distance between the dumb shows as described in print and the dumb shows as potentially performed; the descriptions of the dumb shows are sufficiently detailed to facilitate a rough mental version of what they might have looked like (and to some degree, even sounded like). That this imagined version might be understood as impoverished relative to the sensory richness of performance does not undo its potency or importance for readers. As subsequent portions of this chapter will make clear, encouraging readers to think of reading plays as a kind of performance while also reminding them that reading is fundamentally *unlike* seeing a play becomes a distinguishing feature of paratexts towards the end of the sixteenth century.

Further, it is important to note that these kinds of descriptive excursions continue to pervade what we think of as modern editions of plays, although they are located in different, predominantly marginalized spaces on the page or within the book. Reliance on descriptions and narratives can also be located in those streams of performance criticism that proceed from a belief that textualizing a performance can make that performance meaningfully present for readers, and more importantly, open up that perpetually absent but imaginatively and memorially recaptured performance for critical analysis.[12] This is precisely what the descriptions of the dumb shows attempt to do for the readers of O1 *Gorboduc*, concluding as they do with what are in effect instances of performance criticism that carefully circumscribe the dumb shows' meanings; the first description ends as follows:

> Hereby was signified, that a state knit in vnytie doth continue stronge against all force. But beynge deuyded, is easely destroied. As befell vpon Duke *Gorboduc* deuidinge his Lande to his two sonnes which he before held in Monarchie. And vpon the discention of the Brethrene to whome it was deuided.

In this way, the conspicuous deficiencies of attempting to "Sett forthe" in print the play as it "was shewed" are partially recuperated as the ineluctable textuality of the book of the play becomes a means of representational potency and a vehicle for interpretive insight. The printed play's unavoidable recourse to mere words upon words when accounting for performance is at once its most glaring weakness and its greatest strength, yielding unique readerly information to compensate for performative data that remains both irrecoverable and of a different order.

Of course, since *Gorboduc* was designed for private performance during the Christmas and New Year revels of 1561–2 (first at the Inner Temple, and then later before the Queen at Whitehall), few potential readers would likely have been familiar with the play as performed. With the rise of the public theaters towards the end of the sixteenth century, however, those purchasing printed plays might very likely possess memories of specific performances, leading to the interconnectedness of textual and performed modes of dramatic production gaining further layers of complexity. Peters suggests that "by the later sixteenth century...[printing] conventions had begun to harden" and "printers seem to have come to rely on a readership familiar with both the theater and the typographic conventions of the drama" (24). Indeed, as Mark Bland has argued, it seems probable "that the opening of the Rose Theatre in 1587 and subsequently the Swan implicitly brought with

them a greater potential demand for printed playbooks, both as literature and as records of performance" ("Appearance" 106).

Few plays at the Rose were evidently as memorable as Marlowe's two-
part *Tamburlaine*, which was first performed perhaps as early as 1587[13]
and frequently revived during the 1590s. The play's popularity with
readers mirrors its success on the stage: after its initial publication in
a black-letter octavo in 1590, the two plays were reprinted (in various forms) in 1593, 1597, and 1605–6, an impressive feat, considering
Blayney's calculation that "fewer than 21 percent of the plays published
[between 1583 and 1642] reached a second edition inside nine years"
(389).[14] On stage and in print, Marlowe's *Tamburlaine* was a revelation, a commanding presence possessing a seemingly limitless rhetorical
power unique to English drama; the character's potential for provoking
wonder in both mediums was recognized by O1's printer and publisher,
Richard Jones.[15] Jones's epistle "To the Gentleman Readers" is a concise, though calculated effort to straddle page and stage, positing the
printed *Tamburlaine* as able to retain the vitality so essential to the
play's success at the Rose, while also explicitly distinguishing the play
as printed from the play as performed. The epistle is regularly touted as
being instrumental in assigning drama a literary authority that it had
previously lacked, thus helping to create a rift between page and stage
that would only become more pronounced in the seventeenth century.
Kirk Melnikoff has recently challenged this claim, believing that Jones
was not a "literary pioneer," but was instead "very likely fashioning
his *Tamburlaine* for the established print market of collected poetry
and chivalric literature—a market that he had done much to shape"
(209). Melnikoff's contextualization of *Tamburlaine* within Jones's
larger publishing career provides an important corrective for how to
read the epistle, but it goes too far in discounting Jones's campaign to
position the printed play in relation to how its potential readers might
have remembered it in performance. While Jones might not be attempting to put forth the play as what Melnikoff calls "dramatic literature"
(209), he does, in my view, fashion the reading of *Tamburlaine* as an
experience that, while distinct from the play's theatrical existence, is
fundamentally linked to it.

Jones's target market for "the two tragical Discourses of the Scythian
Shepherd" includes those familiar with the play in performance: "My
hope is that they wil be now no lesse acceptable vnto you to read after
your serious affaires and studies, then they haue bene (lately) delightfull
for many of you to see, when the same were shewed in London vpon
stages" (A2r). In tapping into the memories of *Tamburlaine*'s popularity

in performance, Jones claims to be putting forth a play that is both like and unlike the one theater audiences have come to know. In one sense, what is being presented is "the same" as what was "shewed" to London's theatergoers; at the same time, however, Jones is candid about the fact that the printed play represents a distinct mode of representation, the content of which he has deliberately altered in order to distinguish it from its performative iterations:

> I haue (purposely) omitted and left out some fond and friuolous Iestures, digressing (and in my poore opinion) far vnmeet for the matter, which I thought, might seeme more tedious vnto the wise, than any way els to be regarded, though (happly) they haue bene of some vaine co[n]ceited fondlings greatly gaped at, what times they were shewed vpon the stage in their graced deformities. (A2r)[16]

Significantly, then, Jones's epistle is an admission of editorial activity: he is presenting a text he claims to have improved over the version of the play that was performed on stage. What, if anything, Jones excised from *Tamburlaine* cannot be determined; it is equally unclear whether the "fond and friuoulous Iestures" in question were authorial in nature or the result of actors' interpolations that were absorbed into a theatrical document informing Jones's copy-text. Whatever the case, the reality or actual content of the deleted portions are less important than Jones's claim itself: he is constructing a distinctive text for his clientele—a streamlined version designed for discerning readers, one apparently devoid of the clownish elements that "to be mixtured in print with such matter of worth, it wuld prooue a great disgrace to so honorable & stately a historie..." (A2r-A2v).

The play can be read, offers Jones, after one's "serious affairs and studies," and he is confident that the play in print will be no less "delightfull" than it was "in London vpon stages" (A2r). That Jones draws on *Tamburlaine*'s success in the theater suggests his treatment of stage and page is not strictly hierarchical: performed and textual modes can both give pleasure, but the respective pleasures—while connected—are different, and they are produced by different means. Theatergoers are fashioned as a relatively passive audience: they merely "see" the play rather than subject it to "serious" scrutiny; the "co[n]ceited fondlings" amongst them "greatly gape" at the "fond and friuolous Iestures," an image that figures certain portions of the audience as empty receptacles, inertly consuming whatever is presented to them. Conversely, Jones references readers' "wisdomes" and appeals to their "learned censures," implying that it will take some interpretive labor to delight in the play in its printed form. One cannot discount the entrepreneurial puffery that Jones is espousing in all of this, flattering potential customers into buying his product, but it must also be said that the epistle prefaces a play exceptionally suited to pronouncements of bold, unique ways of affecting audiences. The Prologue to the first part of *Tamburlaine*, recognized by one editor as a kind of "challenge, almost a manifesto" (Dawson xi), echoes Jones's epistle in championing the play as a "matter of worth" by accentuating its distinctive, elevated language:

> From iygging vaines of riming mother wits,
> And such conceits as clownage keepes in pay,
> Weele lead you to the stately tent of War,
> Where you shall heare the Scythian Tamburlaine:
> Threatning the world with high astounding tearmes
> And scourging kingdoms with his co[n]quering sword.
> View but his picture in this tragicke glasse,
> And then applaud his fortunes as you please. (1–8)

Similar to Jones's epistle, Marlowe's Prologue explicitly brings certain performance conventions to mind only to undermine their currency and deny their appropriateness, yet does so while nevertheless embracing the potential wonders and delights of staged spectacle ("View but his picture.../ And then applaud his fortunes as you please"). Spoken at the Rose, the Prologue anticipates the theatrical effectiveness of Marlowe's creation and locates the authority for that effectiveness in the playwright's attempts to create a "textually determined purpose of playing," a "verbal picture of an imaginary world" (Weimann 56, 57). When published and read, the Prologue resonates differently, now *recalling* Tamburlaine's spectacular presence and inviting readers to experience his "high astounding tearmes" in a printed form.[17]

Jones's epistle ultimately seeks to define *Tamburlaine*'s readers (and those readers' interpretive skills) in relation to theater audiences and the power of the play in performance. Such a strategy becomes more commonplace in the early seventeenth century, and it comes to be articulated most explicitly and forcefully not by publishers but by playwrights involved in seeing their works into print. While playwrights contributing prefatory material to their printed works are engaging with potential readers, like Jones's paratext, these engagements often remain linked to the play's life in the theater, identifying readers by contrasting their position with "the social institution of the theater, the physical space and the people who inhabited it" (Farmer and Lesser 92). In certain instances, the link between text and performance was maintained precisely because a playwright sought to deny or diminish it, championing the legitimacy and potential appeal of a printed work by denigrating theater audiences who had failed to respond to it properly. John Webster is one such playwright whose printed plays maintain a complicated— even paradoxical—relation to performance.[18] The chronological shift from Marlowe's *Tamburlaine* to the work of Webster is a sizable one, but it yields a productive juxtaposition of strategies for formulating the interconnectedness of page and stage, and these strategies subsequently encourage different imaginings of performance on the part of readers. Consider the title page to the first quarto printing of *The Duchess of Malfi* (1623), for example, which proclaims the book of the play to be "*As it was Presented priuately, at the Black-friers; and publiquely at the Globe, By the* Kinges Maiesties Seruants," while adding that the book is "The perfect and exact Coppy, with diuerse *things Printed, that the length of the Play* would not beare in the Presentment." This would have it both ways: the text that follows is the play as it was presented on stage; the text that follows is the play that, because of "diuerse *things Printed*," has technically never been performed. What constitutes the *Duchess of Malfi*? The title page suggests that the play is what Webster conceived and wrote (some of which was not performed), what private and public audiences were presented with (some of which was not written by Webster, as evidenced by his marginal note next to the song in 3.4, "The Author disclaimes this Ditty to be his" (H2r)), and also what the reader now holds in hand—it was all of these things and somehow more, the sum of the play being greater than its constituent manifestations.

Webster's first solo playwrighting effort was, by his own admission, a failure. In an address "To the Reader" of the first quarto of *The White Devil* (1612), Webster initiates the play's life in print by coming to terms with its death on stage:

> *In publishing this Tragedy, I do but challenge to my selfe that liberty, which other men haue tane before mee; not that I affect praise by it, . . . onely since it was acted in so dull a time of Winter, presented in so open and blacke a Theater, that it wanted (that which is the onely grace and setting out of a Tragedy) a full and vnderstanding Auditory: and that since that time I haue noted, most of the people that come to the Play-house resemble those ignorant asses (who visiting Stationers shoppes their vse is not to inquire for good bookes, but new bookes) . . .* (A2r)

The rancor in Webster's epistle is undeniable, his intense bitterness produced not just by the play's short run at The Red Bull, but also by the fact that the play's sudden and absolute failure was so cruelly disproportionate to his own labors: "*I was a long time in finishing this Tragedy*" (A2v). Webster describes the play's utter lack of success in language of exposure, focusing on inauspicious elements both natural and human. The play, he claims, "*was acted in so dull a time of Winter, presented in so open and blacke a Theater, that it wanted . . . a full and vnderstanding Auditory.*" This suggests that harsh, gloomy weather prevented or discouraged individuals from making their way to the theater (or perhaps from staying for the length of the performance); or perhaps Webster is implying that unforgiving weather interfered with the ability of those who braved the open air to fully hear or even see what was being performed. What Webster makes unmistakably clear is that those who made up the audience did not much like or comprehend what they saw: they were not "*vnderstanding*," they were "*ignorant asses*," they were "*vncapable*" (A2v). His formulation of the play's original playing space and audience is put forth to support his belief that his work was thoroughly muddled by a distracting and distracted theater.

Webster presses on, providing one final blast against those who so completely failed to appreciate his work: even "*should a man present to such an Auditory the most Sententious Tragedy that euer was written,*" he rails, "*the breath that comes fro*[m] *the vncapable multitude is able to poison it*" (A2r, A2v). Such a statement formulates the theater as a space of extreme sensory stimulation; in addition to foul weather, the noxious air steaming from the audience—the symbolic product of their lack of refinement and interpretive shortcomings—can engulf the stage, contaminating performance.[19] Cumulatively, these images of exposure and contamination in Webster's epistle call forth an imagined *scape* of a theater tainted by forces beyond its control, which is implicitly juxtaposed against the inherent stability and ostensible unambiguity of the *scape* of the page. That is, relative to the sounds, smells, and general confusion of the "*open*" theater, the clarity and stasis of the printed play become interpretive catalysts, textual properties that allow for Webster's work to be experienced in a more controlled and productive way. The epistle concludes with Webster explicitly stating the terms and contexts in which he wants his printed work to be received. He refers readers to

> *that full and haightned stile of Maister* Chapman, *the labor'd and vnderstanding workes of Maister* Iohnson, *the no lesse worthy composures of the both worthily excellent Maister* Beamont *& Maister* Fletcher, *and lastly*

(without wrong last to be named) the right happy and copious industry of
M. Shake-speare, M. Decker, & M. Heywood,

adding that, in printing his play, he is *"wishing what I write may be read by their light."* To situate his works in relation to these other writers and to ask readers to do the same is to embrace the qualities of printed play-texts that make such comparisons and juxtapositions possible. Again, Webster's understanding of his printed play can only be gleaned tangentially, but against the ephemerality of the performed play, the epistle—with its brief foray into performance history, Latin quotations, and references to successful playwrights—adumbrates a book that is present and permanent in ways that a production at The Red Bull could never be. The epistle's final statement (taken from Martial), is, quite fittingly, an assertion of immutability: "non nurunt, haec monumenta mori"—"these monuments know not death."

Despite his resentment over the play's failure and his championing of its merits in print, however, Webster does not entirely discount the potential of theatrical representation; in a footnote at the end of the playtext, he makes a point of praising those who originally performed his play:

> For the action of the play, twas generally well, and I dare affirme, with the Ioint testimony of some of their owne quality, (for the true imitation of life, without striuing to make nature a monster) the best that euer became them; whereof as I make a generall acknowledgement, so in particular I must remember the well approued industry of my freind *Maister Perkins*, and confesse the worth of his action did Crowne both the beginning and end. (M2v)[20]

Such a conspicuous addendum regarding the quality of the acting subtly reasserts his claim in the prefatory epistle that the original audience was to blame for the play's failure. Webster thus frames the book of *The White Devil* with efforts to differentiate textual and performative modes, but ultimately these efforts simultaneously enclose his playtext within recollections of the limitations—*"so open and blacke a Theater"*—and the potency—"the true imitation of life"—of the play's incarnation at The Red Bull. In the end, readers of *The White Devil* are positioned within a participatory system—"the play"—that is connected to the logic of both the page and the stage, with the printed playtext subtly acknowledging its roots in the performed event even as it actively seeks to minimize them.

This complex differentiation of textual and performed modes also informs Webster's playtext on an elementary level in that the play is printed continuously, a compositional technique whereby "verse lines broken between two speakers are set on one line to create a full metrical unit" (Lesser, *Renaissance Drama* 66). The term "continuous printing" was first used by Greg, who included under its umbrella instances where "each new speech, instead of (as is usual) beginning a fresh line of print, follows on from the last, with the speaker's name (or prefix) within the line" (*Bibliography* I: xviii). Since Greg's definition would thus include compositorial efforts to save space and paper, Lesser modifies his use of the term in order to focus on instances where continuous printing "is clearly used to create a full verse line" (*Renaissance Drama* 66 n23). Lesser's refinement is significant: split verse lines could be set on a single line when a compositor or printer was intent on cutting the not insignificant costs of paper, or when the manuscript copy had been inaccurately cast off and a compositor had to cram lines together, but plays systematically featuring continuous printing appear motivated by aesthetic, rather than economic concerns. Such a stylistic choice was meant to present the printed playtext in a conspicuously literate form and distance the book of the play from its theatrical heritage. Plays printed continuously were literary objects, with the space of the page manipulated so as to distinguish the reading of works like *The White Devil* from the experience of reading other non-continuously printed plays. Lesser argues that the process was

> a means of creating a group of select plays. And while not obvious to the buyer, a reader would surely have remarked it, since the change of speaker in mid-line can be jarring until it becomes familiar. Once bought and read, then, continuous printing, marking the play as literary, may have added cultural capital to the play, making it more valuable to its owner, and therefore more desirable for others. (*Renaissance Drama* 70)[21]

The implementation of such a strategy bespeaks an awareness of the interpretative and affective ramifications that can be produced by altering the *scape* of the page. The fact that this reversion to a more condensed appearance functioned as a sign of a "literary" play, distinct from other plays in the bookshop, is indicative of just how well established it had become to utilize white space in printed plays to distinguish between speakers and speeches. Continuous printing would not have conferred any literary valence or other "cultural capital" if non-continuous printing were not the predominant way of producing and reading a play.

Further, the deliberate minimization of white space magnifies the capabilities of the book of the play to serve as a discrete arena for producing the work, a mode of production that can be differentiated from performed modes by altering the way in which information is presented to readers—in this case, increasing the textual density of lines on the page. If, as Worthen argues, we as modern readers "now expect plays to deploy the (white) space of the page to register the drama's theatrical identity, to insert a sense of the temporality of the playing into the readerly text of the play" (*Print* 77), the nascent forms of this position in the early seventeenth century would have been undermined by continuously printed plays like *The White Devil*, which were designed to de-emphasize substantive linkages between viewing and reading experiences.

In setting broken verse lines as unified, full lines, continuous printing infuses the page with a textual logic that impels readers to consider verse exchanges between characters as mutually constitutive and synergetic; in performance, verse exchanges might not necessarily resonate in the same way. Continuous printing, then, along with other typographic features like act and scene divisions, contribute to what Turner refers to as the "conceptual unity" of the printed play; Turner continues:

> Redistributed across the page in deliberately segmented units of action, the newly unified "work" makes possible a completely different sense of space from that which predominates on the stage: it allows the reader to project across the play in its entirety a homogeneous, unbroken, "containing" space that is imagined to link or underlie the various "places" of the fiction, whether these be onstage or off, "within" or "without". (180)

In addition to encouraging readers to conceive of the work comprehensively, the printed play often asks its readers to negotiate this unified space in specific ways, reminding them that they as readers are actively involved in utilizing the stability of the page to make meaning(s). Some paratexts concede that transferring a play from manuscript to print introduces errors into the text, with the corollary of this concession being that the interpretive burden is shifted toward readers, affording them more responsibility in correcting mistakes. In a postscript to the epistle prefacing the corrected version of his *Parasitaster, or The Fawn* (Q2, 1606), for instance, John Marston remarks, "Reader, know I have perused this coppy, to make some satisfaction for the first faulty impression: yet so urgent hath been my business, that some errors have styll passed, which thy discretion may amend" (A2v). In a similar vein, readers of the 1634 edition of *Philaster* are lauded as the play's "skilfull Triers and Refiners," with the actors rather casually dismissed as nothing more than "laboring Miners"

(A2v). The final page of Thomas Dekker's account of James's coronation pageant, *The Magnificent Entertainment* (1604), contains a note "To the Reader," which instructs that "Some errours wander vp and downe in these sheetes, vnder the Printers warrant: which notwithstanding may by thy Authoritie be brought in, and receiue their due Correction" (I4r). While these examples seem to draw a distinction between page and stage—indeed, Marston's postscript adds that "*Comedies* are writ to be spoken, not read: Remember the life of these things consists in action"—other plays deliberately conflate the acts of textual production and reception with performance and theatrical activity. Francis Beaumont, in a commendatory poem to John Fletcher's *The Faithful Shepherdess*, refers to the printing of the play as "a second publication" (¶3v), with the first being an apparently short run in the theater (due to the audiences' confusion as to what they should expect from Fletcher's "pastorall Tragie-Comedie" [¶2v]). An errata sheet precedes the play-text of Dekker's *Satiromastix* (1602), to which the playwright appends this message: "In steed of the Trumpets sounding thrice, before the Play begin: it shall not be amisse (for him that will read) first to beholde this short Comedy of Errors, and where the greatest enter, to give them in steed of a hisse, a gentle correction" (A4v). Peters helps to elucidate instructions such as Dekker's, which "theatricalise the convention [of readers acting as correctors] in order to stress the active role of the reader, present to the reading, which becomes an alternative kind of performance" (133). Other references to readerly participation conflate reading and performing even more explicitly. John Ford lauds Philip Massinger's *The Roman Actor* (1629), claiming that although the characters and plot were known to audiences before Massinger's play, they

> ...meerly were related
> Without a Soule, Vntill thy abler Pen
> Spoke them, and made them speake, nay Act agen
> In such a height, that Heere to know their Deeds
> Hee may become an Actor that but Reades. (A4v)

Where Ford transforms Massinger's readers into actors (and it is not clear if Ford means that readers "become" the classical figures represented in the play, the stage performers, or both of these at once), George Chapman champions Ben Jonson's *Sejanus* (1605) as

> *Performing such a liuely Euidence*
> *in thy Narrations, that thy Hearers still*
> *Thou turnst to thy Spectators; and the sense*

That thy Spectators haue of good or ill,
Thou iniect'st jointly to thy Readers soules. (¶4v)

One assumes that Jonson, who acknowledges that the "voluntary Labours of my Friends, prefixt to my Booke, haue releiued me in much, whereat (without them) I should Necessarilie haue touched" (¶2r), approved of Chapman's appraisal that reading *Sejanus* constitutes a unique form of spectatorship, especially since, toward the end of his epistle "To the Readers," the playwright is determined to excise any memorial remnants of *Sejanus*'s performance history. "I would informe you," writes Jonson, "that this Booke, in all nŭ[m]bers, is not the same with that which was acted on the publike Stage, wherein a second Pen had good share: in place of which I haue rather chosen to put weaker (and no doubt lesse pleasing) of mine own, then to defraud so happy a *Genius* of his right, by my lothed vsurpation" (¶2v). Unlike playtexts that claim to recapture or contain a play's collaborative processes, Jonson's "Booke" of *Sejanus* seeks to deny the validity of the play in performance coming to bear on a reader's interpretive and imaginative activity. The play as it existed on the "publike Stage" represents a different version of the work, one that Jonson is seemingly intent on positioning in the past. In deliberately reshaping the text of the play and customizing an explicitly literary epistle, Jonson ensures that, in Orgel's words, "the drama of *Sejanus* no longer requires the mediation of an acting company for its realization. The play is now a transaction between the author and the individual reader, and the only performance takes place in the reader's imagination" (*Imagining* 2). Orgel is striking at the heart of the matter, but his formulation, while accurate, raises a larger question: given Jonson's ongoing project of shifting authority from the unruly ways of the theater to his printed texts, what kind of performance are his readers being asked to imagine?

The short answer is that there is not just one answer: *Sejanus* represents a moving target in that the extant printed versions of the play appear driven by different objectives. The quarto edition of the play, in addition to being printed continuously (a stylistic reinforcement of Jonson's literary pretensions that, as we have seen in the work of Webster, proved influential), is bordered by relentless marginalia that reference Jonson's Latin sources. The marginalia provide another layer of literary gloss to a playtext that Jonson wants readers to conceive of as a "Booke," although there are two other, related, factors that should also be noted: the play's lack of success in the theater and the potential parallels that could be drawn between *Sejanus*'s conspiratorial themes and the contemporary political scene. Jonson claims that he has included the notes "onely... to shew my integrity in the *Story*, and save my selfe in those common Torturers, that bring all wit to the Rack" (¶2v), but, having already been questioned by the Privy Council after a performance of the play in 1603, he would have had good reason to ensure that his subject matter was not misconstrued once disseminated in print; alternatively, if Jonson did intend for *Sejanus* to be subversive, the notes serve as an effective material alibi. Either way, it is both the manipulability and the relative fixity of the printed page that allow him the opportunity to dampen the potential of unintended, dangerous readings. Jonson supplies the abbreviated authors' names, titles, and page numbers of his Roman sources to shape and control the tangential moves that can be made away from the playtext; by framing his pages with information of his choosing, Jonson suppresses the possibility of contemporary allusions being made as he entrenches a reader's engagement with the play in classical precedents and texts. The notes that border the quarto text of *Sejanus* are designed to create more of a literate conversation between playwright and reader than to cultivate an imagined performance: as Jonson admits, "Whereas, they are in *Latine* and the worke in *English*, it was presupposed, none but the Learned would take the paynes to conferre them" (¶2v). Jonson writes sardonically in his epistle of erasing the collaborative relationship with his co-author; in its place, his extensive notes establish a carefully managed collaboration with the reader, an esoteric exchange between Jonson as author/editor and those learned enough to navigate his marginalia. Jonas Barish writes of Jonson's shift from "publike Stage" to private "Booke" that the actor's voice represented "an unpredictable and untrustworthy element over which he had too little control; print offered an escape into a stabler medium" (qtd. in Weimann 36). I would concur that Jonson is invested in an "escape" from the theater into the ostensible stability of print, adding that Jonson is much less intent on utilizing his *mise en page* to foster or inspire a return voyage back from the book to an imagined realization of the play as performed. As John Jowett explains, the marginal notes "destroy the horizontal axial emphasis" of a standard "play quarto's page layout" ("Fall" 286); by precluding a reader's rhythmic engagement with the dialogue, the marginalia undermine the "deployment of words and actions in time and space" (287). The *scape* of the page takes precedence over the *scape* of the imagined scene.

This dynamic between page and stage changes significantly, however, in the folio version of *Sejanus*. Jonson maintains his firm control over the appearance of the printed text, this time by removing the referential marginalia that so distinguished the quarto edition of the play; the margins of the folio text of the play are thus largely bare, save for occasional stage directions, many of which are not found in the quarto text. Critics have long wondered about Jonson's decision to remove his marginalia, since compiling the notes for the quarto must have been a laborious task. Clues as to the motivations behind Jonson's textual alterations are provided by the title page of the folio text, which differentiates itself from its quarto predecessor in a conspicuous way. The quarto title page locates its authority exclusively in its claim to be "Written by Ben Ionson," while the folio title page, before recognizing Jonson as "Author," recollects *Sejanus*'s (apparently short) performance history: "Acted, in the yeere 1603. / By the K. MAIESTIES / SERVANTS" (355). There are other noteworthy differences: both texts contain a long, detailed argument outlining the plot to follow, but only the quarto text, so concerned with delimiting the horizon of readings, attaches an interpretive postscript, "This we do aduance as a marke of Terror to all *Traytors, & Treasons . . . ,*" and only in the folio text is it deemed necessary to set "*THE SCENE*" as "ROME" (359).

The most meaningful difference, however, is found in the folio's margins. The folio's sporadic stage directions encode the playtext as just that—a *play*text. Characters are given a certain level of mobility: "*Drusus passeth by*" (362), "*They passe over the stage*" (364); interlocutors speak to one another in particular ways: there are multiple directions in which characters "*whisper*" (362, 413); and other directions give specific performance cues: "*He turnes to Seianus clyents*" (366), "*He turns to Laco and the rest*" (411), "*He salutes them humbly*" (423). Cumulatively, stage directions such as these provide a more nuanced understanding of the play's performance potentialities. Where the quarto's supplementary information denied the possibility of meaningful *performancescapes* by directing readers away from the play-as-performed, toward texts and narratives of Jonson's own choosing, the folio text offers intermittent opportunities to imaginatively engage with matters of performance by marking its margins with directions that situate the reader in the interpretive, transitional, and meaning-making space between page and stage. That Jonson is committed to sharpening his readers' visualization of a play that had not been performed in some time is evidenced by the fact that stage directions are added to the text even when the surrounding dialogue renders them superfluous, as in act 5, where a direction is given, "*The Senators shift their places,*" followed immediately by Arruntius's comment that "The place growes hot, they shift" (430).

Side by side, the quarto and folio texts demonstrate Jonson experimenting with the appearance of the page to customize texts in accordance with what he believes to be the needs of his intended readership. What Barish might call Jonson's second "escape" to the stability of the printed folio page takes on a richer connotation in that the folio text utilizes the typographical marker of the stage direction to gesture outside the bounds of the book, back at the forever absent and ephemeral play-as-performed.

The final verso page of the folio text of *Sejanus* mirrors the claims made on the title page—"This Tragedie was first / acted, in the yeere / 1603. / By the Kings Maiesties / SERVANTS" (438)—and strengthens the printed play's connection to its performance history by naming "The principall Tragaedians" in a list that includes "WILL. SHAKE-SPEARE," "IOH. HEMINGS," and "HEN. CONDEL." These three figures are of course more famously linked by Shakespeare's own Folio of dramatic works, with Heminge and Condell apparently serving as the primary organizers of the collection. The impact of Jonson's and Shakespeare's Folios on conceptions of dramatic authorship and the legitimization of the literary qualities of drama is well established, and I do not believe it is necessary for me to return to such matters here.[22] What bears reasserting is that the publication of Jonson's *Workes* in 1616—"a culminating achievement of writing and patronage" (Bergeron 129)—fundamentally altered the way that printed playtexts could be encoded for readers. Where a playwright's body of work would have previously only been available in a range of heterogeneous, largely perishable individual units produced by printers and compositors possessing varying levels of skill and care for the material at hand, Jonson's *Workes* offered his collected plays (as well as certain poems, masques, and entertainments) in a systematically arranged and relatively uniform manner, and presented them to readers as dignified, permanent, and definitive.[23] Moreover, Jonson's Folio was designed and engineered to put forth a totalized understanding of his life's writing: from its title page featuring a proscenium stage, triumphal arch, obelisks, laurels, inscriptions, and statues, to its dedicatory poems (some of which are entirely in Latin), to the dedications accompanying each play, it is clear that the folio is intended to position Jonson and his work within enduring, classical contexts. Jonson's Folio has been described as possessing a textuality that is "antioccasional" and "antitheat[rical]" (Lowenstein, "Printing" 182); indeed, given some of Jonson's prefatory efforts to disassociate his printed plays from the theater, the "antitheatrical" label is one that is assigned to Jonson with great frequency. Yet, as I have argued, Jonson's alterations to the folio text of *Sejanus* reveal a playwright who was not above utilizing and manipulating the space of the page to substantiate links between the play as printed and the play as (potentially) performed.[24] Shakespeare's Folio followed Jonson's example in seeking to account for his canon in a cumulative way, although rather than emphasizing classical associations, Shakespeare is memorialized in Heminge and Condell's epistle to readers as an author "Who, as he was a happie imitator of Nature, was a most gentle expresser of it" (A3r). Later in the century, a folio collecting works attributed to Francis Beaumont and John Fletcher reflects and refracts its predecessors in intriguing ways by projecting itself as a veritable archive of writing for the stage; the more explicit gestures toward the stage in the Beaumont and Fletcher Folio are perhaps not altogether surprising given that it was produced during a period when public performances of the playtexts it collects were no longer an option. Despite the different motivations and forces behind the Shakespeare and Beaumont and Fletcher Folios (to which I now turn), they, like Jonson's *Workes*, suggest that spectres of performance continue to haunt the production of dramatic texts even after plays are collected and styled as authorial and literary, and despite the predominantly textualized ways that readers were asked to conceive of plays when encountering them in collected forms. All playtexts tell a different story, but the underlying pattern that I am highlighting is that the codes and rhetorical framing devices that attempt to mark printed plays as a distinct form of dramatic production often accomplish this differentiation by way of the impossible and the paradoxical: by claiming to recount and record the absent performances and potentialities that are immune to stabilization. An invitation for readers to remain cognizant of performed modes of realization is thus an attribute of printed drama with a long and diverse ancestry.

Intersections of Literary and Theatrical Logic in Shakespeare's First Folio

That the Shakespeare Folio, is, as Kastan remarks, a "book [that] presents itself as literary" (*Book* 72) is beyond dispute. The most heavily mined source of the Folio's pretensions is the prefatory note "*To the great Variety of Readers*," where it is apparent that Heminge and Condell's sense of the work they are collecting is a textual one. The Folio's value, they propose, is not conferred by encapsulating or memorializing specific performances (a claim made by many individually printed plays in the period), but by the texts' proximity and fidelity to Shakespeare's original writings: "His mind and hand went together: And what he thought, he vttered with that easinesse, that wee haue scarse receiued from him a blot in his papers." Heminge and Condell imply that Shakespeare's work ("what he thought")—a concept that Peter Shillingsburg understands as possessing "no substantial existence" (43)—took on a material form in his unblotted manuscript papers. Further, Heminge and Condell formulate the Folio as a transmitter of this work, one absolutely free from distortion: the volume contains not just Shakespeare's "writings," "perfect of their limbes, and...absolute in their numbers," it also represents these writings "as he conceiued the[m]." Heminge and Condell implicate themselves in the perpetuation of Shakespeare's creative efforts, and the lineage that they sketch— from thoughts to papers to print—strictly concerns itself with textual purity and stability, excluding the potential influences and interpolations of theatrical collaborators and performances.

An effacement of performance also characterizes their (in)famous statement that

> as where (before) you were abus'd with diuerse stolne, and surreptitious copies, maimed, and deformed by the frauds and stealthes of iniurious impostors, that expos'd them: euen those, are now offer'd to your view cur'd, and perfect of their limbes, and all the rest, absolute in their numbers, as he conceiued the[m].[25]

Again, Heminge and Condell concern themselves with the texts of Shakespeare's plays, this time the extent to which they have previously been "maimed" and "deformed." Their concern for what has been presented to readers in a damaged form surely refers not to the physical vessel that contains the text—i.e. the *document* (what we would retrospectively identify as a "good," "bad," or "short" quarto, scribal copy, or whatever)—but to the *text* (the intended order of words and punctuation) contained in that document. The claim of having cured and perfected the previously marred texts is founded on their apparent access to the purest wellspring of Shakespeare's genius—his "papers"—which allows them to reproduce more faithful texts of Shakespeare's works. Any involvement on the part of individuals involved in the theatrical production of the plays is excised from their equation.

That Heminge and Condell, actors both, would not disparage the theater when narrating Shakespeare's history in print is to be expected.

What is, as Kastan remarks, somewhat more "surprising" is their overall "disregard for the theater in the commemorative volume" (*Book* 71). According to Kastan's reading of the Folio's preliminaries,

> One might think that they would emphasize the fruitful collaborations of playwright and actor, the popularity of the plays among audiences of all ages and social classes, or even suggest, as some play texts did, that the true life of drama is on the stage. But they make only a single gesture to the theatrical auspices of what is published. In their dedication to the Herberts they comment that so great was their Lordships' "likings of the seuerall parts, when they were acted" that even before it was published "the Volume ask'd to be yours." But rather than suggest the aesthetic priority of the staged play, here its priority is merely temporal; and indeed the play as performed is imagined not as the essential experience that the published play can only and belatedly approximate but as a more ephemeral form of the volume itself. (*Book* 71–2)

Kastan's point is true to the mark: given Shakespeare's long and intimate association with London's theatrical scene, the Folio's lack of direct engagement with the economic and collaborative realities of dramatic production is striking, and the latter portion of Kastan's claim effectively captures the transitory nature of performance within Heminge and Condell's paratexts. Regarding Heminge and Condell's "single gesture" to the theater, however, Kastan overstates his case: in identifying conspicuous absences from their writings, he neglects more subtle links to theater and performance in Heminge and Condell's epistle and in other sections of the prefatory matter (which one assumes Heminge and Condell had some organizational involvement in). From a broad perspective, the decision to group Shakespeare's plays generically, though it necessitated forcing certain works (like *Cymbeline*) into misleading categories, might, as Orgel suggests, "have had the attraction of classical forms for Shakespeare's first editors, conferring the dignity of ancient drama on the work of their fellow actor" (qtd. in Murphy, *Print* 42). Similarly, the inclusion of "The Names of the Principall Actors in all these Playes" could serve as a general reminder that "these Playes" did exist and thrive elsewhere, outside the bounds of the printed book, subjected to the interpretive labors of professional performers. The list of actors is not a hasty snapshot of the company's makeup, but instead appears thoughtfully designed to encompass, at least in part, what was in actuality a fluid membership; S. P. Cerasano identifies "roughly four 'generations' of players" (331) that are recorded, from the company's first sharers to those who were members when the King's Men received their final patent in 1619. Subtly then, the list of actors connects the Folio's play-texts to an extended history of collaborative theater practice by identifying many of the individual performers who brought the plays to life. The list obscures much more than it reveals, however, and it will sustain a glance toward performance for only the briefest of instances; it is, as Cerasano remarks, above all "a memorial record, enshrining the names of key players but in no way characterizing the qualities that made them distinctive" (343).

To counter Kastan's claims more specifically, the writings of Heminge and Condell in fact reference two contemporary theaters by name in the epistle, one of which, the Blackfriars, assumed a central position in the latter stages of Shakespeare's career; they inform readers that

> Censure will not driue a Trade, or make the Iacke go. And though you be a Magistrate of wit, and sit on the Stage at *Black-Friers*, or the *Cock-pit*, to arraigne Playes dailie, know, these Playes haue had their triall already, and stood out all Appeales...

In one sense, this passage differentiates the interpretation of Shakespeare's printed texts from interrogations of live "Playes"—what follows in the Folio need not be subjected to the same kind of scrutiny that is applied to contemporary performances in the leading private theaters; but in another sense, the passage also establishes for readers of the Folio that the success of the collected plays has already been proven and validated by their previous "triall(s)" in the public theaters. In one fell swoop, the fate of plays in performance is both marginalized and recognized as primary and integral to success in print.[26] A similar figurative mixture of page and stage lingers in Heminge and Condell's instructions to "Iudge your sixe-pen'orth, your shillings worth, your fiue shillings worth at a time, or higher, so you rise to the iust rates, and welcome." Like so many passages in the epistle, this hierarchizing of readerly judgement is open to interpretation. On the surface, the passage applies the shifting price scale to the Folio itself, which perhaps suggests that Heminge and Condell are asking that readers proceed through the Folio in incremental units, play by play, in order to produce their money's worth of enjoyment and then respond with the requisite amount of appreciation.[27] Yet as Hackel points out, "The instructions [also] evoke the language of the playhouse, where admission prices did, in fact, operate on a sliding scale" ("'Great Variety'" 144). Hackel supports her reading with a quotation from the Induction to Jonson's *Bartholomew Fair*, in which the Scrivener "grants the audience the right to judge the play according to their investments":

> It shall be lawful for any man to judge his six pen'orth, his twelve pen'orth, so to his eighteen pence, two shillings, half a crown to the value of his place: provided always his place get not above his wit. . . . marry, if he drop but sixpence at the door, and will censure a crown's worth, it is thought there is no conscience in that. (qtd. in " 'Great Variety' " 145)

Heminge and Condell thus blur the distinction between reading and theater audiences, implying that their respective investments in dramatic works provide similar opportunities for commendation or criticism. To claim that Heminge and Condell are positing reading and theater-going as equivalent activities would be to push things too far, though clearly images and metaphors of the theater informed their thinking as they endeavored to sell their collection of plays.

The epistle to readers ends with a tantalizing remark from Heminge and Condell: "And so we leaue you to other of his Friends, whom if you need, can bee your guides." One might be tempted to take them literally here and ascribe to the dedicatory poems that follow a concerted, systematic effort to direct readers' negotiations with Shakespeare's printed texts. As enticing as this sounds, the temptation must be resisted, not only because the spirit of Heminge and Condell's piece is ultimately commercial rather than exegetical ("what euer you do, Buy") but also because the poems themselves prove to be more concerned with lauding Shakespeare's career and mourning his death than they do with providing interpretive guidelines. What the dedicatory poems do contain, nevertheless, are the explicit theatrical gestures that Kastan identifies as missing from Heminge and Condell's prefatory material. Hugh Holland, for example, deploys a pun to acknowledge the theater most often associated with the playwright: "His dayes are done, that made the dainty Playes, / Which made the Globe of heau'n and earth to ring." Other prefatory pieces offer more complex assessments. Jonson's poem concludes by way of referencing *"the drooping Stage; / Which, since thy flight frŏ[m] hence, hath mourn'd like night, / And despaires day, but for thy Volumes light."* Hitting a similar note, Leonard Digges first stresses the permanence of the Folio—*"This Booke, / When Brasse and Marble fade, shall make thee looke / Fresh to all Ages"*—before lamenting the impoverished stage that Shakespeare has left behind:

> *Nor shall I e're beleeue, or thinke thee dead*
> *(Though mist) vntill our bankrout Stage be sped*

(Impossible) with some new straine t'out-do
Passions of Iuliet, *and her Romeo*;
Or till I heare a Scene more nobly take,
Then when thy half-Sword parlying Romans *spake.*

James Mabbe's contribution, which figures Shakespeare as an animated (and animating) presence behind performed and textual modes of producing his works, is worth quoting in full:

Wee wondred (Shake-speare) *that thou went'st so soone*
From the Worlds Stage, to the Graues-Tyring-roome.
Wee thought thee dead, but this thy printed worth,
Tels thy Spectators, that thou went'st but forth
To enter with applause. An Actors Art,
Can dye, and liue, to acte a second part.
That's but an Exit *of Mortalitie;*
This, a Re-entrance to a Plauditie.

Collectively, the dedicatory poems are, like Heminge and Condell's epistle to readers, concerned with Shakespeare as author and creator, but all of them situate Shakespeare's writings as existing within, and between, the bounds of both the book and the stage.

All this is not to say that Kastan is incorrect in pointing out the ephemeral position that performance occupies in the Folio: the implicit, indirect nature of many of the references I have touched on essentially prove his point. When it comes to the playtexts collected in the Folio, Heminge and Condell's narrative involving Shakespeare's unblotted pen and exclusive authority actually misrepresents two collaborative processes—that of performance and of print production—both of which inevitably transform playtexts as they descend in any number of permutations from manuscript (perhaps through the theater) to print. In emphasizing Shakespeare as sole author, Heminge and Condell minimize the contributions of his various collaborators in the creative process: not just actors but also other playwrights now recognized as determining the shape of plays ascribed only to Shakespeare (such as Middleton in *Macbeth* and *Timon of Athens*, Fletcher in *Henry VIII*). Also elided from Heminge and Condell's description of the plays' transition to the Folio are scribes and compositors, whose work with playtexts and their paratextuals impinge on the way in which printed plays demarcate and negotiate the space between page and stage. In Worthen's words, "For while punctuation, capitalization, exits and entrances, the placement and variation of speech prefixes are surely not the stuff of drama, by representing a relationship between writing and performance, the material properties of printed plays inevitably represent the identity of drama in the age of print: they frame the mise-en-page as a site of performance" (*Print* 11). It is via the informational structure of the play on the page that textual theorists and editors attempt to trace the origins of printed playtexts and estimate the extent to which they have come into contact with, and been transformed by, the contingencies of performance. The editors of the Oxford Shakespeare, for instance, distinguish between the vestigial markers of authorial foul papers, such as "loose ends, false starts, textual tangles...inconsistency in the designation of characters in speech prefixes...[and] 'ghost' characters called for in stage directions," and the remnants of textual modifications produced during a play's realization in the theater, like stage directions that are "more systematically supplied...[and] more practically...worded," and "characters [that are] more consistently identified in speech prefixes" (*Companion* 9, 12). The distinction between relatively private and relatively socialized versions of playtexts, though it can "easily harden into a misleading dichotomy" (*Companion* 12), nevertheless allows for an understanding of reciprocity between written, printed, and performed modes of production: an original manuscript version of a play with the potential to guide performance is subjected to the interpretive labors of various individuals and institutions, from which demonstrably different versions of the original play are produced.

Challenging this established model, Lukas Erne has endeavored to prove that "Shakespeare's 'long' plays"—most of which are found in the Folio—"were not performed in anything close to their entirety in the sixteenth and seventeenth centuries" (*Literary Dramatist* 174), a point that has huge ramifications for his understanding of the nature of many printed texts prepared for readers. Shakespeare, argues Erne, wrote "much material that was never, nor was ever intended to be, performed" (136). Erne believes that the longer texts (found in the Folio or in "good" quartos) "correspond to what an emergent dramatic author wrote for readers in an attempt to raise the literary respectability of plays," while the "short, theatrical texts...record in admittedly problematic fashion the plays as they were orally delivered on stage to spectators" (220). Erne focuses on the variants between long and short versions of *Henry V*, *Romeo and Juliet*, and *Hamlet*, believing that the conspicuous differences between them "bespeak the different media for which they were designed" (223). There are difficulties with Erne's larger claims,[28] but one thing he does particularly well is demonstrate how the presence or absence of paratextuals—particularly stage directions—can communicate information about performance in different ways, thus altering the imaginative demands made of readers. As an example of the kinds of conclusions Erne draws, consider his reading of (theatrical) quarto and (literary) folio versions of the entry of the French Herald during the battle of Agincourt in *Henry V*, after King Henry has discovered the slaughtered English boys. Erne notes that both texts are essentially the same save for one important difference. After the stage direction marking the Herald's entry (he is *"Mounioy"* in the Folio), the Folio text includes an exchange between Exeter and Gloucester that is not present in the first quarto:

> *Exe.* Here comes the Herald of the French, my Liege.
> *Glou.* His eyes are humbler than they v'sd to be.

The significance of these lines, according to Erne, is "that they can be *acted* and therefore do not need to be *spoken*. In performance, the words would unnecessarily reiterate what the actor conveys through body language" (222). Referencing Berger's "imaginary audition," Erne states that "the two lines present in the readerly but absent from the theatrical text...allow a reader to imagine a point of stage business that could otherwise only be conveyed in performance" (222). Erne's description of the way in which the printed text allows for a reader to imaginatively engage with the play as performed—in this instance encouraging readers to picture a noticeably subdued Mountjoy making his way towards Henry's forces, a detail that impacts on not only the way one pictures Mountjoy's body language, but also the manner in which he subsequently speaks— resonates with my descriptions of *performancescape* in chapter 1. I am thus in accordance with his fundamental argument that the manipulation of paratextuals (and the *mise en page* in general) can potentially influence a reader's ability to approximate performance. I do, however, wish to address his assertion that some of Shakespeare's plays were designed to "function according to a 'literary' logic" (23). This chapter has put forth that a strict division between types of dramatic signification is not what is encoded on the early modern page; instead, what printed playtexts tend to record is a diffusion of dramatic modes in which readers are frequently confronted with the opportunity to imaginatively engage with theatrical action and the indistinct shadows of performances past. I contend that the connections between stage and page as they are recorded in print are more dynamic, more synergistic, than a binary that opposes "literary" and "theatrical" logic will support, and a brief examination of a play first printed in the Folio will help illustrate my point.

The play is *Cymbeline*, which is admittedly an unlikely piece to bring to the discussion: it exists in only one extant state, it is not burdened with contentious textual cruces, it is (and has always been) a play of middling popularity. *Cymbeline* is extremely long, exceeded in the Folio only by *Hamlet, Richard III, Troilus and Cressida,* and *Coriolanus,* and, according to Erne, thus much too lengthy to be performed in its entirety in the seventeenth century.[29] I am interested in the play's fifth act, specifically the battle between the invading Romans and the British/Welsh soldiers, and the ensuing description of this battle by one of its key participants, Posthumus. The battle itself, like most extended action sequences in Shakespeare, lacks a certain vitality or intensity when apprehended by way of the printed page. Where a theater audience is presented with physical markers of dissonance—active bodies confronting one another, the grunts and moans of actors, the clamor of weaponry—readers have to make due with inert markings on the page, signs representative of theatrical potential and/or convention. Which is not to say that the stage directions in the Folio text of *Cymbeline* meant to account for the frenetic climax are not helpful: in the eyes of one editor, the directions for most of the fifth act seem " 'literary,' descriptive rather than theatrical," aimed at "help[ing] a reader visualize what is going on, and perhaps to reflect a contemporary staging" (Warren 72).[30] Curiously, after (in rapid succession) the defeat of Jachimo by Posthumus, the capture and rescue of Cymbeline, and the turning of the tide through the sheer will and valor of Belarius and the two hidden princes, what immediately follows is a long narrative description by Posthumus of the events that have just taken place on stage. Roger Warren notes that "there is no sign of textual disturbance at this point, so it is probably [safe] to conclude that the duplication is deliberate, Shakespeare choosing to show the audience the battle from the outside and then from the viewpoint of a participant" (74).

Warren is thinking specifically of the effects of the doubled-perspective on theater audiences, but what of readers? More specifically, what of readers encountering *Cymbeline* for the first time as it is printed in the Folio? They are first faced with the opportunity to, as Erne puts it in his discussion of *Henry V,* "imagine a point of stage business that could otherwise only be conveyed in performance" (222). As mentioned, the stage directions add touches that seem to go beyond merely recording theatrical detail; 5.2 opens with this direction:

Enter Lucius, Iachimo, and the Romane Army at one doore: and the Britane Army at another: Leonatus Posthumus following like a poore Souldier.

They march ouer, and goe out. *Then enter againe in Skirmish Iachimo and Posthumus: he vanquisheth and disarmeth Iachimo, and then leaues him.* (TLN 2892–7)

The direction allows readers to position figures on an imagined stage and approximate their movements; the "*Skirmish*" between Jachimo and Posthumus is especially provocative, with "*he vanquisheth and disarmeth Iachimo, and then leaues him*" adding subtlety to a confrontation that could easily be condensed into a more simplified form. The next direction in the scene appears similarly aimed at readers:

The Battaile continues, the Britaines fly, Cymbeline is taken: Then enter to his rescue, Bellarius, Guiderius, and Aruiragus. (2908–10)

Again, that Belarius and company not only "*enter*," but "*enter to his rescue*" amidst a backdrop of a continuing battle facilitates a (relatively) more detailed readerly awareness of the moment's enactment on stage. As helpful as the stage directions might be in producing *performancescapes* (of Posthumus "vanquishing" Jachimo, of a continuing battle), however, they do not provide nearly enough information to fully flesh out how the scene might be communicated by actors' purposeful, active bodies. "*Then enter againe in Skirmish*" is richer than just "*enter againe*," and the same can be said of "*vanquisheth and disarmeth*" as opposed to something like "*Jachimo falls*," but the details that are supplied inevitably hint at the vast range of information that is missing. How long does the skirmish last? How, precisely, does Posthumus vanquish and disarm Jachimo? Does Posthumus linger over his prone victim (*is* Jachimo prone?), and if so, to what effect? Even if the text provided answers to these questions, the end result would be to produce more lacunae that a reader of the text would need to fill. The stage directions close the gap between page and stage, but they also help to constitute that gap, reminding readers that it can never be completely closed.

A much different scene follows: after "*They* [Belarius and his adopted sons] *Rescue Cymbeline*," Posthumus re-enters and begins to recount his version of the encounter to a "*Britane Lord.*" While Posthumus's recollection follows hard on the heels of the staged representation of warring British and Roman soldiers, his retelling of the battle moves further and further away from the kinds of detail that could be communicated in performance. He speaks of "the Enemy full-hearted, Lolling the Tongue with slaught'ring" (2935–6), of a lane, "ditch'd & wall'd with turph" (2942), of emboldened British soldiers who began to "grin like Lyons /

Vpon the Pikes o'th' Hunters" (2966–7), and of numerous dead and wounded: "some mortally, some slightly touch'd, some falling / Meerely through feare" (2937–8). In short, Posthumus's description expands beyond the possibilities of the stage: he details a battle that can only be realized by the imagination, infusing it with metaphorical and sensory details that no reading or performance of the previous scene can produce. The situation in *Cymbeline*, with an extended narrative deployed to recast a moment that has just been staged, brings to mind Worthen's claim that "insofar as performance transforms the language it uses into action, even descriptive words must be made to do something beyond what they say. For this reason, assigning a 'literary' origin to language describing action depends on a limiting misconception of the work of words in performance" ("Intoxicating" 324). Posthumus's narrative privileges the literary over the theatrical, poem over play, but this does not mean that the literary assimilates performance, or, returning to Erne, that the literary is efficiently compensating for information that could otherwise only be communicated through the actor's body (how does a lion grin?). In fact, the scene in question is introduced by yet another reminder of the incongruity of textual and performative modes. The entry direction to the battle scene had identified Posthumus as a "*poore Souldier*," but in the narrative scene he enters (merely) as "*Posthumus.*" The shift in the paratextual description poses readers with a challenge that audiences will not face, since the actor playing Posthumus will likely make it clear—through his posture, gait, intonation, etc.—if the character should still be understood to be in a physical and emotional state akin to the last time he was seen on stage. In other words, an audience will not have to decide if Posthumus is still "*poore*"—the decision will have been made for them.

To reverse field, consider Posthumus's narrative from the perspective of a theater audience. Warren writes in a commentary note that "the audience has already seen what he describes" (224), but this oversimplifies the matter: they have and have not seen what Posthumus recounts. For one thing, the six-line, nationalistic rallying cry that Posthumus attributes to Belarius—"Our Britaines hearts dye flying, not our men, / To darknesse fleete soules that flye backwards; stand, / . . . Stand, stand" (2952–3, 6)—is not found in the previous scene, only the more fragmented (and politically neutral) "Stand, stand, we haue the'aduantage of the ground, / The Lane is guarded: Nothing rowts vs, but / The Villany of our feares" (2911–3). Further, the narrative itself hints at just how far Posthumus's retelling of the battle deviates from a performance of it. There is a metatheatrical nod to limited numbers of live actors standing in for vast armies in Posthumus's praise for the "Nobleness" (2961) of Belarius and the princes: "These three, / Three thousand confident, in acte as many: / For three performers are the File, when all / The rest do nothing" (2956–9). His claim that "Some slaine before, some dying; some their Friends / Ore-borne i'th'former waue, ten chac'd by one, / Are now each one the slaughter-man of twenty" (2975–7) similarly gestures at the finite numbers of human bodies that make up all acting companies—"each one the slaughterman of twenty" is a figurative remembering true to the world of the play that nevertheless bespeaks the imaginative participation required by audiences of the play in the world.

Whether in print or in performance then, these two scenes in *Cymbeline* are marked by the intersections *and* divergences of page and stage. Text and performance interpenetrate and inform one another, and in so doing, each mode of production reveals the limitations of the other. The literary and the theatrical intermix so innately that even portions of playtexts that seem designed to privilege reading audiences are imbued with the potential to produce imaginative engagements with performance potentialities. Yet the negotiations of text and performance need not be distilled into a binary of literary texts intended for readers versus scripts meant for performance; rather, it seems more useful to speak of the printed page as shaping and stabilizing a confluence of information that blends literary and theatrical elements. As Michael Dobson expresses in a wonderfully concise paradox, "If it is true that performance by its very nature exceeds the Shakespearian text . . . then we still need to acknowledge that the Shakespearian text exceeds any given performance" ("Writing" 160). From its texts to its paratexts, Shakespeare's Folio corroborates Dobson's assessment, recording the intricate convergences and divergences that constitute as well as complicate the conceptual framework linking printed and performed modes of dramatic realization.

Echoes and Reflections in the Beaumont and Fletcher Folio

Textual negotiations of performance are reconstituted in another major folio from later in the seventeenth century collecting the *"Comedies and Tragedies"* of Francis Beaumont and John Fletcher (1647). Although the Folio presents and markets Beaumont and Fletcher as collaborators responsible for its entire contents, it has been established that this is far from accurate—the stationer Humphrey Moseley, in fact, tips his hand in the Folio's preliminaries, where he admits to including "some

Prologues and *Epilogues*...not written by the *Authors* of this *Volume*" (g2r). Beaumont's share in the Folio is relatively small, with G. E. Bentley noting that "[t]he evidence is overwhelming that Beaumont had nothing to do with most of the plays" attributed to both playwrights (qtd. in Brooks 145). The precise breakdown of attributions in the Folio is beyond my purview; my interest in the Beaumont and Fletcher collection instead stems from the ways in which its paratextuals actively recall the theater even as they champion the plays' transition into print.[31] Marvin Carlson writes of "something in the very nature of the theatrical experience itself that encourages...a simultaneous awareness of something previously experienced and of something being offered in the present that is both the same and different, which can only be appreciated by a kind of doubleness of perception in the audience" (51); the invitation for early modern readers to indulge in what Carlson would term a "kind of double vision" (51), to recognize and attend to both printed and performed modes of dramatic realization, is what I have been attempting to highlight throughout this chapter, and it is an invitation that extends across much of the prefatory framework introducing the Beaumont and Fletcher Folio.

Those involved in compiling the Folio are upfront about its emulation of Heminge and Condell's collection: the dedication to Philip Herbert, also one of the dedicatees of the Shakespeare Folio, references "*the example of some, who once steered in our qualitie, and so fortunately aspired to choose your* Honour, *joynd with your (now glorified)* Brother, Patrons *to the flowing compositions of the then expired sweet* Swan *of* Avon SHAKESPEARE" (A2r). More subtle echoes of the Shakespeare Folio can be heard in Moseley's claim that Fletcher "never writ any one thing twice,...never touched pen till all was to stand as firme and immutable as if ingraven in Brasse or Marble" (A4v), which recalls Heminge and Condell's assertion that "we haue scarse receiued from [Shakespeare] a blot in his papers." As in Shakespeare's Folio, the dedicatory poems to the Beaumont and Fletcher Folio avow that collecting and printing plays bestows deserved immortality on both the author(s) and the works themselves.

The prefatory material to the two folios differ in that the latter collection is more explicit in its pronouncements regarding the actual reading experience the plays make possible, especially in terms of the texts' relations to the plays as performed. The apparent desire to create substantial links to the plays in performance is largely explained by the Folio's publication during the Interregnum, when the production of plays at public theaters was no longer a reality. James Shirley's epistle "TO THE READER" acknowledges the absence of public performances, but reconfigures the quiet of the theaters into the Folio's major selling point:

> *And now Reader in this* Tragicall Age *where the* Theater *hath been so much out-acted, congratulate thine owne happinesse, that in this silence of the Stage, thou hast a liberty to reade these inimitable Playes, to dwell and converse in these immortal Groves, which were only shewd our Fathers in a conjuring glasse, as suddenly removed as represented, the Landsc*[ape] *is now brought home by this optick, and the Presse thought too pregnant before shall be now look'd upon as greatest Benefactor to Englishmen, that must* acknowledge *all the felicity of* witt *and* words *to this Derivation.* (A3r–A3v)[32]

Shirley navigates the painful emptiness of the theaters by minimizing the representational power of the plays in performance. The emphasis on the impermanence of performance—*"as suddenly removed as represented"*—sets off the interpretive and affective potential provided by the relative fixity of the printed page. The Folio allows for a more meaningful encounter with the dramatic works in question, one that is very much a product of the book's ostensible stability; the value of the book's permanence is expressed most provocatively in Shirley's claim that the authors' printed works will bear the impressions of their readers: he informs readers they will be able to *"stand admiring the subtile Trackes of your engagement"* (A3v). The printed volume is thus figured as an interpretive space that makes possible forms of active, readerly participation (*"finding your self at last grown insensibly the very same person you read"* [A3v]) that are more present and enduring than the inevitably transitory significations of theatrical performance. In many ways, Shirley's epistle to readers foreshadows Harry Berger's binary of the "Slit-eyed Analyst and the Wide-eyed Playgoer" (xiv) and the prominence he assigns to the reading experience, to "how much is withheld from an audience that can only hear and see, how much is occulted in the text they cannot read" (149). Revealingly, the Folio's ability to capture the richness of Beaumont and Fletcher's creations is put forth in spatial and ocular terms: readers are enticed with the possibility that they can *"dwell and converse in these immortal Groves,"* an opportunity denied the plays' first generation of interpreters since the works *"were only shewd our Fathers in a conjuring glasse."* Where theater audiences were witnesses to mere representation, readers are able to situate themselves in the works, their gaze refined by the *"optick"* that is the Folio.

The promised end of readers' negotiations with the printed "*Derivation*" of the plays is immersion in a vivid, imagined land*scape*, a formulation that, as I have been arguing, is itself suggestive of the generative capabilities of printed drama.

Shirley's articulation of loss in the face of the silent public theaters is reasserted in a number of the Folio's dedicatory poems, as are his claims that reading the Folio offers a superior means of realizing the plays. The attempt to put forth the printed plays as capable of replacing any and all of the significations of performance often results in figurations that conflate acts of reading with acts of theatrical participation. James Howell remarks "Vpon Master *FLETCHERS* Dramaticall Workes," asserting that although "*the Stage is down . . . / And . . . we cannot have Thee trod o'th' stage, / Wee will applaud Thee in this silent Page*" (b4r). Robert Gardiner boasts that the Folio "*at last unsequesters the Stage, / Brings backe the Silver, and the Golden Age*" (c2r). Jasper Maine styles Beaumont and Fletcher's shared pen as "*part Stage and Actor*" (d1r). In John Web's commendatory poem, stage and book, actors and readers all become indistinguishable:

> *What though distempers of the present Age*
> *Have banish'd your smooth numbers from the Stage?*
> *You shall be gainers by't; it shall confer*
> *To th' making the vast world your Theater.*
> *The Presse shall give to ev'ry man his part,*
> *And we will all be Actors; learne by heart*
> *Those Tragick Scenes and Comicke Strains you writ,*
> *Vn-imitable both for Art and Wit;*
> *And at each* Exit, *as your Fancies rise,*
> *Our hands shall clap deserved Plaudities.* (c2v)

The excerpt from Web's piece is particularly suggestive in that it seeks to distinguish unique properties of printed playtexts, such as stability that can sustain prolonged and repeatable engagements—readers can "*learne by heart*" lines or entire scenes—while enfolding these attributes of print in extended metaphors of performance and theatrical participation. The notion that "*The Presse shall give to ev'ry man his part*" starkly contrasts the widespread dissemination of ostensibly uniform copies of an entire volume of plays against traditional "parts" distributed to actors—handwritten fragments of a greater whole, designed to be absolutely unique. As Peters observes of paratextuals such as those found in the Beaumont and Fletcher Folio, "the commentaries on print and performance repeatedly draw attention to their own paradoxes, implicitly recognizing, at the same time that they attempt to define separate media, the limits of medium distinction. Like theater, print is fixity and unfixity, it is accuracy and error, it is enlightenment and obscurity, it is order and chaos..." (111).

The mutability of playtexts is a point that the Folio's stationer, Humphrey Moseley, finds himself compelled to address at length. Humphrey's remarks on earlier incarnations of Beaumont and Fletcher's plays in a prefatory letter addressed to readers have become central to reassessments of the transmission of dramatic texts. Moseley first stresses that "You have here a *New Booke*; I can speake it clearely; for of all this large Uolume of *Comedies* and *Tragedies*, not one, till now, was ever printed before"; he then proceeds to clarify this issue in a passage that has drawn much attention:

> One thing I must answer before it bee objected; 'tis this: When these *Comedies* and *Tragedies* were presented on the Stage, the *Actours* omitted some *Scenes* and Passages (with the *Authour's* consent) as occasion led them; and when private friends desir'd a Copy, they then (and justly too) transcribed what they *Acted*. But now you have All that was *Acted*, and all that was not; even the perfect full Originalls without the least mutilation; So that were the *Authors* living (and sure they can never dye) they themselves would challenge neither more nor lesse then what is here published; this Volume being now so compleate and finish'd, that the Reader must expect no future Alterations. (A4r)

Thus, while admitting that the plays collected in the Folio likely exist in various, conspicuously different versions, and positing the source of these variants as the contingencies or "occasion[s]" of the theater, Moseley fashions his Folio as the endpoint of any further proliferation: it is "compleate and finish'd." The printed text, that is, reins in the unruliness of the theater and the slipperiness of the written word. Though (or perhaps *because*) the source of the actors' copies is not clear—are they copying from memory? from written texts? from some combination of the two?—textual theorists have seized on Moseley's description of actors' transcriptions of playtexts. Scott McMillin, for instance, positions Moseley's comments as central to his theory of actors collectively dictating plays to scribes,[33] and Erne utilizes the passage to underline his distinction between shorter theatrical texts and longer literary ones—Moseley's address suggests, according to Erne, that the practice of actors producing abridged texts of plays was "well established" (261).[34] Peter Blayney's reading of Moseley, if true, offers a more profound hypothesis: assuming that a reconstruction by actors of a shortened performance text "might emerge noticeably garbled," Blayney concludes that "what Moseley has been trying to tell us since 1647 is, I believe, the commonplace and innocent origin of the kind of text that Pollard called a Bad Quarto—but we have been too busy chasing imaginary pirates to listen" (394). Edward Pechter is more cautious in his assessment: "[Moseley] is referring not to a general category of text, only to instances in which some of 'these plays,' the ones included in his Folio, might be said to have been published before" (24). Rather than scrutinize the plausibility of these conjectures, I wish instead to note that the range of scenarios to which the Moseley passage has been put is a function of Moseley deliberately situating the Folio amidst competing forms of authority. Whether he is espousing the predictable rhetoric of a bookseller merely hawking his wares or transmitting a rosetta stone for early modern textual scholars is secondary to the fact that printed plays in his narrative are assuming a mediating role between the written and the performed. Moseley's apparent fidelity to "the perfect full Originalls" privileges text over performance, but the two modes of production are nevertheless innately and inextricably linked: Moseley's copy-texts are perfectly full not because they exclude the influences of the theater and its practitioners but because, impossibly, they encompass performance history and performance potentialities, "All that was *Acted*, and all that was not."

Moseley reasserts the Folio's connections to both page and stage more explicitly in a distinctive poem that functions as a transition piece from the commendatory verses to the plays. The poem, under the heading of "THE STATIONER," reads as follows:

As after th' *Epilogue* there comes someone
To tell *Spectators* what shall next be shown;
So here, am I; but though I've toyld and vex't
'Cannot devise what to present ye next;
For, since ye saw no *Playes* this Cloudy weather,
Here we have brought Ye our whole Stock together.
'Tis new, and all these *Gentlemen* attest
Under their hands 'tis Right, and of the Best;
Thirty foure Witnesses (without my taske)
Y'have just so many *Playes* (besides a *Maske*)
All good (I'me told) as have been *Read* or *Playd*,
If this Booke faile, tis Time to quit the Trade. (g2r)

Moseley here provides one final reminder of the heightened possibilities and limitations of printed drama during a period in which the performance of plays is prohibited. The poem epitomizes the spirit of the Folio's paratextuals; as Brooks explains, "by enacting within print a now prohibited bit of theatrical ritual, Moseley briefly reminds his readers of that which has been taken away from them, and simultaneously implies he can provide the next best thing" (149–50). But Moseley is not quite finished. He actually creates one final textual interstice in a "POSTCRIPT" below his poem that makes a number of hasty claims, most of which indicate an awareness of the shape and organization of the page affecting the reading experience: some of the prologues and epilogues to playtexts found in the Folio were not written by Beaumont or Fletcher; the Commendatory Verses prefacing the playtexts have a "different Character" because they were "(for expedition)" sent to "severall Printers"; and despite the use of several printers for the verses, the work itself is uniform, "one continued Letter."[35] Ultimately then, the postscript "struggles to account for two sets of collaborations—one in the printing house, the other in the playhouse" (Brooks 150). In essence, this chapter has been devoted to the site of the struggle Brooks highlights: the early modern printed page and the ability it is presumed to possess in representing meaningful connections to drama's performed modes.

The Beaumont and Fletcher Folio embodies many early modern formulations of page and stage, making, as it does, competing claims about what is being presented to readers: on one hand, the accuracy and completeness of the collected plays are championed, with the Folio put forth as a permanent record of authorially intended texts. On the other hand, the printed plays are figured as intimately connected to a past in which a vibrant, collaborative theater first brought them to life, with the Folio channeling the necessary energies to animate them once more. The Beaumont and Fletcher Folio thus records inherent tensions between textualized and performed modes of realization, offering readers the best of both worlds: the "perfect full Originalls" and works that are essentially performed when read, replacing the vacuum of the age's silent stage. Poem and Play are in perfect, conflated harmony. The subsequent printing history of the works of Beaumont and Fletcher is neither extensive nor diverse enough to trace this conflated authority through to any great effect. When considered in light of the edited afterlives of Shakespeare's texts, however, the Beaumont and Fletcher Folio's complicated and contradictory assessment of a printed playtext's ability to engage with performance—its awareness of itself as both an archive and portal through which performance can be imagined—proves prescient. Echoing Brooks, I would contend that all printed drama reminds readers of what has been taken away from them, though these reminders can be more implicit than Moseley's; further, as my remaining chapters will demonstrate, editors at the forefront of shaping Shakespeare's drama in print have employed a number of strategies that go a long way towards compensating for what has been lost.

CHAPTER 3

Performance and the Editorial Tradition

Thus Conscience does make Cowards,
And thus the healthful face of Resolution
Shews sick and pale with Thought:
And enterprises of great pith and moment,
With this regard, their currents turn awry,
And lose the name of action.

In any other passage, in any other play, the changes might go unnoticed, but in what has become the most famous speech in Shakespeare's most famous work, the alterations, though subtle, are impossible to miss. The quotation remains instantly recognizable as the conclusion of Hamlet's "To be or not to be" speech; the "native hue" of Resolution so familiar to modern eyes and ears, however, has become "the healthful face," and this face is no longer "sicklied o'er with the pale cast of thought" but rather "Shews sick and pale with Thought." The modifications, which are printed in a 1676 quarto of the play, were made by William Davenant, Restoration theater manager of the Duke's Men, one of two companies supported by royal proclamation when the public theaters reopened in 1660. The title page to *The Tragedy of Hamlet, Prince of Denmark* declares the text representative of the play "As it is now Acted at his Highness the Duke of *York*'s Theatre," and the Players' Quarto, as it is frequently called, is understood to be a fairly accurate reflection of *Hamlet* as it was performed in the latter half of the seventeenth century. Davenant's efforts to render the final portion of Hamlet's famed speech more readily intelligible might be conspicuous, but other forms of mediation on Davenant's part are equally profound; the justifications for his treatment of the play are communicated in a stark prefatory note "To the Reader":

> *This play being too long to be conveniently Acted, such Places as might be least prejudicial to the Plot or Sense, are left out upon the Stage: but that we may no way wrong the incomparable Author, are here inserted according to the Original Copy, with this Mark " (A2r)*

Those passages distinguished by quotation marks are not insignificant: around 800 lines of the Q2 text were evidently cut from performance, including most of the play's political undercurrents (the Danish ambassadors, most mentions of Fortinbras before the final scene), roughly half the "O, what a rogue and peasant slave am I" speech, all of Hamlet's advice to the players, and the entirety of Hamlet's final soliloquy.[1]

The implications of Davenant's address to readers, as well as the appearance of the quarto's pages—a record of lines that simply did not exist when cut from performance, "a synoptic vision of Shakespeare's play, book and performance side by side, each commenting upon the other" (Taylor, *Reinventing* 49)—must not be overlooked. The Players' Quarto is designed to mark its deviations from the play as performed, to encode the printed play with a means by which to recognize, and perhaps even interrogate, the distance between printed texts and performance texts. Davenant's address to readers is intriguing not because it acknowledges a gap between text and performance—from its first incarnations in print, *Hamlet* has registered such a rift, with Q1 (1603) championing the play "As it hath beene diuerse times acted by his Highnesse seruants in the Cittie of London: as also in the two Vniuersities of Cambridge and Oxford, and else-where", and Q2 (1604) locating its authority in a superior text, "Newly imprinted and enlarged almost as much againe as it was, according to the true and perfect Coppie"; rather, what is significant about the 1676 quarto is the implication that the printed page can both represent *and* mend the rift, and in the process become a meaningful site of exchange between the two modes of production. The introduction of a relatively simple bit of code into the text—quotation marks identifying lines *not* spoken in the theater—affords readers the opportunity to utilize the *scape* of the page to produce more accurate imagined approximations of the play as interpreted and staged by the Duke's Men.

Despite the significance of the way in which the Players' Quarto negotiates text and performance, Davenant is not regarded as a major figure in the establishment of editorial principles related to the Shakespearean text, and strictly speaking, he is not; as Marcus Walsh writes of the performance editions that began to proliferate in the next century and applied similar strategies for identifying the reduced texts used in the theater, "The eighteenth-century theatre texts are functional reprints rather than works of scholarship,... bearing virtually no signs of editorial intervention in terms of commentaries, glossaries, or introductions" (126). It is true that performance editions, for the reasons Walsh outlines, have had a minimal impact on the development of editorial practice; interestingly, however, Davenant's Player's Quarto can, from certain angles, be seen to be doing what we now think of as editorial work. Consider again the passage that opened this chapter: the insertion of "the healthful face" and "Shews sick and pale with Thought" were changes meant to facilitate the apprehension of theater audiences, but when recorded in the printed play, the alterations are akin to editorial mediations meant for readers. In Gary Taylor's words, "What later editors and commentators will put into the footnotes—paraphrases that explain Shakespeare's meaning—Davenant simply sticks into the dialogue itself" (*Reinventing* 47–8).[2] Any readerly engagement with performance is of course inherently incomplete and fragmentary—no text can record the myriad forms of nontextual labor required to actually stage a performance; despite these limitations, the marginal code in Davenant's edition, in providing performative data in a textually distilled form, nevertheless functions as an interpretive catalyst that reacts with, and alters, the reading experience. While the Players' Quarto is not governed by a systematic, rigorous methodology aimed at such things as elucidating textual variants present in earlier printings or resolving textual cruces, it does offer a striking example of how the malleability of the printed page can render awareness of performance practice an integral, and indeed inevitable, condition of the reading experience.

Davenant's edition, moreover, was known by those editors of the early eighteenth century who laid the cornerstones that have shaped editorial procedures related to the Shakespearean text ever since—Nicholas Rowe, for one, follows certain cuts and additions that Davenant had implemented in his version of *Hamlet*.[3] It is to the founding texts of the editorial tradition that I now turn, to critical editions of Shakespeare that are governed by discernible strategies related to emendation and elucidation. The work of editors like Rowe, Alexander Pope, Lewis Theobald, Edward Capell, and Edmund Malone is, quite rightly, usually studied in relation to their alterations of playtexts that were increasingly understood as discrete, literary objects; retrospective assessments of their work tend to focus on matters of emendation, textual commentaries and glossaries, modernization, and adjustments to punctuation, lineation, and meter. The overriding concern of these editors was with recognizing Shakespeare's plays "as constituting a body of literary work, within a literary context, recoverable and interpretable by the scholarly study of that context" (Walsh 124). Without denying their disproportionate interest in Poem over Play, my focus will shift attention to a different, related issue: how do the strategies of Shakespeare's early editors—which often display a lack of concern with or even explicit dismissal of performance potential—represent for readers the dynamic relationship shared by page and stage? Throughout, I will be considering "performance potential" in its broadest sense: not as an attempt to record or recapture the details of a specific performance, but in terms of textual representations of the possibilities of performance. In Davenant's case, he is recording stage conventions in his printed text, but the act of importing information from stage to page *changes* that information even as it shapes the reading experience. What the reader encounters is less an archive of stage history than mediated imprints of performance marking textual pathways along which imaginative engagements with the stage might follow.

That representations of performance in early critical editions ranged so widely—from excision and marginalization of what were deemed to be theatrical interpolations (Pope), to esoteric symbols meant to encode staged action into the text (Capell)—indicates that from the outset, editorial engagements with Shakespeare involved utilizing the manipulable space of the page to configure some sort of harmony between text and performance. Moreover, given the scholarly endeavors to recover, restore, and authenticate Shakespeare's plays in print and the concurrent preference for heavily adapted and transformed versions of Shakespeare in the eighteenth-century theater, when critical editions from the period do gesture toward the stage, these gestures tend to be in terms of idealized, imagined performances figured as being located *in* the literary text; that is, the editions more often than not imply that performance potentialities are "contained" in the text and that the imagined performances that reading can produce are thus merely realizations of the text's instructions. Although not referring specifically to eighteenth-century editorial practice, Worthen makes use of an apt metaphor, that of the text as "blueprint": "It implies on the one hand that the performance will materialize the implications of the text in a very different form, and that the materialization will necessarily specify and particularize the design; on the other hand, it also implies that the final performance is prescribed, that its structures and mechanics have already been laid down, and that performance is merely following the directions" (*Print* 172). Worthen's point is that this blueprint analogy persists in many current formulations of page and stage, but the metaphor is also applicable to the earliest incarnations of critical editions of Shakespeare, where certain forms of editorial mediation allow for an awareness of performance contingencies to be built from the text and its apparatuses. Indeed, by the latter half of the eighteenth century, Davenant's codified engagements with performance evolve into Capell's attempts to condense a range of stage actions into an entire system of printed symbols—quite literally, performance as, in Capell's words, "punctuation," a descriptor that is simultaneously evocative and impossible.

The "Impressions" of Rowe

The subcurrent of attention directed toward matters of performance, largely subsumed by more prominent and powerful streams of attention devoted to emending and modernizing the text, is exemplified in the work of Rowe, the first Shakespearean editor to be individuated for his efforts. As Rowe makes clear in the dedication to his six-volume collection of Shakespeare's works (1709), he understands his central task to be "to redeem him from the Injuries of former Impressions" (vol. 1, A2r).[4] "Impressions" has here a strictly textual emphasis: Rowe is not seeking to counter the adaptive impulses of the contemporary theater, but instead refers to the lineage of Shakespeare's texts; the "Injuries" in question have been incurred in the process of printing, not in the theater.[5] Further, Rowe's redemptive energies are clearly fuelled by authorial and literary concerns: "I must not pretend to have restor'd this Work to the Exactness of the Author's Original Manuscripts: Those are lost, or, at least, are gone beyond any Inquiry I could make; so that there was nothing left, but to compare the several Editions, and give the true Reading as well as I could from thence" (vol. 1, A2r-v). Rowe thus situates himself within a history of textual dissemination in writing and in print that can be traced (albeit only in theory) back to Shakespeare's originary creative acts. Rowe delves no further into his strategies, but he succinctly identifies the major obstacles facing any editor of Shakespeare: the prevalence of errors that have been introduced to the texts, authorial manuscripts that can be reconstructed only via a combination of interpretive and imaginative work, and the existence of extant versions that are connected in uncertain ways. Rowe's account does not specifically acknowledge the influence that the play as performed might have on either the printed versions produced for readers or on the reading experience itself—the "true Reading(s)" that he seeks to restore can presumably be attained without recourse to the exigencies of performance. The edition's investment in the materiality of printed playtexts is further demonstrated in the piece following the dedication, "Some Account of the Life" of Shakespeare, where Rowe occasionally references other pages in his multi-volume collection; in his discussion of *The Merchant of Venice*, for example, he remarks on "two Passages that deserve a particular Notice. The first is, what *Portia* says in praise of Mercy, *pag. 577*; and the other on the power of Musick, *pag. 587*" (vol. 1, p. xx). Comparisons of this sort have become absolutely commonplace in editorial practice, but the implications of such a move are worth remembering: not only is Rowe implying that exemplary passages can be appreciated when removed from their general context but his comments also attest to the fact that these passages (and their respective contexts) can be accessed readily by readers. Singling out passages in this way utilizes the material features of his printed text: Rowe's edition is searchable; noteworthy passages can be flagged; disparate passages can be juxtaposed; readers can navigate the edition in any direction and at any speed.

Rowe's prevailing concern with printed "Impressions" of the plays is echoed in most retrospective assessments of his edition, which often emphasize the prolonged influence that Rowe's work has had on the shape of subsequent editions of Shakespeare. His most conspicuous alterations to his copy-texts have to do with modernization and standardization: Rowe updates spelling and punctuation to conform to contemporary standards, divides plays into acts (and usually scenes as well), provides each play with a list of *dramatis personae*, inserts exits and entrances where they had not been previously marked, and begins each play with a brief reference to its location (doing the same for some, but not all, subsequent scenes in each play). Holland, writing in the introduction to a facsimile of Rowe's edition, has gone so far as to claim that Rowe's edition "was the single greatest determinant on the way Shakespeare's plays appeared in collected editions, in some respects even more important than the early quartos or the First Folio" (vol. 1, p. vii). It is thus crucial to observe that Rowe—himself a playwright attuned to the realities of the eighteenth-century stage—utilizes the page to imprint performance in significant ways; his approach to things like scene locations and stage directions is not entirely systematic, but the noteworthy ways in which he altered the shape of texts (relative to their previous incarnations in the seventeenth-century folios) are informed by considerations of theatrical possibility. Somewhat ironically then, given Rowe's emphasis on the materiality and textuality of the plays, "The editorial virtues of his text derive in large part from his theatrical background" (Taylor, *Companion* 53). Rowe remains such a significant and contentious figure not only because he was the "first" editor of Shakespeare's collected works but because he was the first critical interpreter of Shakespeare whose extended engagement with both text and performance was worked out on the space of the page. That is, the very means by which he made the texts more reader-friendly are also the means by which he facilitated readers' imagined approximations of performance. Crucially, Rowe's strategies for enabling readers to engage with, and imagine, printed playtexts *as drama* gave them a literary form that misrepresented performance in fundamental ways.

Rowe uses the Fourth Folio (1685) as the basis for his own collection, thus working from the most recent edition and following what was standard practice (F4 was based on F3, F3 on F2, F2 on F); his decision to use a received text rather than extensively collate extant materials was repeated by subsequent editors of Shakespeare, until Edward Capell's edition in 1768.[6] Rowe's rather underwhelming assessment of his editorial efforts in his dedication—he has taken "some Care," and has worked "pretty carefully"—seems, in retrospect, to be honest and accurate. It has been documented that he consulted printed editions other than F4, predominantly other Players' quartos from the Restoration, though his consultation of earlier versions of texts is far from comprehensive.[7] Barbara Mowat assesses the impact of Rowe's practice of conflation:

> It was Rowe who began the scholarly tradition of combining Folio and quarto texts to make what we now call conflated texts, and it was Rowe who established the practice of combining them with no signal to the reader that the editor had found lines and passages in different "editions"—as Rowe called them—and that the editor had himself been responsible for putting them together to make a text of his own. ("Rowe" 319)

It is difficult to argue with Mowat's critique, though her summation that "what Rowe constructed was a conflated text that hid the fact of its constructedness" (319) is anachronistic in that it holds Rowe to modern standards that he did not concern himself with. Mowat's complaint that Rowe combines Folio and quarto texts "with no signal to the reader" discounts Rowe's mention of his effort "to compare the several Editions"—perhaps this is all the signal that Rowe deemed necessary to account for his haphazard consultation of other printed texts. Rowe, simply put, was not invested in collating procedures that have since become integral to the editorial process. Furthermore, the dedication's bevy of first-person pronouns ("I have taken," "I must not," "beyond any Inquiry I could make," "I could," "I have"), combined with numerous verbs representative of editorial work ("restor'd," "compare," "give," "endeavour'd," "render'd"), yields a statement that is not quite an admission of his own complicity in constructing Shakespeare's text, but does reveal an awareness of his influential role in the reproduction of Shakespeare's "Work" for readers. The most provocative piece of evidence suggesting that Rowe was aware of his influence over the shape of the printed page is the existence of a trial sheet for his edition, dated 1708. Consisting of the title page and the first eight pages of text from *The Tempest*, the sheet is described by Holland as "an experiment in setting, establishing both the format for the page and significant elements of the house style that would be used for the full edition" (Holland, "Modernizing" 25). Holland identifies numerous subtle differences in spelling and punctuation between the 1708 trial sheet and the 1709 collected version of the play; the trial sheet, unlike the edition proper, is based on F2—likely a "convenient presence on Rowe's shel[f]" (27)—and Rowe follows this earlier folio in printing the classical "Actus Primus. Scæna Prima." rather than the more contemporary "ACT I. SCENE I.," which would become his standard in 1709. "This trial sheet," writes Margaret Jane Kidnie, "makes one aware, in a very concrete way, of the constructedness of an editorial tradition that can otherwise seem transparent, or 'natural'. Rowe *experimented with* possible formats" ("Staging" 164, emphasis in original).

Rowe's most prominent means of (re)constructing Shakespeare's works involve his manipulation of paratexts, particularly lists of *dramatis personae*, scene locations, and stage directions. His deployment of these editorial apparatuses, though undeniably influential, is not entirely consistent in that a range of information is communicated to readers across the edition, often differing from play to play. The majority of the lists of *dramatis personae* provide comparable amounts of information related to social standing and relationships amongst characters. The most scant list, that of *Troilus and Cressida*, identifies all male characters as only "Trojan" or "Greek"; other lists encode fragments of narrative, hinting proleptically at developments in the play's action: Saturninus in *Titus Andronicus*, for example, is *"Son to the late Emperor of Rome, and afterwards declar'd Emperor himself,* while Bassianus is *"Brother to* Saturninus, *in Love with* Lavinia."[8] General scene locations found under the *dramatis personae* also vary greatly: rather than attempt to detail the dizzying changes in *Antony and Cleopatra*, Rowe describes the scene as "*Several Parts of the Roman Empire*"; the locations of *Julius Caesar*, however, receive a more expansive treatment, with "*the first three Acts and beginning of the Fourth in* Rome, *for the remainder of the Fourth near* Sardis, *for the Fifth in the Fields of* Phillipi." That these scene indicators introducing each play are meant to provide readers with nothing more than rough mental maps helps to explain how plays as disparate as *A Midsummer Night's Dream* and *Timon of Athens* inhabit nearly identical imagined spaces: "Athens, *and a Wood not far from it*" and "Athens, *and the Woods not far from it,*" respectively. Rowe's treatment of localities is instrumental in formalizing an influential editorial precedent: readers are invited to visualize what Erne calls "the represented dramatic fiction" rather than "the theatrical representation" (*Modern Collaborators* 80).[9] It is not that fictionalized localities completely cut readers off from visualizing the stage, only that the process of encoding information likely to be more readily available in the theater transforms that information in fundamental ways as editors mediate potential significations of performance within the bounds of the book. The printed codes targeted at readers, in other words, are of a different order than what is received and processed by theater audiences. Where spectators are cued by things like costumes, stage props, or painted flats, the fictionalized localities of the sort that Rowe helps to popularize firmly situate a reader's participation with the play on the page.

At the same time, however, the areas of the playtext that Rowe is best known for purposefully manipulating—the *dramatis personae*, scene indicators, stage directions—remain the surest means of facilitating readers' navigations between *mise en page* and *mise en scène* and thus sharpening *performancescapes*. Rowe's added stage direction in *Timon of Athens*, for example, that Timon scatters the "detested Parasites" at his fateful banquet by "*Throwing the Dishes at them, and drives 'em out*" (vol. 5, p. 2196), funnels a reader's imagination toward a very specific range of possibilities; the Folio versions of the play contain no such direction, meaning that readers receive no information supplementary to the dialogue as to what, if anything, Timon is throwing. Editors have continued to tinker with this particular moment in *Timon*: subsequent editions have sometimes specified that Timon first throws hot water and then hurls stones at his dinner guests, interpolations that absorb and modify Rowe's, producing a *performancescape* that invites readers to envision Timon's explosion of hostility (and its potential ramifications) in a different way. The shift from no direction to dishes to stones likely has no great bearing on one's overall assessment of the play, but considering that Timon is also physically repelling callers after he retires to his cave outside Athens, an editor's treatment of the banquet scene can resonate much later. Though the Folio text does not contain a stage direction, the dialogue implies strongly that Timon fires a stone at Apemantus during the climax of their verbal sparring in the fourth act: "Away thou tedious Rogue, I am sorry I shall lose a stone by thee" (TLN 2009–10); an editor inserting directions for a stone (or stones) to be thrown at the banquet and then later at Apemantus can provide a consistency to Timon's violent misanthropy that is otherwise not necessarily available to readers of the play. Rowe himself does not make such a link, but his willingness to introduce paratextuals that govern a reader's engagement with the Shakespearean text essentially instituted the practice that make such a link possible.

The other influential practice initiated by Rowe's edition was its inclusion of engravings depicting particular scenes from each play.[10] While the claim that "all of [Rowe's] engravings depict early-eighteenth-century costumes, scenes, and staging techniques" (Dugas 145) overstates the case (one need only look at the first engraving in the collection prefacing *The Tempest* to realize that the illustrations are not bound to the possibilities of theatrical representation),[11] it is clear that many of the illustrations do reflect the contemporary stage. The ghosts tormenting Richard in the final act of *Richard III*, for instance, seem to be emerging from a trap door in the floor, while the engraving of the assassination scene in *Julius Caesar* appears to use as its background a Roman cityscape on painted flats (the likes of which had been popularized on the Restoration stage). Other engravings are even more nuanced in their approximations of performance: an overturned chair is prominent in the foreground of the illustration of the closet scene in *Hamlet*, an acknowledgement of the actor's point popularized by Thomas Betterton (?1635–1710), who abruptly recoiled at the reappearance of the Ghost (see Figure 3.1).[12] Even though no engraving can be linked to a specific performance, the cumulative effect of the illustrations is that the "Imagination is subordinated to a realistic portrayal of the modes of the contemporary theatre" (Jackson 470). Stuart Sillars offers compelling remarks as to how a frontispiece such as the one supplied for *Hamlet* engages what he refers to as "the reader's progress through the dramatic continuum" (4):

> For the reader who witnessed the performance, the engraving may function as a memorial trigger; for the one who has not, it may suggest a response of great immediacy. But in itself it remains essentially distanced from these events, because of the change in medium the moment has undergone. (8)

Figure 3.1 The frontispiece to Rowe's edition of *Hamlet* (1709). By permission of the Folger Shakespeare Library.

The engravings can thus be understood as a means by which the plays are made *present* for readers—in the full sense of both contemporary and visible. In no way can the engravings be understood to recapture or freeze performance, but what they offer is a kind of portal through which to conceptualize the interpretive space between disparate modes of realization.

The ruffled curtain draping the upper corners of more than a dozen engravings, for instance, functions as what Sillars terms a "metaphor of the theatre" (44) and as part of a system that "infuse[s] in the reader an awareness of the difference between page and stage as visual and experiential media" (45). The prominence of powdered wigs, three-cornered hats, and immense head-dresses are, along with Rowe's treatment of punctuation and spelling, part of an effort to modernize Shakespeare's text; the engravings also carry with them the potential to ground readers' imaginings of particular incidents, a point that would have been especially important for those plays that had yet to enter the eighteenth-century repertory, like *All's Well That Ends Well* and *The Comedy of Errors*. Since they carry no identifying tags or cross-references, the engravings cannot always be matched to specific acts, scenes and line numbers—T. S. R. Boase remarks that "Troilus and Cressida are frankly taking a curtain call" (86–7), though it seems more likely that what is being depicted is Cressida passing Troilus's sleeve to Diomedes. Though the engravings range widely in terms of the relative dynamism of the moments they capture, their comprehensiveness (one for each play, including the six apocryphal works that Rowe imported from F4) and consistent placement (before the *dramatis personae* of each play) create a conduit that runs throughout Rowe's edition, one that allows for symbiotic exchanges between textual and performed modes. More specifically, the inclusion of the engravings originate a systematic practice that facilitates visual representations (or approximations) of performance coming to bear on readers' engagements with Shakespeare's printed texts. A revealing example is provided by the engraving introducing *A Midsummer Night's Dream* (see Figure 3.2), where the fractured state of Oberon and Titania's relationship is rendered strikingly: two rival factions of fairies stretch across the page, centered by the confrontation of their respective leaders; Oberon and Titania each carry scepters that they rather ominously point at one another, the tips of which are almost, but not quite, touching; a moon is shaded by a passing cloud in the sky of the flat-like background. It is not that the engraving is absolutely true to a specific performance, nor that the engraving totally determines a reader's imagining of Oberon and Titania's meeting, nor that it is impossible for a reader to produce a similarly symbolic visualization of the meeting without a suggestive illustration. What the engraving represents is the potential of a paratext to enhance the text proper and enrich the reading experience. A reader moving through 2.1 of Rowe's text of the play might recall or make reference to the engraving,

Figure 3.2   The frontispiece to Rowe's edition of *A Midsummer Night's Dream* (1709). By permission of the Folger Shakespeare Library.

and in doing so, encounter an image that stimulates or enhances an awareness of certain lines ("the Forgeries of Jealousie"), images ("the Moon . . . / Pale in her Anger, washes all the Air"), or matters of tone and tension (Titania's summation of the "Progeny of Evil" that are the result of "our Debate, ... our Dissention"). Combined with the text, the engraving serves as a resource from which the reader's imagination can extrapolate more vivid and resonant *performancescapes*. Many of the engravings found in Rowe's edition now appear remarkably stilted and static, though this is due in large part to the fact that high-quality photographs have come to pervade Shakespeare editions of the past 50 years; these photographs, though usually more provocative than an engraving, are performing the same role of mediating page and stage.

Pope's "Reprobation": The Porter in *Macbeth*

Rowe does not explicitly position his edition relative to live performance and theatrical history; as my reading of his edition has shown, the manner in which his editorial strategies constructed the links between text and performance must be inferred from his treatment of paratextuals like stage directions and scene locations. Rowe's successor, Alexander Pope, is much more forthcoming in his edition (1723–5) about his understanding of the relationship between Shakespeare's plays in print and on stage. Pope demonstrates a greater interest in, and familiarity with, the early quartos, though his consultation of texts that predate the Folios is far from comprehensive or systematic; significantly, his desire to canvass early editions in search of alternate readings is driven by an unequivocal distrust of the First Folio. For Pope, the theater is a poisonous influence on Shakespeare's written works that subsequently contaminates the transmission of these works into print. Particularly damning for the First Folio (in addition to being compiled by two actors, Heminge and Condell) is that, in Pope's estimation, it contains an accumulation of "trifling and bombast passages ... For whatever had been added, since those Quarto's, by the actors, or had stolen from their mouths into the written parts, were from thence conveyed into the printed text ... " (vol. 1, p. xvi). Pope is intent on removing the taint of theatrical interpolation, though this is not to say that the purified text that Pope is interested in producing is intended to be entirely Shakespeare's, or even Shakespeare in his entirety. Pope does consult the early quartos that he can get his hands on, but he is uninterested in judging their relative authority or delving into stemmatics; instead, matters are straightforward: all early texts are potentially corrupted, which allows him the freedom to "unsystematically ... pick and choose among variant texts as some particular readings appealed to him more than others" (Murphy, *Print* 65).[13] This approach to variant readings and theatrical interpolations is, not surprisingly, a key determinant in the shape of Pope's edition.

Tellingly, Pope claims that "one may look upon [Shakespeare's] works...as upon an ancient majestick piece of *Gothick* Architecture, compar'd with a neat Modern building: The latter is more elegant and glaring, but the former is more strong and more solemn. It must be allow'd, that in one of these there are materials enough to make many of the other" (xxiii). The metaphor is revealing: beyond fashioning Shakespeare's works as an enduring creation worthy of reverence, it also betrays Pope's willingness to subject these works to his own system of editorial architectonics. If Shakespeare's plays are a "majestick piece of *Gothick* Architecture," then they are also in need of continual upkeep and refinement, even large-scale reconstruction. Pope may elide his influence by claiming to have "discharged the dull duty of an Editor, to my best judgement, with more labour than I expect thanks, with a religious abhorrence of all Innovation, and without any indulgence to my private sense or conjecture" (xxii), but his *mise en page* tells a much different story. "[P]ointing out an Author's excellencies," writes Pope, "[is] the better half of Criticism" (xxiii), and to this end he devises a number of strategies for signalling readers: "Some of the most shining passages are distinguish'd by comma's in the margin; and where the beauty lay not in particulars but in the whole, a star is prefix'd to the scene" (xxiii). Distinguishing what he deems exemplary portions of text in these ways proves to be relatively unobtrusive: noteworthy passages marked by marginal commas run from just a few lines (Cleopatra's "Peace, peace! / Dost thou not see my baby at my breast, / That sucks the nurse asleep"), to much longer speeches (Mercutio's Queen Mab speech and Prospero's summation of his magical achievements, "Ye elves of hills, brooks, standing lakes and groves..." are among those recognized), and as Pope explains, extended sequences worthy of a reader's attention are identified by an innocuous star prefacing the scene—the post-assassination confrontation between Brutus and Cassius in *Julius Caesar* (4.3 in Pope's edition) is an example of a scene evidently worthy of this distinction.

Much more significant—and conspicuous—are the textual ramifications of Pope's anti-theatrical bias. His claim that there are "almost innumerable Errors, which have risen from one source, the ignorance of the Players, both as his actors, and as his editors" (xiv) is no mere flourish; rather, this position determines on a fundamental level the manner in which Pope's edited text is presented to readers. When it comes to the influence of the theater, he takes an uncompromising stance: "Some suspected passages which are excessively bad, (and which seem Interpolations by being so inserted that one can intirely omit them without any chasm, or deficiency in the context) are degraded to the bottom of the page; with an Asterisk referring to the places of their insertion" (xxii). What is important to understand about Pope's strategy of marginalizing "theatrical interpolation" is that despite being the product of an anti-theatrical stance, it nevertheless represents a conscious, systematic *engagement* with performance. The deep irony of Pope's intention has never been sufficiently addressed: in removing what he understands to be the "excessively bad," interpolated passages, Pope draws attention to the very influences that he seeks to suppress. An examination of Pope's edition reveals an ostensibly discriminatory strategy that seems to subvert itself as soon as it is put in motion, with "degraded" passages set off in the margins in a reduced font, distinguished in a manner not unlike Pope's use of commas or stars to identify exemplary passages. Thus, in the very act of attempting to strip what he considers to be theatrical interpolations of their authority, Pope simultaneously *confers* a certain measure of authority on particular passages in his inability to do away with them entirely. Paradoxically, the more egregious and expansive the supposed influence of the players, the more conservative Pope becomes in his alterations to the playtext and his *mise en page*: a marginal note to 1.2 of *The Two Gentlemen of Verona* explains that

> *This whole Scene, like many others in these Plays, (some of which I believe were written by* Shakespear, *and others interpolated by the Players) is compos'd of the lowest and most trifling conceits, to be accounted for only from the gross taste of the age he liv'd in…I wish I had authority to leave them out, but I have done all I could, set a mark of reprobation upon them, throughout this edition.* †††(vol. 1, p. 157)

Thus the most severe mark of Pope's dissatisfaction with theatrical interpolation—that of the triple daggers—is reserved for entire scenes that can only be made to disappear by way of wishful thinking. Significantly, when smaller passages are removed from the text proper, Pope more often than not supplies readers with the means to *undo* the divisions that his strategy introduces: the "low and vicious parts and passages" (xxi) that he "sifts" from the text are not scattered to the winds but shifted to a different site on the page, and readers are given specific instructions as to how they can blend two otherwise discrete elements into a fuller version of the playtext. It is worth noting that

Pope explains his asterisks as marking not the deletion or excision of passages, but "the places of their insertion" (xxii), a rhetorical move that seems to give readers an implicit invitation to reconstitute that which has been sundered. Ultimately then, although text and performance are separated and placed in discrete segments of the page, in a strange and surely unintended way, Pope's edition exemplifies what Edmund King terms "dramatically informed anti-theatricalism" (4) in that it has the potential to foster readings that put the opposed elements of Poem and Play into meaningful contact with one another.

In order to gauge Pope's insistence that Shakespeare's printed plays are comprised of a heterogeneous mixture of literary and theatrical elements from which Poem and Play can be tagged and separated, it is worth considering an example of his policy of "reprobation" in more detail. Pope has little patience for crude humor or elaborate word-play—*Love's Labour's Lost*, for instance, is heavily cut, while the quibbling of Viola/Cesario and Feste in 3.1 of *Twelfth Night* (a play that is otherwise largely spared Pope's censure) is an example of a scene given the triple-dagger mark of disapproval. It is unsurprising then that the opening 40 or so lines of the Porter scene in *Macbeth* (2.4), which include the Porter's ruminations on the knocking at the gate and his initial exchanges with Macduff on the effects of drunkenness, are confined to the margins. Given that the Porter scene was not performed in the Restoration or eighteenth century, Pope's handling of the Porter is in sync with contemporary performance practice.[14] It is thus ironic that Pope's unique strategy of textual hierarchization could leave readers, rather than theater-goers, with a greater appreciation for the Porter's performance potential and the character's temporary authority over the play. The degraded passage begins the scene in the Folio, meaning that Pope's edition of the Porter scene begins not with the Folio's direction for a "*Knocking within*," but with an emended entrance, "*Enter* Macduff, Lenox *and Porter*" followed by Macduff's "Is thy master stirring?" Although it is entirely plausible that a reader would completely ignore the cut passage and proceed directly from the end of 2.3 (page 541 in the edition) to Pope's revised starting point for 2.4 (which is conveniently located overleaf at the top of a new page, 542), it is also plausible that a reader would finish reading 2.3 and follow the asterisk after a concluding "*Exe*[unt]" to the bottom of page 541, where the cut passage is reproduced (see Figures 3.3 and 3.4). To be sure, Pope intends for a reader making this tangential move to view the bits with the Porter as uncouth humor unworthy of serious consideration, the unfortunate by-product of Shakespeare's obligations "to please the lowest of people, and

The Tragedy of M A C B E T H.   541

How is't with me, when every noise appalls me?
What hands are here? hah! they pluck out mine eyes.
Will all great *Neptune's* ocean wash this blood
Clean from my hand? no, this my hand will rather *
Make the green ocean red ——·

Enter Lady.

Lady. My hands are of your colour; but I shame
To wear a heart so white. I hear a knocking   [*Knock.*
At the south entry. Retire we to our chamber;
A little water clears us of this deed.
How easie is it then? your conftancy.
Hath left you unattended —— hark, more knocking!   [*Knock.*
Get on your night-gown, left occasion call us,
And shew us to be watchers; be not loft
So poorly in your thoughts.

Mach. To know my deed, 'twere best not know my self.
Wake *Duncan* with this knocking: would thou couldst! [*Exe.* *

                                                     S C E N E

* ——will rather
Thy multitudinous sea incarnadine ;
Making the green one red.
Enter Lady. &c.

* —— wouldst thou could'st!

                    S C E N E IV.

                    Enter a Porter.

                                        [*Knocking within.*
Port. Here's a knocking indeed: if a man were porter of hell-gate, he
should have old turning the key. [*Knock.*] Knock, knock, knock. Who's
there, i'th' name of *Belzebub?* here's a farmer, that hang'd himself in th' expectation of plenty: come in time, have napkins enough about you, here
you'll sweat for't. [*Knock.*] Knock, knock. Who's there in th' other devil's name? faith, here's an equivocator, that could swear in both the scales a-
gainst either scale, who committed treason enough for God's sake, yet could
not equivocate to heav'n: oh come in, equivocator. [*Knock.*] Knock,
knock, knock. Who's there? faith, here's an *English* tailor come hither for
stealing out of a *French* hose: come in taylor, here you may roafty our goose. ·
[*Knock.*] Knock, knock. Never at quiet! what are you? but this place is too
cold for hell. I'll devil-porter it no further: I had thought to have let in some
of all professions, that go the primrose way to th' everlasting bonfire. [*Knock.*]
Anon, anon, I pray you remember the porter.

                                                     Enter

Figure 3.3 The end of 2.3 in Pope's edition of *Macbeth*. By permission of Bielefeld University Library.

to keep the worst of company" (vol. 1, p. ix). Yet Pope's treatment of the degraded passage is noteworthy: not only is it reproduced in its entirety but it appears in an edited form that is commensurate with the text proper. He maintains the use of regularized speech prefixes and retains stage directions found in the Folio (the "*Knocking within*" that begins the scene and various "*Knock*[s]" throughout the Porter's first speech). Pope is thus careful not to damage or significantly alter the portion

542   *The Tragedy of* M A C B E T H.

S C E N E   IV.

Enter Macduff, Lenox *and Porter.*

Macd. Is thy mafter ftirring?
---- Our knocking has awak'd him; here he comes.
Len. Good morrow, noble Sir.

Enter Macbeth.

Macb. Good morrow both.
Macd. Is the King ftirring, worthy *Thane?*
Macb. Not yet.
Macd. He did command me to call timely on him,
I've almoft flipt the hour.
Macb. I'll bring you to him.
Macd. I know this is a joyful trouble to you :
But yet 'tis one.
Macb. The labour we delight in, † phyficks pain;
This is the door.
Macd. I'll make fo bold to call, for 'tis my limited fervice.
                                                    [*Exit* Macduff.

Enter Macduff, *and* Lenox.

Macd. Was it fo late, friend, ere you went to bed,
That you do lye fo late?
Port. Faith, Sir, we were caroufing 'till the fecond cock:
And drink, Sir, is a great provoker of three things.
Macd. What three things doth drink efpecially provoke?
Port. Marry, Sir, nofe-painting, fleep, and urine. Letchery, Sir, it pro-
vokes, and unprovokes; it provokes the defire, but it takes away the perfor-
mance. Therefore much drink may be faid to be an equivocator with letche-
ry; it makes him and it mars him; it fets him on, and it takes him off; it
perfwades him, and difheartens him; makes him ftand to, and not ftand to;
in conclufion, equivocates him into a fleep, and giving him the lie, leaves him.
Macd. I believe drink gave thee the lie laft night.
Port. That it did, Sir, i' th' very throat on me; but I requited him for
his lie, and I think, being too ftrong for him, though he took up my legs
fometime, yet I made a fhift to caft him.
S C E N E, *&c.*   † *heals or cures* pain.

4   *Len.*

Figure 3.4   The beginning of 2.4 in Pope's edition of *Macbeth*. By permission of Bielefeld
University Library.

of text being amputated; the cut passage remains intact, meaning that
a reader shuttling between the text proper and Pope's unique form of
paratext can reattach it rather seamlessly—the degraded passage carries
over to the next page, ending with an "*&c*" that directs the reader back
up to the text proper and Pope's preferred starting point for the scene.

What is Pope removing from his version of *Macbeth* in marginalizing
the role of the Porter? What might readers who engage with the degraded

passage be made especially aware of? For one, the Porter's discourse on the dangers of "equivocation" is absolutely in tune with the larger thematic concerns of a play steeped in matters of doubleness and double meanings. The opening of the Porter scene may not be integral enough to its immediate context or the play as a whole for its removal to create what Pope refers to in his preface as a "chasm" or "deficiency" (xxii) in the playtext, but the bulk of the Porter material has its echoes elsewhere in the work—the Porter's rant against "an equivocator, that could swear in both the scales against either scales, who committed treason enough for God's sake, yet could not equivocate to heav'n" (541) finds a more succinct formulation in Macbeth's paranoia over "th' equivocation of the fiend / That lies like truth" (593).[15] With the role of the Porter fully intact, concerns over equivocation and doubleness can be seen to pervade the world of the play from its highest levels of leadership to its most base attendants.

Thinking specifically in terms of the dynamic interconnections of text and performance, the Porter scene—and Pope's treatment of it—becomes even more resonant. It has often been noted that the Porter (who asks, "Who's there i'th' name of *Belzebub?*... Who's there in th' other devil's name?") might have been intended to recall devil-porters at the gates of Hell in medieval miracle plays; indeed, the character claims at one point that "I'll devil-porter it no further."[16] Though this trace of a medieval theatrical type might not be readily apprehensible for eighteenth-century or modern audiences, the character of the Porter does appear to be linked to a mode of playing founded on physicality and histrionics.[17] The Porter is curiously positioned in the play, buffering the Macbeths' responses to Duncan's murder and the visceral reactions to the horrific scene of his death that follow the arrival of Macduff and Lennox. The abrupt shift in tone that accompanies the Porter—whose commentary is rife with English proverbs and perhaps even veiled references to current events— can be understood to momentarily suspend the intensity of the imaginative effects that surround him, allowing the world of the play to be temporarily subsumed by the play in the world.[18] The passage itself, in other words, dramatizes the tension between text and performance that is typographically and spatially represented on Pope's hierarchized page. The necessities of plot and action demand that Macduff and Lennox enter, so that Duncan's corpse can be discovered, so that Macbeth can be crowned, so that the play can advance toward its conclusion, but the Porter stems the dramatic tide in refusing to answer the knocks at the gate for as long as he can. In not only denying the knocking but seeking to define for the audience what (and how) the knocks might signify, the Porter momentarily asserts the authority of the performer over defining stage space and staged meaning. When the scene is communicated in print, the text of the Porter's dialogue (a digression that begins, "Here's a knocking indeed") and certain instructions for performed actions (the stage directions for "*Knock*[ing]") are typographically interwoven. As a result, readers of Pope's edition, though encouraged to discriminate against the transformation of the text into staged action, are still privy to instances such as this scene from *Macbeth* in which the printed play can operate as a generative interpretive space offering conceptual linkages between page and an imagined stage. Pope renders the Porter's ribald philosophizing discrete, but this cuts both ways: it removes the "bad" passage from Pope's best-text of the play, but it also makes this passage conspicuous on the page. Paradoxically, the Porter's clowning—and the prominence of this clowning, given his position in the play—becomes both muted and accentuated. Due to Pope's manipulation of his *mise en page*, readers might very well find themselves drawn to, rather than repelled from, the significance of the stage business involving the Porter and the rich conflation of textual and performed modes that inheres in the differentiated passage.

Theobald and the "True Reading"

Pope's aesthetic sensibilities and perception of the corrupted nature of Shakespeare's extant printed plays mean that he is doubtful of the possibility of efforts to "repair the deficiencies or restore the corrupted sense of the Author" (vol. 1, p. xxiii). The title selected by Lewis Theobald for his book-length assault on Pope's edition— *Shakespeare Restored* (1726)—thus immediately marks his distance from Pope (and from Rowe as well—Rowe, you will recall, claimed that "I must not pretend to have restor'd this Work to the Exactness of the Author's Original Manuscripts" [vol. 1, A2r]).[19] By way of an introductory essay and a detailed critique of Pope's treatment of *Hamlet* (as well as an appendix challenging Pope on a variety of textual issues from other plays), *Shakespeare Restored* cultivates Theobald's strategies for engaging the Shakespearean text, planting seeds that would eventually blossom into his own critical edition of the plays (published in 1733). Theobald subjects Pope's edition to remarkable scrutiny, repeatedly faulting Pope "where he has *maim'd* the Author by an unadvis'd *Degradation*; where he has made a *bad* Choice in a *Various Reading* and degraded the better Word; and where he, by *mistaking* the *Gloss* of any Word, has given a wrong Turn to the Poet's Sense and Meaning" (*Restored* 134).[20]

Unlike Pope, Theobald does not believe that it is incumbent on an editor to bring Shakespeare into line with contemporary tastes and literary fashions—which is not to say that Theobald is above emending or altering Shakespeare's text; rather, his editorial principles, combined with a more powerful authorial orientation than either Rowe or Pope had exhibited, lead him to ensure his emendations are founded in a defensible methodology. Unlike his predecessors, Theobald had read extensively in the English Renaissance—not just dramatic texts other than Shakespeare, but prose and poetry as well as crucial reference texts like Hall, Holinshed, and Plutarch; for Theobald, this broad reading both authenticates the editor's commitment to his primary material and legitimizes any emendations that are made: "An Editor...should be well vers'd in the History and Manners of his Author's Age, if he aims at doing him a Service" (vol. 1, pp. xlv–xlvi).[21] Greater familiarity with Shakespeare's context, contemporaries, and sources enables Theobald to emend and gloss corrupted and obscure readings that Rowe and Pope had left unchanged. Theobald also displays a greater concern for the authority of the early quartos; his belief (which echoes Pope's) is that Shakespeare's works were contaminated by "Mutilations or Additions made to them" (I. xxxviii) in the theater, and these corruptions have become further ingrained with each printed incarnation:

> To these obvious Causes of Corruption it must be added, that our Author has lain under the Disadvantage of having his Errors propagated and multiplied by Time: because, for near a Century, his Works were republish'd from the faulty Copies without the assistance of any intelligent Editor... (vol. 1, pp. xxxviii–xxxix)

Where Theobald differs from Pope is in his willingness to assign at least part of the blame for textual corruption on the realities of early modern printing house practice; theatrical interpolations may have introduced "Mutilations" to Shakespeare's works, but Theobald is simultaneously aware that those transmitting these works in print have not done enough to heal the textual scars. A more nuanced understanding of the early quartos is a point of pride for Theobald: "I have thought it my Duty, in the first place, by a diligent and laborious Collation to take in the Assistances of all the older Copies" (xlii).

Theobald's collation is certainly more extensive than anything that had yet been attempted, but he is far from consistent in how he employs his bibliographic knowledge, often making decisions based on his own aesthetic preferences (despite his prefatory convictions to the contrary).[22] Because of his more detailed engagement with primary and secondary texts, Theobald's *mise en page* is relatively full of conspicuous annotation. Theobald defends his copious notes by suggesting that they in fact stabilize his edition: "a Note on every [obscure or emended passage] hinders all possible Return to Depravity; and for ever secures them in a State of Purity and Integrity not be lost or forfeited" (vol. 1, p. xlv). The idea that the text can be "secured" by surrounding it with editorially prescribed paratexts is absolutely central to Theobald's programme. If Theobald's edition exemplifies a turn in Shakespearean editorial practice, it is toward utilizing verifiable documentary records to temper an editor's aesthetic impulses when making decisions regarding textual variants and cruces. David Greetham makes the point that "the archive of public memory and the archive of documentary record often bear an uneasy, shifting relation to each other" (5), but near the midpoint of the eighteenth-century, editorial procedures exhibit no real anxiety in regard to hierarchizing these two modes of memorialization. The staged performance (a locus of public memory) and the printed book may have been acknowledged as different though nevertheless connected ways of producing the same dramatic work, but the book was given precedence. Samuel Johnson, for example, is willing to accept that "a play read, affects the mind like a play acted," but it is clear that in his mind, a performance merely activates that which is textual: "a dramatick exhibition is a book recited with concomitants that encrease or diminish its effect" (vol. 1, p. xxix). In Theobald's case, securing his emendations and paratextual negotiations with Shakespeare by linking them to other material records—a move produced by his desire for "a State of Purity and Integrity" that is exclusively textual and literary— means that he turns away from more intangible archives constituted by performance histories, memories of performance, and the repertory. In juxtaposing disparate pieces of text to establish things like poetic tendencies and habits of figuration, Theobald's work highlights the stability conferred by the printed page—in his hands the edited text becomes a massive source of data that makes rapid retrieval and cross-references a necessary means of defending editorial emendation. Theobald's marginalia becomes a kind of latticework that interweaves playtext, editorial commentary, collations of alternative emendations, and other textual sources (most of which are Shakespearean, though Theobald does reference the work of other Renaissance playwrights as well); unlike those in Pope's edition, Theobald's margins are not a site of degradation but of elucidation—what Theobald writes in the margins is meant to contribute to the reading experience rather than remain distinct from it. Theobald's edition is not intended to produce especially vivid *performancescapes* precisely because of where he locates meaning and value: imaginative reconstructions of the ephemeral, collaborative elements of a play's potential realizations on stage are not what his manipulation of paratextuals is meant to account for.

Theobald's commitment to stabilizing the text and his disinterest in engaging with performance potentialities become most apparent when he is dealing with moments of complicated or ambiguous stage action. A revealing example is his treatment of the monument scene in *Antony and Cleopatra*, where the mortally wounded Antony is carried on to the stage and somehow lifted to his lover on an upper-stage or structure above. Michael Neill describes the staging of this moment—particularly the matter of hauling Antony's body aloft—as "especially awkward" and "difficult to resolve" (363).[23] In fairness to Theobald, at the time of preparing his edition a "straight" version of *Antony and Cleopatra* was not a part of any repertory; John Dryden's interpretation of the story, *All For Love*, was first produced in 1678 and was the preferred version until the early nineteenth century. Dryden's version does not involve the hoisting of Antony's body implied by the Folio text (in fact, Dryden alters the ending of the play to have the dead bodies of Antony and Cleopatra on stage together), so Theobald likely had not confronted the scene as we are familiar with it today. Theobald's received text (which he collates below the text proper) provides this reading:

[Ant. *I am dying, Ægypt, dying; only yet*]
I here importune Death a while, until
Of many thousand Kisses the poor last
I lay upon thy Lips.
Cleo. *I dare not, dear,*
Dear my Lord, pardon; I dare not,
Least I be taken.

Theobald adds this comment:

...how inconstantly is the Lady made to reply? *Antony* says, he only holds Life 'till he can give her one last Kiss: and She cries, She dares not: What dares She not do? Kiss *Antony*? But how should She? She was above lock'd in her Monument; and He below, on the Outside of it. With a very slight Addition, I think, I can cure the whole; and have a Sort of

Warrant from *Plutarch* for it into the Bargain. [. . .] Now *Plutarch* says, "*Antony* was carried in his Men's Arms *into the Entry* of the *Monument*: Notwithstanding, *Cleopatra* would not *open the Gates*, but *came to the high Windows*, and cast out certain Chains and Ropes, *&c.*"—So that *Antony* might very reasonably desire her to come down; and She as reasonably excuse herself, for fear of being insnared by *Caesar*. (vol. 6, pp. 313–4)

The issue for Theobald (as it is throughout his edition) is to elucidate the text where he perceives the sense to be muddled, to provide what he calls "a real Restoration of the true Reading" (vol. 1, p. xl). To rectify the perceived corruption, Theobald adds the purely conjectural "Come down" to the end of Antony's speech in the exchange, so that what Cleopatra is refusing is not a kiss, but the request that she descend from the monument. As this example makes clear, Theobald's understanding of a "true Reading" exists on an exclusively textual, literary continuum: his emendation of the text (dubiously rooted in a reference to Plutarch) is not required to adhere to potential stage practice, nor is it meant to enrich or even facilitate a reader's imaginative approximation of the play as performed. Theobald's edition includes the direction, "*They draw* Antony *up to* Cleopatra" (the Folio direction reads "*They heaue Anthony aloft to Cleopatra* [TLN 3045]) but otherwise passes over the issue of Antony's body being raised up. If anything, Theobald's commentary only exacerbates any potential confusion as to the staging of the scene by basing his emendation on the physical separation of Antony and Cleopatra and raising the possibility of Cleopatra possessing "certain Chains and Ropes."

Capell: Performance as "Punctuation"

Edward Capell's ten-volume edition of Shakespeare, published some 35 years after Theobald's, involves a much different rendering of the scene from *Antony and Cleopatra*, in terms of both the methodology driving Capell's practice and the appearance of his edited pages. Capell's edition is immediately striking in its uncluttered margins: he reserves his commentary and notes for a completely separate three-volume publication, *Notes and Various Readings to Shakespeare* (1779–83), which means that the pages of his edition appear remarkably stark in comparison to other eighteenth-century editions. Extensive marginal commentary had persisted in editions of Shakespeare after Theobald; Samuel Johnson, who believed that "notes are often necessary, but they are necessary evils" and found himself juggling readings by Rowe, Pope, Theobald, Thomas Hanmer, and William Warburton, had included in the famous preface to his edition the invitation for readers to "read every play from the first scene to the last, with utter negligence of all his commentators" (vol. 1, p. lxix). What Johnson laments but cannot do without, Capell adopts a deliberate policy to counter: the relative bareness of Capell's pages is a powerful response to what he calls the "the paginary intermixture of text and comment" (vol. 1, p. 30). His edition has been hailed as "a revolutionary achievement" (Taylor, *Companion* 55) primarily because Capell deviates from the received-text tradition—he is the first editor to build his edition from scratch rather than annotate the printed text of his predecessor. While he is best known for his refined bibliographic understanding, Capell also deploys a markedly unique way of accounting for performance potentialities on the page that is deserving of consideration, and this distinct approach is on display in his handling of the monument scene in *Antony and Cleopatra*.

Capell in fact possessed a special familiarity with bridging the gap between the text and performance of the play: in 1758 David Garrick had commissioned Capell (who was already at work on his edition of Shakespeare) to prepare a streamlined version of *Antony and Cleopatra* for performance at Drury Lane.[24] Ten years later, when his complete edition of Shakespeare's works was published, Capell included his treatment of "*Antony*'s death" in a prefatory list of "additions" or "insertions" that he made to Shakespeare's text that "may, possibly, merit the reader's thanks, for the great aids which they afford his conception" (vol. 1, p. 27). It is clear then that Capell was concerned with the manner in which the death scene was presented to readers and the resulting ability of those readers to imagine how the Folio's cryptic stage direction might possibly work itself out on stage. His most significant alteration is to the scene's central direction: in Capell's text, the direction reads, "Cleopatra, *and her Women, throw out Certain Tackle, into which the People below put* Antony, *and he is drawn up*" (vol. 8, p. 102)—this is the same direction that he had employed in his adaptation for Garrick. The fuller direction includes—relatively speaking—more information than users of the text might otherwise bring to their reading, and this information has the potential to sharpen—again, in relative terms—their imaginings of the moment as it could be performed. Capell's text, in other words, is designed to offer richer *performancescapes*. While it is more detailed than what is found in the texts of either the Folio or any of his predecessors, Capell's emendation nevertheless raises as many questions as it seems to answer: What kind of "*Tackle,*" and who lifts him up? Cleopatra asks that her attendants "Help me," so perhaps she, Charmian, and Iras all heave together? Is the direction in a suitable place, or could it come later in the scene? Is Cleopatra meant to be in an upper gallery or on a special structure representing the monument? These unanswered questions (and one could easily think of dozens more) reassert basic incongruities of reading versus seeing, but they need not lead to understandings of the printed page as being disengaged from performance. Capell's stage direction remains a fragmentary and incomplete thing, but *performancescapes*—no matter their relative vividness—are always fragmentary and incomplete. Any printed text is necessarily unable to recapture in full the nuanced sensory experience of live performance; what Capell's paratextual adjustments demonstrate is the ability of the printed page to frame the interpretive gap between page and stage and consequently heighten readers' awareness of the interpretive labors required to transition between one mode and the other.

While the incremental benefits of Capell's more detailed direction for imagining performance are open to debate, it is useful to consider the subtle differences in interpretive demands that his direction makes. The raising of Antony up to whatever is serving as the monument is something that takes a certain amount of time for actors to accomplish, to say nothing of the way in which those involved in a performance may wish to slow the moment down to ensure communication of its symbolic import—as Leslie Thomson observes, the design of the monument scene actualizes "the related ideas of weight, bearing, drawing, rising and falling that fill the play" (qtd. in Neill, *Anthony* 366). What is true of any stage direction meant to account for the moment (and true of most stage directions in general) is that it will not take nearly as long to *read* the direction as it would to enact it on a stage. The same can be said of envisioning a performance: there is a disconnection between the time it takes to read a moment comprised of a portion of playtext and its accompanying paratextuals (stage directions, speech prefixes, scene locations) and how long one *imagines* it would take to perform this moment; put a different way, there exists a tension between the temporal dimensions of reading a playtext and what Keir Elam calls—in reference to the perpetual "presentness" of dramatic action—the "discourse time" (*Semiotics* 117) of a play.[25] Theobald's "*They draw* Antony *up to* Cleopatra" or the Folio's "*They heaue Anthony aloft to Cleopatra*" are both sparse enough that they can be, and perhaps are prone to being, processed at the speed of reading; by this I mean that in eliding detail, directions such as these simply do not provide much in the way of firm footing upon which to ground imaginative extrapolations.[26] Although it must be said that a reader is under no obligation to interrogate the feasibility or level of detail in each and every stage direction he or she encounters, when it comes to fostering considerations of the drama's potential for representation on stage, not only does Capell's direction add information, it also has sequential actions embedded within it: Cleopatra and company make some sort of rigging available, Antony is (somehow) attached to it, and then he is subsequently borne aloft. Such a formulation certainly does not supply all of the specifics (what stage direction could?), but it does go further than earlier editions in inviting readers to consider the movement of Antony's body as resulting from a series of events that take time to be realized in performance. There is nothing inherently revolutionary about the kind of direction Capell chooses to provide; extant early modern plays often deploy directions indicative of sequential actions that highlight the rift between time-spent-reading and time-spent-seeing/imagining—indeed, the Folio text of *Antony and Cleopatra* includes this direction earlier in the play: "*Camidius Marcheth with his Land Army one way ouer the / Stage, and Towrus the Lieutenant of Cæsar the other way: / After their going in, is heard the noise of a Sea-fight. / Alarum. Enter Enobarbus and Scarus*" (TLN 1973–6). While a reader might process this as a single direction or discrete paratextual unit within the printed text, the direction is structured in such a way that it makes apparent the impossibility of its constituent elements occurring simultaneously on any stage, real or virtual. What makes Capell's modification to the monument stage direction noteworthy is that it is meant to actuate what he calls a reader's "conception" at a point in the text where "conception" might otherwise lack instigation.

Capell's attempts to grapple with performance within the margins of his text go further than making alterations to stage directions. His reworked version of *Antony and Cleopatra* was published in 1758, just ahead of Garrick's production, and this publication served as a kind of testing ground for a system of symbols meant to highlight and encode details of performance within an edited playtext. The symbols first implemented in 1758 are subsequently deployed throughout the ten volumes of his complete edition of Shakespeare: underscores (_) indicate a change of address within a speech; double quotation marks indicate an aside; crosses (†) denote dramatic gestures, highlighting things pointed to or shown on stage, while double-crosses (‡) do the same for props delivered or presented; finally, a superscript dash is meant to distinguish irony.[27] Capell believes that "the punctuation he has follow'd (into which he has admitted some novelties)" will be of "much benefit to the Author" and result in "profit and understanding" for readers (vol. 1, p. 28). In essence, what Capell develops is a method of shorthand notation for referencing potential points of emphasis in performance. As one critic writes, Capell "hoped...readers would visualize the action in their minds' eyes upon an invisible stage, with the result that the print would take on an active as well as a poetic life" (Winchester 26). "Punctuation" is indeed an apt descriptor for this effort: his performance-cipher might appear laughably incomplete and even redundant when it is deployed, yet in its very obtrusiveness it is a remarkably efficient means of utilizing the manipulability of the printed page to emphasize performed action.

Capell's system of symbols serve as a reminder that the more nuanced and meaningful the engagements with performance attempted by a printed incarnation of a play become, the more the book of the play will have to amplify the conspicuousness of its own textuality and lean more heavily on some of the fundamental features afforded by print. In chapter 2 I highlighted the tendency of printed playtexts to resort to ekphrastic, narrative digressions to provide readers with details that could otherwise only be communicated in performance; I have also argued in chapter 1 that the relative stability of the printed play—its ability to support decelerated readings and tangential moves away from the playtext—affords readers the opportunity to gain information located elsewhere in a critical edition that can come to enhance *performancescapes*. Worthen writes of "print culture's efforts to imprint the stage, to locate the signs and signals of appropriate, authorial performance within the text itself" (*Print* 85), an assertion that gets to the heart of Capell's undertaking, which is to literally encode performance into the body of the playtext, to capture certain speeches, actions, and behaviors, in standardized (and thus reproducible) printed symbols. Such a plan might well sound misguided and wholly impractical, the epitome of a printed text's inherent tendency to distort the realities of performance. It is crucial to remember, however, that what Capell is offering is a streamlined version of commonplace forms of paratextual mediation: the asides, changes of address, gestures, and manipulations of props that Capell is compelled to codify are otherwise represented by editors within square brackets or silently added to an existing framework of stage directions. But in whatever form these things are expressed, a codification of performance data is the goal. Capell's system is all the more striking because it has the audacity to expose and amplify one of the basic principles upon which all printed drama is based: that elements of performance can, at some level, become a form of "punctuation," encapsulated in print and distributed throughout a playtext in various paratextual formats.

"Proof": Malone and His Influence

The last great edition of the eighteenth century, while indebted to Capell's bibliographic achievements, is in some ways its antithesis—at least in terms of its formal structure: Edmund Malone's ten-volume edition of Shakespeare (1790) synthesizes emendatory activity with archival impulses, submerging the plays in the documentary record to produce a staggering collection of information related to the playwright, the production of his works, and his historical milieu. It is for this diverse and extensive ancillary material that Malone is best known; "it is not in his achievements as an editor" that he accomplished most, writes one critic, "but in the elaboration of a larger context for the practice of textual scholarship, ... [in making] Shakespeare's work more accessible in a historically distant context" (Bristol 84, 85). Malone's edition involves the reproduction of important documents as well as a number of original essays that extrapolate from this documentary record: the plays are printed after the transcription of things like Shakespeare's will and a list of "Dramatick Pieces on Which Plays were Formed by Shakspeare," as well as lengthier investigations such as "An Attempt to Ascertain the Order in which the Plays of Shakspeare Were Written" and "An Historical Account of the Rise and Progress of the English Stage." Critics have interpreted Malone's undeniably influential collection in vastly different ways: it has been hailed as "the culmination of the eighteenth-century editorial tradition" (Murphy, "Birth" 105), but has also been put forth as a discernable break from what had come before, "a striking example of how the Enlightenment represented its constructs as Truth, inscribing factual objects and autonomous subjects (each grounded in the other) in the process of reproducing Shakespeare" (de Grazia, *Verbatim* 226).[28]

However construed, Malone's volumes certainly offer ancillary information that is much more detailed than anything found in previous editions. In his preface Malone argues that "mere assertion" will no longer carry the day and that in its place must stand judgements and interpretations "substantiate[d] by proof" (vol. 1, p. xx). This overriding concern with matters of proof and completeness powers everything in

Malone's edition: his desire to establish a chronology of Shakespeare's plays; his inclusion of the Sonnets (Malone's is the first collected edition to do so); his unique and exacting standards of collation, which he explains as involving "every proofsheet of my work read aloud to me, while I perused the first folio" or the relevant "first quarto copy" to ensure that "not a single innovation, made either by the editor of the second folio, or any of the modern editors, could escape me" (vol. 1, pp. xliv-xlv); even his marginal commentary on the plays themselves— which is bursting with Malone's suggestions interwoven with readings proposed by previous editors—is meant to be a site where "conjecture and emendation have given way to rational explanation" (vol. 1, p. lvi). Malone expresses some concern over the sheer mass of material that often crowds out the edited playtext on the page, indicating that he has actually been quite selective about the information that he includes: "I have in general given the explication of a passage, by whomsoever made, without loading the page with the preceding unsuccessful attempts at elucidation, and by this means have obtained room for much additional illustration" (vol. 1, p. liv); despite this claim, the density of his edited pages suggests that Malone was not overly troubled by marginal commentary greatly outweighing playtext so long as, in his mind, the bulk of the commentary concerned itself with fact rather than speculation. As for his treatment of paratextuals such as stage directions and scene locators potentially useful in producing *performancescapes*, Malone claims that

> All the stage-directions throughout this work...I have considered as wholly in my power, and have regulated them in the best manner I could. The reader will also, I think, be pleased to find the place in which every scene is supposed to pass, precisely ascertained: a species of information, for which, though it often throws light on the dialogue, we look in vain in the ancient copies, and which has been too much neglected by the modern editors. (vol. 1, pp. lviii–lix)

Although this seemingly indicates a commitment on Malone's part to utilizing the *scape* of his page to facilitate readers' imaginings of a contemporary theatrical performance, in Malone's hands, particularly in his essay surveying the "Rise and Progress of the English Stage," the stage becomes less an element of imaginative experimentation than it does another site of inquiry that requires fastidious documentation in order to add to the detailed historical framework that the fullest understanding of Shakespeare's works will be built around.

His essay on the history of the English stage is the quintessential survey of the archivist, piecing together as it does excerpts from other writers, records of performance (Malone is the first editor to make significant use of Henslowe's diary), records related to the payment of playwrights and actors, information from early maps of London, and biographies of assorted actors—chiefly those listed in the First Folio. To point out that conceptualizations of live performance are rendered somewhat sterile or even completely marginalized by the narrative patchwork of documentary history is not to denigrate Malone's achievement: the scope of the "meticulously documented" (Schoenbaum 127) piece remains astounding and, at the time, it was unprecedented. As promised by his title, Malone extends his gaze from the English stage's medieval origins right through to contemporary practice, lingering, of course, over the Elizabethan period. Worth noting, though, are Malone's attempts to place textual and performed modes of dramatic representation in a fixed hierarchy, with textual modes in the position of greater influence and importance. As the essay enters the eighteenth century, for instance, Malone remarks that

> From 1709, when Mr. Rowe published his edition of Shakespeare, the exhibition of his plays became much more frequent than before. Between that time and 1740, our poet's *Hamlet, Julius Caesar, K. Henry VIII. Othello, K. Richard III. King Lear*, and the two parts of *King Henry IV* were very frequently exhibited. Still, however, such was the wretched taste of the audiences of those days, that in many instances the contemptible alterations of his pieces were preferred to the originals. (vol. 2, p. 281)

In a similarly revealing passage, Malone associates theatrical success with his own understanding of textually based authenticity. Garrick is the age's finest actor, for example, largely because he is a gifted reader and researcher:

> [Garrick's] good taste led him to study the plays of Shakespeare with more assiduity than any of his predecessors. Since that time, in consequence of Mr. Garrick's admirable performance of many of his principal characters, the frequent representation of his plays in nearly their original state, and above all, the various researches which have been made for the purpose of explaining and illustrating his works, our poet's reputation has been yearly increasing, and is now fixed upon a basis, which neither the lapse of time nor the fluctuation of opinion will ever be able to shake. (vol. 2, pp. 283–4)

Malone's essay on the English stage—and his edition in general—thus registers the tension between the production of critical editions during the eighteenth century that were increasingly intended to be authoritative, and the transformations and adaptations undergone by Shakespeare's works in the theater. While the urgency to adapt for theater audiences what were deemed to be the uncouth or archaic aspects of Shakespeare had largely died down by the time of Malone's edition,[29] his comments on Rowe and Garrick make clear that Malone was still operating at a time when the theater's potential lack of fidelity to textual "originals" remained a sensitive issue; indeed, Malone's praise for Garrick is founded on the actor's representation of the plays "in nearly their original state." For a large portion of the eighteenth century, it was certainly true that "on stage, Shakespeare's words were free to be rearranged, refined and revised, all in the service of keeping them current; on the page, in a different spirit of adulation, they were to be restored to their authentic form" (Kastan, *Book* 95). If Malone's edition is to be understood as the culmination of eighteenth-century editorial practice, it is because his work on Shakespeare represents the most concerted attempt to provide a verifiable historical context for anchoring the desire for authenticity that had haunted printed collections of Shakespeare's drama since the First Folio boasted of providing his works "according to the True Originall Copies." It is not that Malone was oblivious to drama's potential significations on the stage, only that Malone's edition firmly located the authority of collected editions elsewhere. Adopting Taylor's argument that "editing seeks to establish texts that are proximate to a source of value" ("End" 130), then what Malone valued—what he wanted his edition to most accurately reflect and communicate to readers—was Shakespeare as situated in verifiable historical contexts that could be recovered from the documentary record.

Malone's rigorous historical approach casts an imposing shadow over collections of Shakespeare produced throughout much of the nineteenth century; in fact, the editorial tradition after Malone becomes largely derivative for about the next 70 years. George Steevens edited the second edition of Samuel Johnson's text in 1773, and, with the help of Isaac Reed, produced subsequent editions in 1778, 1785, 1793, and 1803. This fifth Johnson-Steevens-Reed collection, along with Malone's 1790 edition, proved popular in reprint well into the 1800s. Both of these heavily reprinted editions eventually ballooned to 21 volumes in length thanks to "a burgeoning accretion of commentary and annotation" (Murphy, *Print* 188).

While derivations of Johnson(-Steevens-Reed) and Malone dominate much of the 1800s, the most influential edition of the century is produced by a team of editors from Cambridge University whose efforts mark a turning point in editorial mediations of Shakespeare. Taylor notes the influence of the institutional, financial, and intellectual resources powering the nine volume edition published between 1863 and 1866: "The Cambridge edition, as its cognomen declares, was the first academic edition of Shakespeare. Shakespeare had until then been edited by poets, barristers, aristocrats, clerics, journalists [. . .]. With the Cambridge edition the professed professionals took over, announcing that Shakespeare was a fit subject for professional academic research" (*Textual Companion* 56).[30] The achievements of the Cambridge editors are monumental. For one, they are the first "To number the lines in each scene separately, so as to facilitate reference" (vol. 1, p. ix); while editors since Rowe had been comprehensive in numbering acts and scenes, the more thorough numeration divides the canon with remarkable efficiency into individual units made up of single lines. The Cambridge edition thus enhances some of the unique interpretive possibilities that printed plays make available: the speed and accuracy of navigating in, and between, plays, is improved, as is a reader's ability to search and cross-reference.

The greatest stride the Cambridge editors made is one rooted in printing history rather than performance history: on the opening page of their preface they reveal that they sought "to base the text on a thorough collation of the four Folios and of all the Quarto editions of the separate plays, and of subsequent editions and commentaries" (vol. 1, p. ix). The unprecedented range of their collation set the standard for future editorial work. Extrapolating from their collated data, the Cambridge editors attempt to distinguish substantive texts from derivative ones, sketching evolutionary descents for Shakespeare's sixteenth- and seventeenth-century editions. Significantly, this sequencing of substantive and derivative printed editions injected notions of scientific exactitude into the subjective decision-making processes of the editor. Proposing lines of textual derivation for the frequently dissimilar versions of Shakespeare's plays is predicated on establishing the most authoritative text (often, though not always, the earliest printed version in the sequence), which an editor can then adhere to as copy-text when faced with variant readings.

The spectre of objectivity so prominently on display in reprints of Malone and the Cambridge edition, while no doubt an alluring possibility, generated potent theoretical responses and refinements in the first half of the twentieth century. Those who led the counter-movement became known as New Bibliographers, and their work shifted editorial values once again, though not yet toward the stage. W. W. Greg—"the hero of the movement" (Honigmann 91)—sought to establish a defensible methodology that allowed for editorial practice to be guided by the pursuit of authorial intentions, yet one that would place limits on the amount of objectivity that the genealogical classification method could provide:

> The genealogical method was the greatest advance ever made in this field, but its introduction was not unaccompanied by error. For lack of logical analysis, it led, at the hands of its less discriminating exponents, to an attempt to reduce textual criticism to a code of mechanical rules. There was just this much excuse, that the method did make it possible to sweep away mechanically a great deal of rubbish. What its more hasty devotees failed to understand, or at any rate sufficiently bear in mind, was that authority is never absolute, but only relative. ("Rationale" 41)

Alarmed by the prospect of an essentially mechanized method of editing, and believing that "it is impossible to exclude individual judgment from editorial procedure" ("Rationale" 48), Greg sought to validate the subjective decisions that all editors inevitably make. According to the New Bibliography, postulating an authoritative copy-text and then slavishly adhering to its readings not only precludes the possibility of incorporating corrected readings from other texts, such a practice also fundamentally distorts what a critical edition should aim to be. Greg and the New Bibliographers thus aimed to defend and legitimize editors' interpretive freedom to enrich their critical editions with substantive readings from other texts. Here is Greg again:

> ... an editor who declines or is unable to exercise his judgment and falls back on some arbitrary canon, such as the authority of the copy-text, is in fact abdicating his editorial function. Yet this is what has been frequently commended as "scientific" ... and the result is that what many editors have done is to produce, not editions of their authors' works at all, but only editions of particular authorities for those works, a course that may be perfectly legitimate in itself, but was not the one they were professedly pursuing. ("Rationale" 50–1)[31]

In other words, if editors essentially abdicate their decision-making duties by adhering to readings from their copy-text simply because it is their copy-text, the ultimate consequence of this practice would be that they end up editing texts of historical documents, not texts of authorial works. Greg views the former as a valuable pursuit in its own right, but he believes that such work should not be conducted under the rubric of an authorial orientation: "A critical edition does not seem to me a suitable place in which to record the graphic peculiarities of particular texts" ("Rationale" 52).

The methods and objectives of the New Bibliography have been scrutinized extensively, and a comprehensive retrospective of their hypotheses and pronouncements is not required here. It will suffice to recall that, in their intention to establish "what the author wrote" ("Rationale" 51), the New Bibliographers attempt to systematize the means of making distinctions between variant readings found in different texts: some differences between texts are "substantive"—"those namely that affect the author's meaning or the essence of his expression"—while some are "accidental"—"such in general as spelling, punctuation, word-division, and the like, affecting mainly [the text's] formal presentation" ("Rationale" 43). Most (in)famously, they are invested in establishing, and experimenting with, interpretive tools that can be used to determine the underlying manuscripts behind printed editions: "if a play was printed from the author's original draft—his 'foul papers' as they were called in the theatre—we may expect to find in it contradictions and uncertainties of action and unresolved textual tangles; if, on the other hand, a play was printed from a theatrical fair copy, we may indeed expect to find such contradictions and tangles smoothed out" (Greg, *Editorial* viii–ix). Having established in their minds the idiosyncrasies of the manuscript which ultimately gave rise to a printed text, editors can then work backwards through the particular printed text that, in theory, best reflects an author's intended meaning.[32] The work of New Bibliographers was undoubtedly affected by their gravitation towards authorial intentions, though it is a mistake to suggest that they necessarily believed an author's intentions to be completely knowable; Greg, for example, states that

> in the case of Shakespeare—and the same applies to the Elizabethan drama generally—we cannot hope to achieve a certainly correct text, not so much on account of the uncertainties of transmission—though they are sometimes serious—*as because the author may never have produced a definitive text for us to recover.* All textual criticism, I suppose, is in a manner tentative; but the conditions that obtain in Shakespeare's plays, in spite of the greater confidence warranted by recent research, still appear such as to make our conclusions even more tentative than usual. (*Editorial* ix, emphasis added)

Greg clearly understood that Shakespeare worked amidst various institutional and social forces, and that the realization of his plays—in print or onstage—could not happen without the involvement of numerous parties. That Shakespeare's intentions might only be partially recoverable, however, did not mean that they were not worth pursuing.

Part of the difficulty in assessing the New Bibliographers is that the designation itself cannot encompass the various interests and tactics of the scholars that have been attached to it.[33] The foundational tenets of Greg were subject to their own evolutionary development as editorial theorists stimulated by his work made increasingly provocative claims of exactitude that surpassed any of Greg's formulations. Elucidating textual transmissions and making informed decisions about copy-texts gave way to Fredson Bowers's claims of stripping away "the veil of print," and of seeking "a scientific basis of factual evidence to assess the influence of the manuscript" ("New Textual" 271, 271–2). In an ironic twist that greatly impacted subsequent assessments of the movement, New Bibliography became associated with the very sort of objective scientific rules that it had originally meant to supplant. New Bibliography as a practice tends to get unfairly painted with a single brush, and comments like Bowers's have long garnered the most attention and criticism. Bowers's contentious remarks likely misrepresent the thinking of many of his peers, but his claims for the exactitude of editorial and bibliographical procedures echo back through the tradition, past the genealogical classification system of the Cambridge editors, past Malone's suggestion that his expertise can "precisely ascertain" (vol. 1, p. lviii) matters for his readers, past Theobald's descriptions of the "Science of Criticism" (vol. 1, p. xl), even past Rowe's attempts to "give the true Reading as well as I could" (vol. 1, A2r-v), all the way back to the hyperbolic claims of the First Folio to represent Shakespeare's works "absolute in their numbers, as he conceiued the[m]."

Though New Bibliography is mistakenly thought of as the most audacious form of a misguided desire for scientific objectivity in editorial mediations, the fact remains that aspirations for objectively "fixing" (in the full sense of the word) the text have lingered throughout Shakespeare's history in print. It must also be said that devoting editorial energies almost exclusively to sorting stemmatic tangles and glossing difficult passages with the utmost precision has a significant impact on an edition's engagement with the plays' performative modes of realization. This chapter has put forth that both the rationale and shape of formative critical editions of Shakespeare were variously modified in order to account for playtexts—though predominantly understood as literary artifacts—having the potential to be transformed by the exigencies of the stage. Admittedly, however, these efforts to address performance potential—ranging in extremes from Capell's esoteric system of codes to Pope's excision of "theatrical interpolations"—tended to be peripheral, indirect, even convoluted. The ultimate decline of the New Bibliography helps to make sense of the quarantined position that performance assumed through centuries of critical editions. Entrenching the editing of Shakespeare in the pursuit of verifiable facts and documentary evidence means that such things as anticipating performance potentialities, supplying performance commentary, or enriching paratexts concerned with performance practice all become much harder to justify as worthwhile editorial pursuits. An overriding emphasis on ostensibly objective engagements with the text—the glossing of words or speeches by way of recourse to parallel passages or by making use of early modern definitions, the recording of alternate readings of other editors—leaves little room for subjective imaginings of performance or for the introduction of less-material forms of performance history that primarily exist only in memory. It is not until notions like authorial intention, textual stability, and historical context are thoroughly troubled in the latter half of the twentieth century that performance histories and performance potentialities—both of which recognize as a matter of course dispersed agencies, collaborative processes, and textual ambiguities—come to be recognized as meaningful variables in editorial practice. Put differently, the vagaries of memory and imagination involved in recalling the ways in which live bodies can enact plays within designated spaces find a central place in the edited Shakespearean text only when meanings inhering in the text itself are brought into question.

The relatively stark attempt to demarcate the transformative processes linking text and performance that opened this chapter—Davenant's method of citing contemporary performance practice by distinguishing lines cut in the theater with marginal quotation marks—has transformed into much more prominent and elaborate forms of editorial intervention. The next chapter concerns itself with more recent incarnations of the impulse to document performance within the bounds of the critical edition. Specifically, the focus shifts to performance commentary, an editorial strategy positioned somewhere between text and performance, materiality and absence, remembering and forgetting.

CHAPTER 4

Performance Commentary: Writing in the Sand

I would like to begin this chapter with what is likely an unremarkable moment early in *Hamlet*, or, more accurately, with what is likely an unremarkable *textual* moment from Harold Jenkins's Arden edition of the play (1982). As planned, Hamlet meets Horatio and Marcellus "Upon the platform 'twixt eleven and twelve" (1.2.252); chilled by "a nipping and an eager air" (1.4.2), the company waits with nervous anticipation for the Ghost of King Hamlet to appear.[1] In the midst of their attempts to establish the precise time of night, we are given this stage direction: "*A flourish of trumpets, and two pieces of ordnance go off.*" If we, like Horatio are confused by the *flourish* and cannon fire, Hamlet reminds us that Claudius had earlier promised this revelling, and the sudden noises "thus bray out / The triumph of his pledge" (1.4.11–12). Now consider Jenkins's commentary note: "It is with an effective irony—which perhaps the audience does not always note—that the cannon by which Claudius celebrates Hamlet's staying on in Denmark are heard by Hamlet at the very moment when he waits for his father's ghost." The note continues: "And the echoes of the new King's revelry will still be in our ears when the ghost of the King he has murdered tells how he got the crown."

I begin with this moment because of the way in which Jenkins attempts to reconcile reading and theater audiences, to engage with both text and performance. He first makes an implicit distinction between readers and theater-goers: a *theater* audience might not always pick up on the irony of Claudius's riotous celebration, but Jenkins is able to highlight the matter for you, the reader, as you diligently navigate the margins of his text. Jenkins then seems to *conflate* readers with theater audiences when he claims that the cannons will still be echoing in *"our* ears" when the ghost of the dead King begins his tale of murder most foul. Readers and spectators become indistinguishable in Jenkins's note, a point that brings with it several implications: Jenkins is suggesting that we can synaesthetically "hear" these cannons as we read (to the extent that they continue to echo 100 or so lines after they first sound), that we as readers can thus partially experience the text of the play as if it were a staged performance, and that such an experience is enabled, at least in part, by his editorial mediations. It is precisely this kind of editorial gesture that this chapter takes as its focus: the impossible attempt to describe or return to the forever-absent play-as-performed.

Rememberings and citations of performance in the margins of critical editions constitute a form of editorial work that, until very recently, has not been subjected to much critical scrutiny. John Russell Brown is among those who have begun to survey the intersections of page and stage as they appear in performance commentary, and he provides a useful summary of the intrinsic limitations of editorial gestures toward the play as it has been, or could be, performed:

> ...no-one can possibly annotate all that has, could, or should happen on stage: the possibilities are infinite, the effects fleeting. Editors can describe a moment in particular performances by quoting brief eyewitness accounts but this involves ruthlessly selecting from among available evidence and presenting it without reference to the moment's place in an entire performance and, usually, without regard for the cultural viewpoint and personal prejudice of the witness. Alternatively, an editor may describe an imaginary performance in terms of movements on stage and physical actions that seem to be called for by the words of the text, although such a speculative account can provide no more than a disembodied staging, more like a diagram than a theatrical happening, a map than a terrain. All these modes of annotation take a reader only a little distance towards a play's theatrical potential and deal with it in fragmentary and abbreviated form. ("Annotating" 157–8)

Brown, aware that performance commentary can potentially misrepresent the plurality of performance possibilities, nevertheless concedes that despite the ways in which the seemingly limitless, fleeting effects of performance are inevitably decontextualized, "disembodied," "fragment[ed] and abbreviated" when recounted by editors, readers can nevertheless reconstitute *something* out of the distorted jumble—not a performance in and of itself, but something that moves "a little distance towards the play's theatrical potential" (158). What Brown figures as a set of loosely connected textual apparatuses and responses—descriptions of particular or imaginary performances; rough, mental "diagrams" or "maps" of staged action; performance fragmented into textual forms—I have attempted to unify under the term *performancescape*. *Performancescape* is meant to substantiate links between an editor's manipulation of textual and paratextual data (the *scape* of the page) and the hypothetical performances that this information can induce (the virtual *scape* of the imagined scene). Performance commentary, because it represents a vital means by which editors can give relative shape and stability to the ephemerality of performance, is a crucial component in the exchanges that *performancescape* seeks to account for. Utilizing the notion of *performancescape* in relation to performance commentary can sharpen one's understanding of its relationship to the edited text as well as the kinds of productive work that this commentary accomplishes within the edition as a whole.

In tracing the "performance" of performance commentary—the ways in which narratives of the play as performed become a part of the edited page and potentially impact the reading experience—it is imperative that I clarify my position regarding an important issue that looms large as soon as one begins to discuss readerly engagements with citations of performance and the concomitant imagined performances that are produced. Throughout this study, I have consciously avoided equating reading with performance, avoided referring to reading *as* a performance, and I want to continue to resist blurring the two modes of production into one another. I am treading a fine line in distinguishing between readers absorbing textualized details of the potentialities of performance and formulating reading itself as a kind of performance, but the distinction is a significant one; the reading-as-performance analogy seems to me to dull what we mean when we write or speak of live performance in a theater. Meisel, for example, posits that stage directions can "make vivid for the reader what the actor must otherwise supply, and incidentally steer the actor to what in the situation waits to be supplied. The result on the page is a melding of reading and performance—a script that becomes performance in the reading" (6); such a proposition, though it usefully acknowledges a symbiotic relationship between page and stage, relies on a significantly scaled-down conceptualization of performance in order to hold true. To my way of thinking,

Worthen's recognition of the fundamental differences between acts of reading and acts of performing is a much more useful proposition to carry forward:

> Whatever we can say about reading, however rich the ambiguities it opens, however readily it might enable the reader to set the play's hypothetical action in the theatre of the mind, a reader does not *use* the text as part of a regime of embodiment, a means of transforming the text into a different mode of publication, in which the words are situated within and conveyed through an event, inflected as living human action, as *behaviour* to an audience of spectators itself engaged in its own complex, reciprocal life. ("Texts" 211)

Simply put, to imagine moments of performance based on a reading of a text is not the same thing as enacting and embodying those moments, and to metaphorically conflate the two muddles the unique interpretive responses that each method of realizing a play demands from its audience.

Keeping this caveat in mind, it can be observed that performance commentary constitutes a form of editorial mediation that major publishers of Shakespeare have increasingly recognized as a valuable means of tapping a play's potential significations on stage. The General Editors' Preface to the Arden 3 series, for instance, contains the assertion that its "notes and introductions focus on the conditions and possibilities of meaning that editors, critics and performers (on stage and screen) have discovered in the play" (Thompson and Taylor xiv); the New Cambridge Shakespeare series similarly promises to be "more attentive than some earlier editions have been to the realisation of the plays on the stage" (Edwards ix), and promises of "an appraisal... of the play's particular effects in performance" with "detailed commentary pay[ing] particular attention to... staging" (Hibbard i) preface each edition published under the Oxford Shakespeare umbrella. As Michael Cordner has pointed out, however, such proclamations are not necessarily indicative of a consistent rationale by which an edition will proceed. Generally speaking, performance commentary is deployed unsystematically, with editions of different plays in the same series varying widely in terms of the attention paid to performance in introductions and notes. In Cordner's words, "a revolution has been decreed without any consistent planning as to how to carry it out" ("'Are We Being Theatrical'" 399). To track the implications of this scattershot revolution, I will focus on performance commentary in recent editions of *Hamlet* and *Titus*

Andronicus. Both *Hamlet* and *Titus* are characterized by textual relationships that make choosing between variants a complicated affair: both exist in versions that reflect demonstrably different incarnations of the work in question: certain early versions seem relatively more authorial and "literary," while others seem to have absorbed elements of performance practice. Tensions between page and stage are thus at the forefront of editorial engagements with each of these plays. Furthermore, dissimilarities in terms of content and popularity (both in print and on stage) yield revealing points of comparison. With its canonical status firmly entrenched since the eighteenth century, *Hamlet* possesses an inexhaustible performance history from which editors can potentially draw. *Titus*'s history in the theater is not as extensive, and to this day many have trouble associating its grotesqueness with Shakespeare;[2] nevertheless, the play's numerous instances of horrific spectacle—indeed, the extent to which the play itself seems to *revel* in horror and trauma—provide editors with opportunities to cite performance by way of references to the complexities of staging, special effects, and influential productions. What *Hamlet* and *Titus* present to editors, then, are much different opportunities for remembering performance, for what Kidnie describes as the act of "sift[ing] through the residue of performance—the stories composed through direct experience of the event, related by spectators, or formulated through investigation of the archives" ("Citing" 122–3).

The "stories" or narrative descriptions that so conspicuously circumscribe medieval and sixteenth-century printed plays have thus in some ways never really gone away, only shifted to different positions on the page.[3] What *has* changed is the general function of the narratives themselves: with coded forms of information (lists of *dramatis personae*, stage directions, speech prefixes) now widely understood and readily decoded by readers, narratives recalling a specific performance or conveying the potential interpretations of performers are no longer utilized to supply an internal logic or consistency to the printed play; rather, anecdotes or citations of performance in modern editions are often a means of demonstrating the myriad uses to which the playtext can be put. Given that editorial annotation represents "a crossing of textual boundaries that undoes the notion of the discrete text itself" (Parker 171–2), then citations of performance potentialities have the ability to significantly "open" up the playtext, leading some commentators to suggest that when it comes to ambiguous moments of staging, editors are best served to do two things: not emend the text, and embrace multifariousness and ambiguity in their marginal notes. It is certainly true that "postmodern" or "open" methodologies can supply readers with the means to entertain interpretations that otherwise might be unclear or unavailable from a reading of the playtext alone. Where I seek to refine current thinking about ambiguity and editorial commentary is in proposing that readers' interpretive freedom is not necessarily precluded by editorial *foreclosures* of ambiguity; rather, performance commentary can function quite effectively—perhaps *most* effectively—when it allows editors to acknowledge the limitations and distortions produced by their own subjective, emendatory acts. "Open" texts are not the only catalyst for producing readerly resistance and meaning-making; texts "closed" by the shaping influence of an editor are nevertheless able to have their readers confront plurality and uncertainty, and performance commentary is often the means by which this is accomplished. Performance commentary can be understood as an interpretive tool that punctures the playtext, linking the printed play to the play as performed and establishing for readers meanings and responses produced in the theater that might intersect with, or might diverge from, their own textual engagements with the play. What results from engaging a text that forecloses rather than accentuates ambiguity is not intrinsically inferior or less useful readerly labor, just labor of a different sort. Readerly participation, upon which all printed texts depend, can be both generated and supported by the interpretive pathways and memorial resonances recorded in performance commentary.

Open Graves and "Open" Texts: Imagining *Hamlet*

The one story that all editors of *Hamlet* inevitably must construct for their readers is also the story that, ironically enough, no one can be sure about: the stemmatic narrative that explains the underlying connections between the original printed texts of the play. The First Quarto (Q1, 1603), the Second Quarto (Q2, 1604), and the Folio text of *Hamlet* (F, 1623) constitute the major pieces of the puzzle, but without definitive evidence explaining how the pieces connect or even what kind of picture the pieces are meant to cumulatively represent, editors are left to make informed hypotheses as to each text's particular provenance as well as to the amount of influence that one text might have had over another. Andrew Murphy writes that "the most complicated issue facing an editor is undoubtedly the business of making sense of the relationships among the surviving early texts of any given play" ("Introduction" 11), and it must be said that *Hamlet* poses as great a challenge in this regard as any play in the canon. Among the issues problematizing an editor's ability to produce a detailed map of the play's authorial, theatrical, and printed streams of transmission is the likelihood that the order in which the plays appeared in print is not representative of their order of composition, as well as the shadow of a lost Ur-*Hamlet* that predates Shakespeare's play and informs it in uncertain and unverifiable ways. The differences between the three early texts have been laid out at great length elsewhere, and providing a comprehensive assessment of the minutiae that distinguish one text from another exceeds the scope of this chapter.[4] For my purposes, it will suffice to recount some of the features that editors and textual scholars generally recognize in each text; I can then proceed to a consideration of how an editor's understanding of *Hamlet*'s textual lineage shapes the horizon of imagined performances that an edition most strongly encourages.

Q1, whose title page announces a printed play "As it hath beene diuerse times acted by his Highnesse seruants in the Cittie of London: as also in the two Vniuersities of Cambridge and Oxford, and else-where," is by far the shortest of the three extant texts. The earliest printed version of *Hamlet* locates its authority in performance practice—"As it hath beene diuerse times acted"—and the playtext itself bears this out: Q1 is undeniably a streamlined version of the play, with a "general emphasis on action and drive" (Dawson, *Hamlet* 27). With its relative brevity, brisk pacing, and a number of unique stage directions—among them, the call for the distraught Ofelia (note the spelling) to enter "*playing on a lute, and her hair down, singing*"—Q1 is widely understood as a "reported" text, though there is little consensus as to why or for whom a reconstruction of the play was produced.[5] Whatever the proximate forces behind its creation, Q1, though "lack[ing] in terms of philosophic range and refinement of language," is now recognized as possessing "an abundance of theatrical energy" (Marcus, *Unediting* 145); the editors of the Arden 3 edition of the play identify three noteworthy characteristics: "(1) the perceived 'theatricality' of Q1 and its links with original staging practices; (2) its speed and narrative drive; (3) its lack of introspection and 'literary' elaboration" (Thompson and Taylor[2] 36).[6]

All of the perceived qualities that mark Q1 as "at once familiar and oddly alien" (Thompson and Taylor[2] 16) are a product of unavoidable comparisons to the other extant texts of the play; for better or worse, one cannot help but interpret and make sense of Q1 relative to Q2 and F, and these much longer texts of *Hamlet* are more representative of the attributes at the heart of modern conceptions of the play and its hero: not action, but introspection; not drive, but delay; not theatricality, but literariness. Q2 is the longest of the three early texts, and the claims of its title page distinguish it sharply from the shorter quarto that had appeared the year before: "Newly imprinted and enlarged to almost as much againe as it was, according to the true and perfect Coppie." With Q2 then, the location of *Hamlet*'s authority is transferred from the stage ("As it hath beene diuerse times acted"), to the page ("the true and perfect Coppie"); editorial practice—itself so long guided by efforts to reconstitute a text representative of something akin to Shakespeare's "true and perfect" manuscript—has leaned heavily on Q2, tending to use it as copy-text in the formation of critical editions. The F text lacks over 200 lines found in Q2, but also adds around 80 lines that are not found in the longest text. F also corresponds quite closely to Q1 in certain areas, which perhaps suggests some connection to a theatrical manuscript, a point that is bolstered by stage directions in F that are sometimes more refined than those found in the longer Q2 text—at the beginning of act 2, for example, Q2's opening stage direction, *"Enter old Polonius, with his man or two* (the adjective *"old"* and the imprecise number of attendants being the kinds of subtleties one associates with authorial foul papers), becomes *"Enter Polonius, and Reynoldo"* in F (Q1 reads *"Enter Corambis, and Montano"*). F, however, also displays "literary" qualities akin to those exemplified in Q2; in fact, F has been described as "tidier" than Q2, "more consistent in its speech prefixes" and displaying a "preference for more capitalization, heavier and more extensive punctuation, and some unsystematic 'modernization' of language" (Thompson and Taylor 484).

What can be made of the intractable tangles of *Hamlet*'s early printing history? Graham Holderness summarizes: "we know that more than one *Hamlet* play appeared on stage and we can with reasonable confidence surmise that as both 'play' and 'text', *Hamlet* existed in a contested multiplicity of modes and manifestations" (180).[7] Holderness's practical assessment speaks to the complexities an editor faces, since the production of a critical edition is driven in large part by the desire to minimize or remove multiplicities and ambiguities. "Editing is by its nature a choosing among available alternatives," writes Leah Marcus, "a setting of limits upon a range of possible forms and meanings" ("Editing" 128). Editors, that is, must wade into the mire to choose a copy-text that befits their orientation. With the approximation of authorial intentions being the guiding principle behind critical editions for most of the twentieth century, editors of *Hamlet* favored Q2 as copy-text since its length, literary richness, and apparent proximity to Shakespeare's primary act of creation made it the most defensible selection. Nailing down intentions is a tricky business, however, and more often than not Q2 was emended and supplemented by readings from F, yielding a conflated version of the play that, in its mixedness, deviated from all three of the original textual witnesses. The conflated text became less prominent in the mid-1980s, when the editors of the Oxford Collected Works—seeking to represent the more socialized versions of Shakespeare's plays, the texts "as they were acted" (xxxix)—used F as their copy text, with substantive Q2 passages shifted to an appendix; this strategy was followed by the editor of the individual Oxford edition, G. R. Hibbard. More recently, the Arden 3 series has produced a two-volume set containing the Q1, Q2, and F texts edited separately, a strategy cultivated by the now widespread understanding that to pursue unified, authorial meanings is to distort a play's distinct textual forms and the historically contingent, fluid interpretations the play has produced.

The publication of the Arden 3 edition of Q1 is indicative of the earliest quarto's changing fortunes. Because of its relative brevity and emphasis on action, Q1 has long been difficult to synthesize with prevailing concerns for intentionality and literariness. Editors have needed to somehow explain Q1 away, recognizing its anomalous properties while simultaneously marginalizing or circumscribing its strangeness. The editor of the New Cambridge *Hamlet*, Philip Edwards, describes Q1 as an "acting text" that represents the play "in a severely truncated form" (61), but goes on to negate Q1's bibliographical and emendatory usefulness for the very reason that it is associated with the stage: in Edwards's mind, once the play falls under the influence of "[Shakespeare's] colleagues who began to prepare it for the stage..., what one can only call degeneration began, and it is at this point that we should arrest and freeze the play, for it is sadly true that the nearer we get to the stage, the further we are getting from Shakespeare" (32). Edwards's position typifies the juggling that editors must do with a text that is recognizable as a version of *Hamlet*, but a version that does not square with entrenched notions of the play's profundity. Further complicating an editor's handling of Q1 is the fact that despite longstanding biases against it, certain portions of the Q1 text—especially those stage directions for which it is the lone source—have been integral to Q2/F conflations of the play on both page and stage; it is not uncommon, for example, for a production or edition of the play to have the ghost of King Hamlet appear in his nightgown in 3.4, though Q1 is the only text that supplies this direction. Hibbard inserts the direction into his edition, adding in a note that it "seems right to preserve [it]," since it "is the only indication we have of how the Ghost appeared in this scene in Shakespeare's day" (282); he goes on to add that "the *night-gown* has at least two functions: it reminds the audience that it is night on the stage; and, in its domesticity, it suggests that old Hamlet is about to play a rather different role from that of the martial figure of the first act. In fact, [the *night-gown*] modifies our previous impression of him greatly by bringing out his humanity" (3.4.95.1n). Hibbard's impulse to include the direction is a reminder of the persistent interdependency of textual and theatrical logic: in his introduction Hibbard describes Q1 as "completely illegitimate and unreliable, . . . having no direct contact with any Shakespearian manuscript" (69), but he is later compelled to recognize Q1's "value," which is that "through the fog . . . one catches glimpses of an acting version of the tragedy current in the seventeenth century" (89).

Thus while editors endeavor to sort out *Hamlet*'s printing history and make careful distinctions between the play's earliest manifestations, when it comes to constructing an edition of the play, these distinctions often lose their rigidity. On one level, distinctions break down whenever an editor imports a variant from another textual version in order to correct or improve what is deemed to be a corruption in the copy-text. On another level (illustrated by Hibbard's adoption of the nightgown direction), the textual incarnations of a play tend to blur together in the margins wherever the performance potentialities of other printed versions are discussed. In other words, the formulation of *Hamlet*'s complex history in print impacts the shape of the edited text of the play as well as an edition's engagements with the play as performed, and a major conduit between textual and performed modes of realization is performance commentary.

The treatment of the graveyard scene (5.1) serves as an especially revealing example of the matrix linking understandings of *Hamlet*'s textual archaeology, the informational structures of the edited page, and imaginings or recollections of performance practice. The graveyard figures as a particularly permeable boundary between stage and page in the play, a site where details found in the early texts are frequently emended to harmonize with engrained opinions of what "should" happen in performance. Perhaps the image of Hamlet meditating with Yorick's skull in hand—surely the most recognizable in Western drama—acts a kind of imaginative epicenter, with an amplified consciousness of the play's realization on stage radiating outward from it; this image has, strictly speaking, no textual basis, at least not as a surviving stage direction. Hamlet's handling of the skull is very strongly implied by the dialogue,[8] and Hamlet is obviously examining the skull closely enough to recoil from its stench—a variation of the familiar "And smelt so? Pah!" (5.1.194) exists in all three early texts. That said, most editors of the play since Capell make matters explicit for readers, adding directions for Hamlet to pick up the skull and then set it back down (in Hibbard's edition, Hamlet "*throws the skull down*" [5.1.191 SD]). *The* iconic image of Hamlet is also the quintessential instance of crossover between the character's textual and theatrical afterlives: the playtext suggests particular interpretive decisions be made in the theater, and this stage practice becomes so firmly established that it in turn comes to inform subsequent printed versions of the text as an editorial emendation.

So familiar is the image of Hamlet with Yorick's skull that the insertion of a stage direction to this effect is hardly the stuff of methodological controversy. Moreover, Hamlet's extended ruminations on "To what base uses we may return" (5.1.196) are in tune with the seemingly more tranquil character who returns from his sea-voyage. As Margreta de Grazia observes, "Modern criticism has taken the graveyard meditation to mark a profound change in Hamlet" (*Hamlet* 129); the character who returns to Denmark in Act 5 that is, tends to be interpreted as a more serene version of the figure whose bitterness and flashes of violence proved so caustic to Elsinore's court for the bulk of the play. Identifying a distinct transformation in Hamlet before and after his self-described "*sudden and more strange return*" (4.7.45), however, is largely contingent upon a staging or imagining of Hamlet's confrontation with Laertes at Ophelia's grave that modifies or ignores an explicit stage direction in Q1: "*Hamlet leapes in after Leartes* [sic]". A physical struggle between Hamlet and Laertes quite clearly occurs in all three early texts, though Q2 and F are unclear as to where this struggle takes place or if Hamlet is brazen enough to instigate a skirmish over Ophelia's corpse—F includes a direction for Laertes to leap into the grave in his fit of mourning, while Q2 does not provide a direction for either combatant. It is not just that editors' representations of Hamlet's confrontation with Laertes can vary, but that editors' strategies at this specific point in the play have a significant impact on the sort of Hamlet they encourage their readers to envision. Further, *performance escapes* at this juncture can accentuate the space of Ophelia's grave as part of an active, imagined topography of the stage, or alternatively, effectively fill it in and render it largely inert.[9]

Marcus seizes on the textual ambiguities surrounding the confrontation between Hamlet and Laertes in the graveyard to advocate an editorial methodology that embraces a postmodern ethos of "perpetual negation," and "stimulate[s] readers to experience elements of undecidability in their reading of Shakespeare" ("Editing" 142):

> Clearly, much is at stake in the editorial decision whether or not to have Hamlet leap into Ophelia's grave after Laertes. Rather than offer a specificity that forecloses interpretive possibilities that two out of three early texts leave open, an editor working with a postmodern textual framework in mind would be likely to leave the matter undecided, weighing the differences among the early texts in a note. ("Editing" 138–9)

Putting aside for now the impossibility of Marcus's call for an editor to leave the matter "undecided," she is quite right to draw attention to the synergistic relationship between text and commentary, the way in which notes can supplement a reading by providing (or dismissing) interpretive options. Surveying the treatment of the graveyard struggle in major critical editions of *Hamlet* from the past 25 years reveals the range of uses to which citations of performance potentialities can be put.

Edwards's Cambridge edition does its best to shift both combatants away from the grave. Although Edwards includes F's direction for Laertes to leap into the grave, immediately following Hamlet's movement out of his hiding spot—"This is I, / Hamlet the Dane" (5.1.224–5)—he adds the direction, "*Laertes climbs out of the grave.*" In a long commentary note, Edwards explains his reasoning:

> Traditionally, Hamlet jumps into the grave at this point, and the two men struggle. The authority for this is the Bad Quarto, "*Hamlet leapes in after Leartes.*" Q2 and F are silent. Shakespeare cannot have intended Hamlet to leap into the grave and so become the attacker. [...] To couple Hamlet's defiant confrontation of Laertes and Claudius with a jump into the grave and a scuffle is unthinkable. Laertes scrambles out of the grave when he sees Hamlet advancing and rushes upon the man who killed his father. (5.1.225 SDn)

Edwards's rationale involves a thorough blending of textual and theatrical logic. Recall that Edwards understands performance itself as a process that essentially amounts to textual corruption: "One can't really complain that the stage debases *Hamlet*: it has to. One can complain about degrees of debasement, however" (66). Q1, given its apparent proximity to an original staging, thus represents the most thoroughly debased text of the play, and Edwards wants little to do with it. His commentary note acknowledges Q1's encounter *in* the grave, but dismisses it in favor of a reading that does not exist in any of the original textual witnesses. Ironically though, Edwards supplements his readings with reference to an *imagined* original staging: in support of his direction for Laertes to enter and exit the grave, Edwards's note directs readers back to the introduction and a series of three drawings by C. Walter Hodges that attempt to recreate an early modern staging of the scene at Ophelia's grave. The illustrations track Laertes's movements into, and out of the grave, as well as Hamlet's advance from behind a pillar; cumulatively, the drawings function as a visual realization of Edwards's imagined performance, with the final illustration clearly presenting Laertes as the instigator: his left hand is grasping Hamlet's neck, and reproduced below is Hamlet's line, "I prithee take thy fingers from my throat" (5.1.227). As much as Edwards dismisses Q1's encounter in the grave because of a comprehensive bias against that text, it is also apparent that the performance that Q1 approximates does not mesh with his own understanding of the scene and its combatants. In fact, despite his principle that "the nearer we get to the stage, the further we are getting from Shakespeare" (32), Edwards appeals to the play's performance history in the conclusion of his note: "Neither [Henry] Irving nor [Edwin] Booth observed the business of leaping into the grave."

Edwards's note, despite explicitly excluding the possibilities available in Q1's treatment of the scene, is not cut off from performance, but rather situates text and performance in a rigid, deterministic relationship. Edwards's comment that "Laertes scrambles out of the grave when he sees Hamlet advancing and rushes upon the man who killed his father" functions as a kind of secondary stage direction, one that supplements his playtext with an almost novelistic description of dramatic action that positions the reader as a spectator. The added details in the note provide the kind of direction that one might expect had Shaw written the play rather than Shakespeare, a snippet of narrative that in Meisel's terms, "make[s] vivid for the reader what the actor must otherwise supply, and incidentally steer[s] the actor to what in the situation waits to be supplied." This secondary direction "goes beyond cueing the bare physical action, to clueing [sic] attitude and expression (the actor's), heightening the reader's/audience's anticipation for what comes next." "The impulsion," writes Meisel, is not just to stage mechanics, "but to the drama itself" (6). When the primary stage direction and secondary stage direction in the commentary work in tandem, a relatively vivid *performancescape* takes shape. Edwards suggests not just that Laertes leaves the grave to assault Hamlet, but also details the manner in which he does so: he scrambles out and begins to rush upon his father's killer at the mere sight of him. The apparent cost of the more vivid imagining of the confrontation is tighter restrictions on a reader's interpretive options—Edwards clears the ground for his imagined staging by asking readers to discount the possibilities recorded in other texts.

Jenkins similarly utilizes a commentary note to dismiss Q1's call for Hamlet to enter the grave in his Arden 2 edition, though the note registers his aversion to the Q1 staging in a more subtle way. Like Edwards, Jenkins includes a direction for Laertes to enter Ophelia's grave; unlike Edwards, however, Jenkins does not go so far as to call a leap by Hamlet into the grave "unthinkable." Rather than a clear direction for Laertes to exit the grave following Hamlet's announcement of his presence, Jenkins inserts a direction for Laertes to begin *"grappling with him."* Does Laertes begin *"grappling"* while he is in, or out of, the grave? Jenkins addresses this matter tangentially: he mentions Hamlet's audacious leap in Q1 in his note, but accepts the argument "that the action requires Laertes, the aggressor, to come out of the grave rather than Hamlet to leap in. Moreover, attendants must be able to part them" (5.1.252n). Why the action "requires" that the skirmish must take place out of the grave, Jenkins (like Edwards) does not say. One must infer that the image of Hamlet attacking Laertes in the grave simply does not conform to Jenkins's image of a protagonist who in the play's final act "perceives in the universe, embracing all its apparent good and evil, a supreme if mysterious design" (157). A Hamlet impulsive enough to leap into Ophelia's grave sharply deviates from Jenkins's understanding of "a man, who after questioning the meaning of creation, comes to accept a design in it beyond our comprehending" (159).

Jenkins's mention of the potential difficulty of separating Hamlet and Laertes should they both be in the grave is a rather unconvincing attempt to envision the complexities of staging the scene in the physical space of an actual theater. The suggestion that Hamlet and Laertes must be out of the grave is in fact invalidated by Ann Thompson and Neil Taylor's Arden 3 volume containing edited versions of Q1 and F; the introduction to this supplementary volume includes a photograph from a 2000 Globe production (based on F), which captures Hamlet and Laertes being hauled out of the grave/trapdoor by attendants. In the primary volume of the Arden 3 *Hamlet* (the edition of Q2), Thompson and Taylor's commentary note on the staging includes the now familiar reference to Q1's direction for Hamlet's infamous leap, but the editors address the physical difficulties of Q1's staging by pointing to a specific moment in the play's performance history: "at the Globe in 2000 Hamlet did leap into the 'grave' made by the trapdoor, and the subsequent fight was not easily visible from the yard" (5.1.247 SDn). Like Edwards and Jenkins before them, Thompson and Taylor do not incorporate the Q1 direction for Hamlet to leap into the grave, although this decision is a direct product of their unique methodology: in producing three separate editions of the play, Thompson and Taylor are under no obligation to unify the early textual witnesses into a single, conflated text. Whenever a copy-text reading (in their Q1, Q2, or F texts) is deemed defensible and plausible (such as Q2's lack of a grave-bound leap for Hamlet), emendation is unnecessary since each of the early texts is being edited as "an independent entity" (92). In their words, "Our editorial approach is to produce a conservative edition of each text, while providing the reader with enough information to entertain a less conservative edition" (510). When it comes to stage directions they explain that "we have refrained from correcting the copy-text when there is no problem of meaning. We have followed the copy-text for stage directions (except where they need amplification or emendation according to Arden conventions, *or when it clarifies the action, or helps the reader to visualize the play in performance)*" (516, emphasis added). What is significant about this latter strategy is that although Thompson and Taylor remain conservative in their treatment of Q2's directions for Hamlet, the graveyard encounter does mark a point of editorial intervention. Q2 lacks a direction for Laertes to enter the grave, and Thompson and Taylor evidently feel the need to rectify a perceived deficiency: they (like Edwards and Jenkins) emend the Q2 text by incorporating the F direction for Laertes to leap into the grave, and then invent a new direction that helps illuminate the action: Laertes *"Leaps out and grapples with him."*

At this stage it is worthwhile to set these combinations of edited playtext and commentary on a sort of continuum and circle back to reconsider Marcus's thoughts on the role of performance commentary in her descriptions of the "postmodern" edition. Edwards, Jenkins, and Thompson and Taylor disseminate what is essentially the same set of data as they manage textual ambiguity in their margins, but they utilize their performance commentary to different ends. Edwards synchronizes his edited text and commentary to argue that the confrontation should only be realized in one way, that alternative stagings must be eliminated from consideration so that a particular arc of realization—Laertes leaping into, then scrambling out of the grave—takes shape. On one level, this is precisely what happens in a performance: textual ambiguities are removed as decisions are made—Hamlet either picks up Yorick's skull or he does not; he either leaps into Ophelia's grave or he does not. Where Edwards distorts matters is in implying that text and performance exist in a one-to-one, deterministic relationship, as if from a range of possibilities one—and only one—choice is possible. Jenkins, too, acknowledges and dismisses Q1's directions for Hamlet, though not in so forceful a manner as Edwards. Jenkins's playtext retains a measure of ambiguity in that it lacks directions that dictate the positioning of Laertes or Hamlet; Jenkins's commentary note, however, serves to remove any uncertainty surrounding their positioning by referring to Laertes as the "aggressor [who] come[s] out of the grave." Thompson and Taylor are, strategically speaking, in a position that most closely resembles Marcus's descriptions of the postmodern editor: because they are editing all three texts "independently," they are able to reference alternatives that destabilize or open up the edited text, thus freeing readers to envision potentialities that the playtext might not make explicit. Their tripartite approach seemingly would enable them to actuate Marcus's postmodern blueprint for handling the scene's assorted leaps: "leave the matter undecided, weighing the differences among the early texts in a note" ("Editing" 139). It is thus extremely revealing that Thompson and Taylor maneuver Laertes in and out of the grave when their copy-text, Q2, does not explicitly do so. "Editors sometimes cannot refrain from providing answers themselves," write Thompson and Taylor in their introduction, adding that "the proliferation of square brackets in our stage directions indicates the frequency with which we, like all editors, have felt the need to fill some of the gaps in the original texts" (134–5).

This compulsion for clarity—to "fill in the gaps"—is why I resist Marcus's suggestion that leaving matters "undecided" is a feasible plan of action for editors to follow or even the most useful strategy if one has a(n inexperienced) reader's best interests in mind.[10] It is certainly true that performance commentary is an editorial tool that allows for the plurality of performative options at any given moment to be integrated into a textual engagement with a printed play. Marcus's point that "a little suggestiveness" in the margins "can go a long way in encouraging readers to generate possibilities for themselves" ("Editing" 140) is crucial: in my mind, the citation of performance potentialities is an absolutely vital element of contemporary editorial practice, even if potentialities are raised only to be dismissed. That being said, the foreclosure of ambiguity is such an intrinsic element of editorial practice that it will be nearly impossible to switch it off completely. The editors of the Arden 3 *Hamlet* have, given their copy-text, no methodological reason for supplying stage directions for either Hamlet or Laertes to leap into the grave other than their desire to clarify stage action, and significantly, Thompson and Taylor emend the Q2 text so that Laertes does leap. Furthermore, even in instances of predominantly "open" texts, "weighing" differences in a note will not present alternatives as a purified pool of data into which readers can innocently immerse themselves. As Kidnie incisively remarks, "editorial annotation has the ability simultaneously to recover and to create" ("Citing" 132), which reminds us that citations like performance commentary are interpretive procedures that shape the information they set forth. The manner in which performance possibilities are communicated could very well place them in a discernable hierarchy, since any details about specific productions or eyewitness accounts that an editor shares will have passed through various interpretive filters. The mention of Q1's unique staging in the Arden 3 commentary note could be seen to backhandedly dismiss the prospect of Hamlet leaping into the grave by drawing attention to visibility problems for many audience members. Had the note lauded Hamlet's leap in the 2000 performance at the Globe as especially effective (as it likely was for some theater-goers whose sightlines were not obstructed), Q1's alternate staging would have been framed quite differently.

All of the commentary notes that I have mentioned above do, in fact, make reference to a particular document that appears to recollect Hamlet's leap as a powerful moment; the anonymous elegy on the death of the most esteemed actor of the age, Richard Burbage (1619), remembers

> ... young Hamlet, old Hieronimo,
> King Lear, the grievéd Moor, and more beside
> That lived in him have now for ever died.
> Oft have I seen him leap into the grave,
> Suiting the person which he seemed to have
> Of a sad lover with so true an eye
> That there, I would have sworn, he meant to die.
> (Chambers, *Elizabethan* vol. 2, 309)

One cannot be certain that the "leap into the grave" refers to Burbage's performance in *Hamlet*, but given the context, this seems the most likely option.[11] That all of the recent editors of the play cite the "leap" portion of the anecdote in their commentary is indicative of the powerful gravitational force that original performance practices exert on editorial thinking. Barbara Hodgdon, surveying recent examples of performance commentary, observes: "Intriguingly, though perhaps not surprisingly, both in past and present climates driven by (differing) notions of authenticity, the performance most regularly and consistently canonized is the absent performance, the 'original' early modern production about which little or nothing is certain (but much imagined) and which is largely irrecoverable" ("Collaborations" 216). Although Hodgdon goes on to argue that resisting the pull of originary moments of performance practice on an open platform stage is necessary to produce commentary that is "attuned to changing spaces and to fluid potentialities of how bodies and texts take on meanings" (217), it is difficult to envision a situation where the imaginative pursuit of original stage practices would not be a valuable exercise for editors, if for no other reason than to provide a kind of baseline from which to measure subsequent performance choices. "Authentic" early modern performances are in no way more recoverable or historically verifiable than ideal, originary texts, though the former are more palatable to those who prefer their authorities socialized and diffuse, their texts pluralized and unstable. Just as imagining an ideal text is often a generative part of the emendation process, so too is imagining performance practices—whether "much imagined" early modern ones, or those partially recorded in assorted historical documents and archives—an integral part of fully engaging with performative modes of production. Whether editors dismiss the Burbage elegy (as Edwards does, substituting in its place his own conception of how original performances might have run), or absorb it (like Hibbard, who believes it lends credibility to the Q1 direction), a commentary note that addresses the anecdote marks a pathway that readers may follow.

The necessity and usefulness of imagining performance practice lead to the other difficulty I have with Marcus's theoretical formulation of the truly postmodern edition: her suggestion that the playtext must remain "open"—that is, the editor refrains, whenever possible, from emending the text to clarify stage action—in order for the performance possibilities cited in the margins to resonate most fully. Marcus implies that, optimally, an editor's performance commentary will be deployed in conjunction with moments of uncertainty and ambiguity in the playtext, thus allowing readers—not editors—to reduce the proliferation of meaning.[12] The examples of performance commentary that I have summarized above, however, suggest that inconsistencies and alternatives in the margins can coexist with the foreclosure of ambiguity in the edited playtext. Granted there are instances where the fluid boundaries shared by text and performance are misrepresented—Edwards's edition is troubling in that his playtext and commentary combine to funnel readers toward envisioning a single performed realization of the text. Here though, I would recall the embedded *escape* in *performancescape*: it is possible for readers to resist or break away from an editor's virtual performance—in the very act of dismissing alternative stagings of the graveyard confrontation in his note, Edwards simultaneously supplies readers with the tools to deviate from his imagined realization. To "escape" from Edwards's imagined staging requires analytical dexterity on the part of readers, but difficult analytical work is also required should an edition pose frequent instances of textual "openness" and ambiguity. The flexing of a reader's perceptual muscles can occur under either scenario—the issue is whether these muscles are used to rein in potentialities in the playtext that have been left exposed by an editor, or to wrest control from an editorially imposed reading that has smoothed over ambiguities in advance.

In truth, openness or foreclosure likely will not be deployed as comprehensive, mutually exclusive strategies by editors; realistically, editors of any stripe will confront moments they are comfortable leaving relatively open, and also find it necessary to foreclose other moments where they foresee ambiguities posing problems for readers.[13] In discussing the preparation of the Arden 3 *3 Henry VI* (coedited with Eric Rasmussen), John Cox lobbies strongly for editors to "reduce sharply or even eliminate completely the stage directions they add to early texts" and in their place "[outline] staging options in the commentary notes" (178). Cox explains that he and Rasmussen intended to add as few stage directions as possible, in the hopes of offering "a text whose openness might approximate the openness of Shakespeare's stage, unencumbered by scenery, elaborate props, or the expectation of verisimilitude," thus presenting readers with "both the information and the freedom to imagine the staging for themselves" (179). Ultimately, Cox regrets that the edition ended up being "a compromise" between this philosophy and "the house style for all Arden 3 editions" (179), which necessitated the insertion of stage directions at points where he and Rasmussen would have preferred only to present options in the notes. I must make clear that I have no quarrel with Cox and Rasmussen's approach per se; asking readers to confront indeterminacies of staging is a worthwhile endeavor that can produce meaningful considerations of the various interpretive (and transformative) labors required to span the gap between a text and an actualized performance. Where I diverge from their position is in my assertion of the effectiveness of performance commentary being used *in combination with* subjective decisions on the part of editors. While Cox rightly points out that "what editors reconstruct through stage directions ... is not the real performance (and never can be)" (178–9), it must also be said that an edited playtext that resolves an indeterminate moment of staging is *like* a performance in that it brings a range of potential meanings and effects to a close. Even the open early modern stage that Cox and Rasmussen seek to mirror would have had to have supplied a specific shape to a text's various staging possibilities during any given performance. What I am suggesting is that the freedom to choose on the part of readers is not precluded by editorial foreclosures of ambiguity. Performance commentary can function quite effectively, it seems to me, when it allows editorial decision making to acknowledge the institutional and collaborative forces that can propel the text in any number of interpretive directions.

The Arden 3 *3 Henry VI* was published the same year as an Oxford edition by Randall Martin (2001), and comparing their respective treatments of an instance of open staging in the Folio text of the play helps to clarify my point. Early in the first scene, the Yorkist forces storm Westminster and eventually seize control of the throne—"the Regall Seat" (TLN 31), as Warwick refers to it. Despite the absence of a stage direction in the F text, at some point during the scene, York evidently seats himself in the throne, for when the Lancastrians finally enter to confront the invaders, King Henry's initial remark is, "My Lords, looke where the sturdie Rebell sits" (TLN 58). At what point, then, if at all, should an editor indicate that York sits down? Cox and Rasmussen, seeking to retain "F's interpretive openness," opt to not provide a stage direction: "Readers of this edition can imagine York seating himself wherever they want to" (Cox 185, 186). Instead of a stage direction, Cox and Rasmussen supply a retrospective gloss on Henry's "look where the sturdy rebel sits": "York has seated himself by this time, perhaps at 44 ["I mean to take possession of my right"] or more climactically at 48 [Warwick's "I'll plant Plantagenet; root him up who dares"]" (1.1.50n). Cox concedes in a footnote to his essay that readers might be confused by Henry's reference to a seated York even though no direction has been provided for York to sit, but he claims that "an editorial stage direction for York to sit seems to reflect editorial yearning for closure rather than a concern for puzzled readers" (193 n26). Martin's edition, however, undermines this argument. He inserts the direction, *"York is seated,"* at the earliest possible instance, adding this bit of staging to an F direction indicating the Yorkists *"goe vp"* (TLN 38) to the raised chair of state. Martin's edition is thus "closed" relative to Cox and Rasmussen's, but it is far from a hermetically sealed space that stifles a reader's freedom. In Martin's opinion, York seats himself in the throne as soon as possible, but his commentary notes reintroduce ambiguity almost as soon as it is removed. Only 17 lines later, at the line from Warwick immediately preceding the entrance of the Lancastrians—"Resolve thee, Richard, claim the English crown" (1.1.49), Martin adds this note: "York may seat himself here, perhaps after hearing the Lancastrians approach, rather than [at the earlier direction in the scene]." Together then, Martin's emended stage direction and commentary note bracket the range over which the actor playing York could settle into the throne. What becomes apparent is that the commentary notes—or strategic lack thereof—in *both* the "closed" and "open" editions are suggestive of the amorphousness of the text before it is shaped by interpretive procedures. That the freedom of Cox and Rasmussen's "open" edition is worth the cost of its ambiguities is far from self-evident. That is, it is not clear to me that Cox's admittedly "puzzled" readers are in a preferable position compared to those readers of Martin's edition who confront the combination of an edited playtext that removes ambiguity and marginal notes that embrace it.

Of course, editorial commentary is not always directed at such conspicuous ambiguities. To this end it is worthwhile returning to Jenkins's edition of *Hamlet* one last time and the textual moment which began this chapter: Hamlet and company waiting on the platform and the sound of cannons exploding in the night. Recall Jenkins's note, which claimed that "the echoes of the new King's revelry will still be in our ears when the ghost of the King he has murdered tells how he got the crown." Jenkins's text (in combination with his commentary) is not encapsulating performance here, or even representing a specific performance in an accurate way—if anything, his *performancescape* seems too limited, since it is equally plausible (and perhaps more likely) that in performance, the King's revelry *will not* be echoing in our ears (metaphorically or otherwise) by the time the ghost "scent[s] the morning air" (1.5.58) and begins to relate the details of his demise. That Jenkins is an editor best known for his exegetical vigilance rather than a profound concern for the nuances of performance is part of the point: the imagining of a staged *Hamlet* that seeps into his commentary suggests that performance is an integral part of even a "literary" editor's thinking, and thus an inevitable condition of the reading experience. What this particular moment represents is an instance of symbiotic exchange between text and performance of the sort that tends to get lost or ignored when the incongruities of the two modes are stressed. The possibilities of the play in performance are informing Jenkins's text, providing it with a certain measure of authority, albeit an absent one—a kind of "dying voice" (5.2.361), to adopt Hamlet's final lines. If the gap between text and performance is insurmountable and the two modes are incommensurable, if, in other words, the rest is silence (I am thinking here of "rest" in the sense of "space" or "interval"), it is a silence that can nevertheless be punctuated by resounding textual materializations of performance potentialities.

Remembering Lavinia

The space separating text from performance can seem a veritable chasm when one moves to consider a play as reliant on gore and visual spectacle as *Titus Andronicus*. In reading *Titus*, one is faced time and again with the fundamental incongruities of page and stage: encountering in print the newly mutilated Titus asking for his family's assistance in lugging away the severed heads and hand that mark their ruin—"Come, brother, take a head, / And in this hand the other I will bear. / And, Lavinia, thou shalt be employed: / Bear thou my hand, sweet wench, between thy teeth" (3.1.280–3)[14]—tends to mute the potentially ridiculous tenderness of the moment when it is enacted on stage (the Andronici share some of the most perversely sweet familial interactions in the canon). Even reading a stage direction as provocative as the Folio text's "*Enter the Empresse Sonnes, with Lavinia, her hands cut off and her tongue cut out, and ravisht*" (TLN 1068–9) fails to convey just how shocking the first appearance of the ravaged Lavinia can be for a theater audience. Such instances of carnage and trauma, as well as the play's investment in elaborate and often emblematic uses of stage space, are constant reminders that the two modes of production can be conspicuously out of sync: the printed stage directions—in any of the early quartos or the Folio, or even those enhanced by editorial emendation—cannot possibly provide all the data necessary to adequately represent the myriad ways that complicated pieces of stage business can be worked out. The preliminary comments of one of the play's most recent editors, Alan Hughes, crystallize matters: "*Titus Andronicus* is not everyone's favourite play. It 'reads badly'; but in comparatively recent years, theatre audiences have been learning that it frequently 'plays well'" (vii).

One might dispute the assessment that the play "reads badly," but what is clear is that *Titus* poses significant challenges to editors who, like Hughes, endeavor to provide readers with "a fuller sense of what is going on in the playhouse" (159). These challenges, it must be said, are different than those presented by better-known tragedies like *Hamlet*. For one thing, *Titus* simply does not occupy a similarly prominent position on the cultural radar. Because of the relatively recent discovery of the play's effectiveness on stage, editors of *Titus* have a somewhat limited performance history against which to trace the foreclosure of various textual ambiguities. The play was immensely popular in its time—Jonson laments in the Induction to *Bartholomew Fair* (1614) that *"Andronicus"* is still considered (by some audience members at least) amongst the "best plays" some "five and twenty, or thirty years" after it first appeared (qtd. in Waith 1); since Edward Ravenscroft prefaced his 1687 adaptation of *Titus Andronicus* by casting doubt on Shakespeare's sole authorship, however, many readers followed suit and did their best to dissociate Shakespeare from a play that can be laughably horrific.[15] Productions of *Titus* tended to be heavily adapted affairs until well into the twentieth century. Many now recognize the 1955 Stratford-upon-Avon production directed by Peter Brook and starring Laurence Olivier as a landmark, even a "major event in theatre history" (Dessen 14), that altered *Titus*'s fortunes and sparked widespread critical awareness of the play's theatrical potential. Deborah Warner's uncut, unflinching, and visceral Royal Shakespeare Company production from the late 1980s—to which Julie Taymor's successful film version (1999) is greatly indebted—offered a much different vision than Brook's heavily stylized violence, but it too helped sustain critical energies for the play. As the remainder of this chapter will make clear, resonant productions like those of Brook and Warner create powerful memorial spectres that can influence the reading of critical editions depending on the extent to which editors choose to invoke them.

The difficulties posed by *Titus* lead Michael Cordner to use the play as a "test-case" ("'Are We Being Theatrical'" 400) for how modern editions of Shakespeare meet the "demand[s] for a new responsiveness to a script's performance implications" (399). Cordner is a prolific evaluator of the limitations and possibilities of performance commentary, and I would like to address his major assertions in some detail before undertaking an examination of editorial engagements with *Titus*'s performance history. In a series of essays, Cordner has detailed various points of crossover between scholarly editing and performance practice, and has made repeated calls for editorial annotation to "avoid prematurely delimiting [the] rich field of [performance] potentiality" ("Annotation" 187).[16] Cordner traces a similar arc in each of his essays devoted to performance commentary: broadly speaking, he examines citations of performance in a sampling of recent editions of a particular play; more often than not, Cordner zeros in on what modern performance commentary *excludes* in order to stress that this form of editorial mediation actually tends to *limit* a reader's interpretive horizons. The basis for Cordner's program is that "at numerous moments actor and reader alike, whatever their choice of edition, will be left without the information they have the right to expect" ("'Are We Being Theatrical'" 402). Given the limited quantity of performance-related information that they can realistically provide, Cordner argues that editors must "[be] explicit about what [they] are doing and why they are doing it as well as about the nature of the evidence from which they are working. Anything less entails in the end systematic misrepresentation of the true situation. It also serves to reinforce the gulf between study and stage" ("'To Show'" 182). Cordner's analysis concerns itself with three key issues that performance commentary raises as a matter of course: the willingness or ability of an editor to be forthright about his or her interpretive shaping of the play in commentary notes, basic spatial restrictions of plays in book form, and the discrepancy between what readers should be made aware of or have the "right to expect" and what editors in fact provide for them. In order to elucidate Cordner's interrogations of performance commentary, his handling of each of these issues must be considered in turn.

Cordner's preferences when it comes to editorial engagements with performance recall Marcus's "postmodern" edition and Cox's "open" text. Whenever he encounters a textual moment that has been, or could be, performed in multiple ways, Cordner stresses that editorial practice must remain true to multifariousness and possibility; as he puts it, "editors should respect the text's openness and not seek to impose their own preferences as if they were the only legitimate interpretation" ("Actors" 195). This inclination for recognizing multiple performance options leads Cordner to formulate the foreclosure of ambiguity in curious ways. The interpretive and subjective forces behind editorial decision making become, in his writings, the products of an overwhelming desire to command an unruly text: "The impulse to control and circumscribe meaning can be a powerful impulse in scholarly activity, and devising the annotation for an ambitious [sic] text provides many opportunities and temptations for an editor to indulge that impulse" ("Actors" 183). Alternatively, but no less strikingly, an editorial insistence on "only one way of imagining" is a "type of colonization of the text," a product of a "territorial imperative" ("Memory and Performance" 104). These references to power and authority recognize the undeniable influence that editors have over the shape of their texts and the readings that their texts most strongly encourage, but Cordner's disparaging tone suggests that he would like to see an editor's interpretive preferences removed from the equation altogether. As appealing and empowering as this might sound, however, it seems to me neither realistic nor practical: it is hard to imagine even the most "open" of commentary notes that does not still present performance options in mediated—even biased—ways. As was seen above, editors colonizing the performative territory of Ophelia's grave formulated potentialities in highly mediated ways regardless of the relative openness of their notes.

Cordner himself walks a fine line between what he believes commentary *should* make available, and what it realistically *can* make available. He is under no illusion that a commentary note could possibly archive all of the relevant performance details at any given moment; performance histories are simply too rich, and there are limits on how much information a commentary note, or even an entire edition, can contain. What Cordner advocates, though—"a sympathetic, ambitious, and historically informed sense of the potentialities of exceptional performance" ("Memory and Performance" 111–12)—is much easier to theorize than it is to exemplify. While Cordner is able to identify instances of performance commentary that are incomplete, misleading, or redundant, he does not provide a clear model of what commentary that will "truly assist in the disentangling of a genuine interpretive problem" ("Memory and Performance" 116) looks like.

"[T]ruly assist" and "genuine interpretive problem" give the game away, since any editorial move to highlight a potential interpretive problem for readers that requires, or could benefit from, performance commentary, is itself the very sort of subjective, preferential act that Cordner finds so troubling. In other words, no two editors will configure the same list of "genuine" obstacles, just as it must be said that no two readers will require identical levels of assistance. An example from Corder's analysis of editions of *Macbeth*, though it takes us further from *Titus*, will allow me to more fully address the ambiguities of his assessments of performance commentary. Cordner takes issue with A. R. Braunmuller's treatment of Macbeth's exit to Duncan's chamber in 2.1 of his New Cambridge edition (1997). Braunmuller supplies a note, "Henry Irving made an actor's 'point' of his exit when he hesitated an unusually long time before leaving the stage very slowly," to which Cordner ultimately has this to say:

> Highlighting Irving's interpretation in this way seems in the end merely anecdotal. If Irving is to be invoked, why not also tell us about the handling of this exit by David Garrick and by Laurence Olivier, by Ian McKellen and by Edmund Kean, and so on, until, at the very least, a representative sampling of different staging options had been laid before

the reader? But what would be the expository purpose of a note which offered such a survey? What problem in the text, likely to cause readers difficulty, would it be designed to unknot? That Macbeth is intended to leave the stage after his soliloquy seems indisputable. How he might leave it is best left to readers—and to actors—to surmise. ("Memory and Performance" 95)

Cordner's *modus operandi* is problematic because of formulations like this one. On one hand, readers face the constant threat of being gulled into having their faculties shackled or manipulated by a misleading or unnecessarily restrictive note, while the same readers nevertheless possess the interpretive wherewithal to foreclose certain ambiguities themselves. Cordner is correct in observing that Braunmuller's note does not solve an apparent problem (though surely an editor's job is not to address only conspicuous problems), but his response to Braunmuller's commentary—the nature of Macbeth's exit "is best left to readers"— speaks to the larger issue of identifying readers and their needs. In exposing the "genuine interpretive problems" in the various editions that he surveys, Cordner simultaneously dictates the capabilities of the "readers" to which he refers. Significantly, Cordner blurs two classes of readers into one: those that will apparently take every suggestion in editorial commentary as legislative and incontrovertible constitute one class, but this group morphs into readers who, when faced with indeterminate information suggesting a wide range of potential meanings, are capable of the "firm, inventive decisions" ("Actors" 194) that imagining performance requires. That the capabilities of all readers appear to change depending on Cordner's own understanding of what constitutes a substantive staging issue not only takes the sting out of some of his criticisms of contemporary performance commentary but also reinforces the fact that any editorial mediation is going to be processed by readers of varying skill sets. It would seem to me that a firm sense of inventiveness can also resist, or deviate from, a reading "imposed" by editorial decision making. In other words, Braunmuller's note on Irving, despite being anecdotal and belying staging *options*, is defensible in my mind, more defensible than excluding it on the grounds of leaving the text "open" at every available opportunity. If certain readers can foreclose the text themselves, it seems likely that these same readers can escape or resist the *performancescapes* that are deployed in the margins. Arguably, supplying the note could help relatively less inventive readers, without necessarily hindering those who are already capable of making inventive approximations of performance. Additionally, adding a note raising only one possibility in performance can *implicitly* raise other options that might be excluded for reasons of space and clarity. Any citation of a specific decision made by a specific performer marks the portion of text being cited as open to interpretation. In this case, that Braunmuller finds Irving's unusually long delay in leaving the stage noteworthy implies that Macbeth need not exit in this manner, and perhaps can even *hurry* off.

Braunmuller himself has raised another issue that looms large in my discussion of performance commentary and readers. Reflecting on the ways in which editors "consciously or unconsciously" (136) shape the Shakespearean text, Braunmuller touches on matters of performance practice (in this case, the confusion surrounding the fainting of Lady Macbeth) and makes a provocative claim:

> An editor might write a note canvassing the [performance] possibilities as that editor understood them and leave the text as is. This choice is utopian because nobody reads notes, and without a visible sign in the text, the line ["Look to the lady"] will remain extremely puzzling. And when I say "nobody reads notes," I especially do not mean undergraduate students or novice Shakespeareans. I mean "nobody." (146)

Braunmuller is, of course, exaggerating: if absolutely no one read notes, no editor in her right mind would craft them with such care and attention, and no publishing house would waste ink on them. That he is exaggerating for rhetorical effect likely does not need to be made clear, but I would like to point out is why Braunmuller's claim is problematic. I, for one, read notes. I have read them faithfully since I was an undergraduate; I have also encountered a number of students who attend to notes (and introductions) with a focus that they do not always bring to the text proper; in fact, there is a category of cunning student that mines notes for critical insights that can be raised during discussions in an attempt to impress peers and instructors. The implication that notes need not be taken seriously or studied closely as to their function within a larger textual machine because "no one" reads them occludes meaningful critical activity on the basis of casual overgeneralization. I would concede that my traverse of performance commentary might be what Braunmuller would call "utopian," and that the particular readerly navigations that I am trying to highlight will, to some eyes, no doubt appear as exaggerated as Braunmuller's "nobody reads notes" assertion. The difference, as I understand it, is that my exaggeration engages a very real part of printed texts, with the intention of sustaining critical inquiry and debate; indeed, much in the same way that notes build—in small increments—an interpretive network bound by their suggestions, gestures, recollections and cross-references, so too does critical activity proceed by way of incremental gains. To dismiss out of hand the great signifying potential of performance commentary because it is not read by a certain threshold of potential readers is dangerously reductive (one assumes that the value of a journal article or book on any topic in the humanities is not quantifiably based on its number of readers). The equivalent counterposition would be me responding to persuasive, thoughtful arguments regarding the potential utility of having readers confront a text's instabilities, ambiguities, and uncertainties head-on, with the following claim: "But no readers—especially inexperienced or unspecialized ones—want to work that hard. They have no interest in answering—or even recognizing—questions that editors have not solved for them." Such a response is critically shortsighted and precludes productive dialogue; moreover, this kind of misrepresentative exaggeration, much like the "nobody reads notes" statement, is simply false, even if we can think of examples of particular readers who might fit either stereotypical profile.

Returning to *Titus*, Cordner observes that the play is "extremely adventurous in its exploitation of the acting and physical resources afforded by late Elizabethan playhouses and their companies. Decoding the details of its intended staging poses many, sometimes perhaps insuperable, problems for the commentator" ("'Are We Being Theatrical'" 407). The first act is especially challenging for editors, as it involves a complicated assortment of entrances and exits involving large groups of actors, movements to and from the upper playing area, various acts of supplication, and large shadows of ambiguity looming over the staging of both Bassianus's seizing of Lavinia and Titus's murder of Mutius—to say nothing of numerous corpses that need to be moved about. In order to help readers better envision the action, modern editors often find it necessary to emend certain stage directions and devote large portions of their commentary to matters of staging. Jonathan Bate stresses that his "admiration for the play's stage qualities" has led him "to include very full stage directions to help the reader visualize it in action" (105), or, as he expresses it elsewhere in his introduction, "to assist the reader in a mental staging of the play" (108). The New Cambridge (1994) editor, Hughes, makes a similar assertion: "In order to clarify the action for the reader I have amplified or added stage directions" (62). An example of a potentially confusing element of the opening act is the question of just how many coffins accompany Titus in his pyrrhic return from warring with the Goths, given that it is clear he is meant to have more than one dead son in tow. Marcus states that Titus is "bearing his valiant sons / In coffins from the field" (1.1.34–5), and Titus himself refers more than once to multiple bodies:

> These that I bring unto their latest home,
> With burial amongst their ancestors.
>
> Make way to lay them by their brethren
>
> farewell to their souls.
> In peace and honour rest you here, my sons;
>
> In peace and honour rest you here, my sons. (1.1.86–7, 92, 152–3, 159)

As the action proceeds toward the internment of Titus's "sons unburied yet" (1.1.90), however, the stage directions contradict the dialogue. Both Q1 and F specify that as Titus makes his first entrance, he is accompanied by, among others, "*two men bearing a Coffin couered with blacke*" who eventually "*set downe the Coffin*" (Q1: TLN 105, 109; F: TLN 84–5, 88–9). When the fallen Andronici are finally entombed, Q1 sticks with a lone coffin—"*lay the Coffin in the Tombe*" (TLN 193)— while F makes a switch that explicitly contradicts the earlier direction— "*and lay the Coffins in the Tombe*" (TLN 175).

With references to numerous corpses and only one coffin (or in the case of F, a single coffin that later multiplies), an editor must decide how to rectify the contradiction. Stanley Wells argues that

> [t]here is no conceivable reason why Shakespeare should have wished to talk of the interment of two (or more sons) yet to provide the means for the burial of only one. A director who is consciously faithful to the apparent discrepancy in the text is taking pedantry to the point of irresponsibility to both author and audience. (*Re-Editing* 92)

Accordingly, Wells conjectures that the first direction should be emended to include the phrase "*men bearing coffins.*" Hughes's Cambridge text goes one step further: citing Wells's conjecture in the collation, Hughes alters the entry direction to specify "*men bearing [two] coffin[s],*" and provides a commentary note that makes no mention of Q1's single coffin. "There must be two coffins," states Hughes, "Titus buries two sons" (1.1.69 SDn). The singularity of Hughes's vision of the action verifies Cordner's warning regarding performance commentary: it *can* misrepresent or unrealistically delimit performance options. For a reader using

Hughes's edition to contemplate the use of a single coffin is not impossible, but since Hughes definitively dismisses performance alternatives at this juncture, such a deviation from the editor's imagining would involve a dextrous navigation of the collation in order to reconstruct the Q1 reading. However, both Bate and Eugene Waith, editor of the Oxford edition (1984), believe Q1's call for a lone coffin is correct, and their use of performance commentary is more in line with how Cordner would like to see it deployed. Bate acknowledges F's pluralized direction, but notes that "Elizabethan staging was often more emblematic than literal" (1.1.72.1–6n), and Waith—who also recognizes the F direction for *"coffins"*—believes that "several coffins . . . would crowd the stage and require more 'extras' in an already large cast" (1.1.149.1n). Neither Bate nor Waith emend Q1's single coffin, and while this decision shuttles readers' imagined approximations of staged action toward an emblematic and symbolic end, both editors identify an alternative reading even as they justify the shape they have imposed on the text.

The list of ambiguous moments of stage action that editors must confront in this play could be multiplied. Without stage directions in the earliest texts, how does one sort out the movements of the various parties in the moments leading up to, and following, Titus's murder of Mutius? What kind of weapon or instrument does Aaron use to cut off Titus's hand in 3.1? Who calls for the ladder enabling Aaron to ascend the scaffold in 5.1? Most editors emend the text so that Lucius gives the order, but Q1 assigns "Get me a ladder" (TLN 2053) to Aaron himself—might the Moor, in an outrageous, defiant act in tune with both the play and his character, *embrace* the prospect of being hanged? What about the absence of a stage direction in the Q and F texts for the eating of Titus's murderous pie? Surveying the performance commentary (or lack thereof) that accompanies these moments would produce a mirror-list, one consisting of examples of commentary that are arguably too restrictive, too open, or somewhere in between. Rather than jump from moment to moment and critique or approve particular editorial decisions, I would like to take a different approach and consider instead the influence that performance histories can exert on editorial practice. By this I mean that certain productions are simply more influential, more resonant—more *memorable*—than others, and this influence will bleed over into editorial streams of thought. Any new critical edition of *A Midsummer Night's Dream*, for instance, would not be doing its due diligence if it failed to make mention of Peter Brook's 1970 white-box production; editions of *A Merchant of Venice* must account for the most provocative interpretations of Shylock, like Charles Macklin's "fierce, relentless" (Halio 63)—but not comic—villainy of the mid-eighteenth century, and Irving's pathos-infused rendition of the nineteenth century. Momentous performances and productions have become an integral part of modern editorial practice; editors, it must be said, are also theater-goers and theater historians, and the most firmly imprinted personal or recorded memories of performance can influence their understanding of the play and, by extension, their treatment of the playtext. In Kidnie's words, "Whether one participates in it as actor or spectator, the experience of a moment is thereafter relived as memory, and it can only be communicated to others through forms of story-telling"; she goes on to remark that "by citing the stories, one enables others to remember, if not performance, then at least the narrativized memories of performance; the uncited performance, by contrast, slides into an oblivion of forgetfulness" ("Citing" 117, 118). Bate in fact grounds his interpretation of the *Titus* coffin/coffins crux in performance history, mentioning that "the Warner production had a single wide multiple coffin; its entry procession was simple but stunning, with Titus sitting on a ladder held horizontally by his sons, the prisoners' heads stuck between the rungs" (1.1.72.1–6n). The reference to Warner sharpens Bate's *performancescape*, the production living in, and giving life to, his edited text.

Memories of Warner's production permeate Bate's edition. By my count, Bate cites Warner's production 21 times in the commentary notes; in contrast, Brook's 1955 production, certainly the most influential version before Warner's, is mentioned only twice.[17] Clearly then, images, narratives, and memories of Warner's production impinge on Bate's imaginings of the play's performance possibilities at numerous points. In his introduction, Bate stresses that Warner's "realism enabled [her] to bring out [the play's] representation of how ordinary human beings can be driven to extraordinary extremities of violence and cruelty on the one hand, resilience and tenderness on the other" (65–6). The play's constant and rapid oscillations between savagery and kindness—so accentuated in Warner's production—are elements that Bate endeavors to make readily available to readers of his edition. Central to Bate's memorial engagements with Warner is the figure, or more accurately, the body, of Lavinia. Lavinia's mutilated body is, without a doubt, a powerful marker of the play's rampant horror and violence; after she is raped and disfigured, her family struggles to make sense of what has been done to her, to understand not only what she is trying to *mean* but also what she has *become*. "This was thy daughter," says Marcus, presenting Lavinia's ravaged body for the first time, to which Titus responds, "Why, Marcus, so she is" (3.1.63–4). The rift between "was" and "is" is produced by the offstage trauma that Lavinia undergoes at the hands of Chiron and Demetrius, and the bulk of the action in the second half of the play involves the efforts of the Andronici to both mend this rift—"who hath martyred thee?" (3.1.81), "who hath done this deed?" (3.1.88)—and respond to it by way of "Mortal revenge upon these traitorous Goths" (4.1.93). Moreover, Lavinia's silent, damaged body becomes a site of interpretation for an audience as well: as Bate puts it, "Lavinia is a 'Speechless complainer' but a bodily presence. Her body is at the centre of the action, as images of the pierced and wounded body are central to the play's language" (36).

To encounter Lavinia within the bounds of a printed text, however, is to not see, and thus not be affected by, her bodily presence. That merely states the obvious, but the fundamental differences between printed and performed modes of realization are, I believe, why Bate references Warner's production as often as he does. After the rape, Lavinia communicates and signifies in a haunting, unspoken language that printed texts cannot reproduce. Titus, striving to "interpret all her martyred signs," claims that

> In thy dumb action will I be as perfect
> As begging hermits in their holy prayers.
> Thou shalt not sigh, nor hold thy stumps to heaven,
> Nor wink, nor nod, nor kneel, nor make a sign,
> But I of these will wrest an alphabet
> And by still practice learn to know thy meaning. (3.2.36, 40–5)

Titus's desperate, impossible boast is, for readers, also a litany of sounds and gesticulations that cannot be replicated in print. Editors cannot reproduce Lavinia's body and her attempts at signification—they can only describe them, transform them (as Kidnie articulates) into narrative. About one-third of Bate's references to the Warner production involve Lavinia; in particular, Bate's commentary focuses on the violence inflicted upon her, and the often unspoken or unseen, otherwise nontextual ways her body communicates throughout the play. As Lavinia is dragged away by Chiron and Demetrius in 2.2, for example, Bate adds this note: "In the Deborah Warner production, Chiron (Richard McCabe) picked her up bodily, obscenely stuffing one hand between her legs; the sounds of rape were heard from offstage" (2.2.186.2n). The next scene begins with the direction, "*Enter the* Empress' Sons *with* LAVINIA, *her hands cut off and her tongue cut out, and ravished*," to which Bate supplies a note indicating that "in the Warner production, Chiron and Demetrius crawled on first, parodying the movement of their mutilated victim" (2.3n). Later in the play, when Marcus presents her mutilated form to Titus, Bate indicates that "in the Warner production, she remained behind Marcus' back" (3.1.58.1n) for as long as the text will possibly allow (until, that is, Titus and Lucius explicitly respond to her presence). Lavinia's powerful silence following her rape is emphasized by Bate: after being discovered by Marcus, eventually "*Lavinia turns*" (2.3.12.1) to face him (an added stage direction unique to Bate's edition), and readers learn that this turn "elicit[ed] a long pause in the Warner production" (2.3.12.1n). Memories of Warner's production even appear to directly influence some of Bate's emendations to his copy-text: he emends Titus's "Hark how her sighs doth flow" (Q1 reading) to "Hark how her sighs doth blow" (F2 reading), noting that "Lavinia's sighs represent the wind (an effect caught strongly by...Warner)" (3.1.226n). When it comes to Lavinia's death at the hands of Titus in the final scene, editors must contend with the Q1 text that provides no stage direction, and the F text which provides the cryptic direction, "*He kils her*" (TLN 2550). At this juncture Bate again references Warner in his notes, this time using the production to explicitly contrast a range of potential interpretations: "In the Warner production, he crisply snapped her neck; at Santa Cruz [a 1998 production directed by Mark Ruckner], she stepped towards him as he held out the knife, actively embracing both her father and death" (5.3.46.1n). Cordner in fact singles out this particular note from Bate for approval: "The implications of that contrast [between productions] is massive, though Bate's non-emphatic way of reporting it calls no special attention to the fact. [...] Both versions meet the script's demands comfortably," he writes, "but, in the process, they tell totally divergent stories" ("Are We Being Theatrical" 413). The "contrast" that Cordner champions constitutes an undeniably effective strategy, though it is one that Bate rarely employs, instead usually choosing to only reference decisions made in the Warner production. Yet, counter to what Cordner would suggest, the commentary's overriding adherence to a single production, while conspicuous, is its most remarkable and effective attribute—the edition is *not* poorer for its overall lack of "divergent stories."

Cumulatively, the fragmented narratives in Bate's edition do not reconstitute or recapture Warner's production (what narrative could?), nor do they even come close to describing in full the nuances of Sonia Ritter's performance as Lavinia (though an illustration of a near catatonic Ritter being examined by Titus (Brian Cox) in the introduction is a useful aid). Bate's recurrent references to Warner's production undoubtedly splinter and distort it, and Bate's selectivity in drawing out certain details dictate the terms of his readers' interactions with it; Ritter and Cox loom large in the notes, for example, while Peter Polycarpou's Aaron is absent from them—might readers infer that his performance was conspicuously unmemorable? Moreover, the inescapable interpretive work of recording and sharing narratives of performance is also at issue, and here we can turn to another example of a potent memory of Warner's production that appears to justify or even motivate an emendation on Bate's part: during Marcus's extraordinary speech in response to first witnessing Lavinia's damaged body, Bate inserts a stage direction of his own creation—"*Lavinia opens her mouth*" (2.3.21.1)—and a note—"spitting blood in the Warner production" (2.3.21.1n)—which together provide a specific visual stimulus for Marcus's "Alas, a crimson river of warm blood, / Like to a bubbling fountain stirred with wind, / Doth rise and fall between thy ros[è]d lips" (2.3.22–4). In a critical study of Warner's production, Dessen writes that the blood escaping from Ritter's mouth at this particular point—in actuality "the only blood of the scene"—"elicited shocked gasps from the audience" (60). Unlike Bate, however, Dessen describes not a "spitting" of blood, but something different: "not a river (or a ribbon) but a trickle" (60). The alternative narrative provided by Dessen thus confirms the moment's memorableness, but it also speaks to the variability of memory, as well as the way in which "the work of memory [serves] not simply to recover an absent event, but to transform it" (Kidnie, "Citing" 129). How does one square Dessen's "trickle" of blood with Bate's "spitting" of it? Is the memory that Bate makes available to his readers inaccurate? Incomplete? There is no recourse to the production itself; it has vanished and is forever inaccessible, existing only in various forms of memorialization—reviews, photographs, director's notes, playbills, Dessen's study, Bate's edition. Even a video recording of a particular night of the production would not necessarily set the record straight: perhaps Ritter spat blood some nights and let it trickle others.

Whatever the case, Bate's addition of the "*Lavinia opens her mouth*" direction, while born of fidelity to Warner's production, certainly circumscribes the performance potentialities that a reader might envision. In Brook's 1955 production, Lavinia's wounds were represented symbolically, with Vivien Leigh's "arms swathed in gauze, [and] scarlet streamers attached to her mouth and wrists" (Waith 55). Bate's graphic *performancescape* involving an open, spitting mouth would seem to preclude a more stylized imagining of Lavinia's violated body. If Bate's use of Warner's production does confirm anything, it is that, as Hodgdon observes, "Writing commentary by the light of admired productions invites visualizing or hearing material particulars that write themselves over text" ("Collaborations" 216). It is important to emphasize, however, that there are positive consequences stemming from the numerous imprints of Warner's production in Bate's edition. Citing performance unrealistically stabilizes and textualizes the inherent impermanence of performance, as well as carves up and decontextualizes performance histories, but these citations of performance can strengthen links between page and stage and aid in readers' comprehension of the interpretive labors of actors and directors that forge those links.

What the narratives of Warner's production accomplish is threefold. First, the connections in the commentary notes establish the production as a memorable conduit of the play's power on stage. The repeated flashes of detail—that Cox "laughed maniacally for a full 10 seconds" (3.1.265n) during the nadir of 3.1, the use of "cheese-wire and an old bucket" (3.1.192.1n) to cut off Titus's hand—serve as constant reminders to readers that the play is more than just an inert text of ink on paper, that what they are reading, while it is a coherent, literary document, will be transformed through its realization by actors in a theater. *Titus* becomes apprehensible as a printed text *and* a performed event; more importantly, these two modes of production are demonstrated to constantly intersect one another—not just by way of the exchange system of Bate's edited text and performance commentary, but by the performance choices that Bate chooses to highlight. Cox's sustained, maniacal laughter is an extreme amplification of an actual line in the text ("Ha, ha, ha!" [3.1.265]), and the horrifyingly creative use of cheese-wire has its origins (however distant) in the earliest quarto: "*He cuts off Titus hand*" ('TLN 1312). Second, Bate's commentary notes, even as they limit multivalence and sidestep "rival versions of equal plausibility" (Cordner, "Actors" 185), add value to the edited playtext. The notes, in other words, which frequently work in conjunction with Bate's foreclosure of textual ambiguity, both reveal and obscure the complexities of performance. In giving textual shape and stability to performance potentialities that are multifarious and rooted in embodied action, Bate provides readers with a firm foundation for their own imagined realizations of particular moments. It must also be said that Bate's deliberate shaping of this foundation is not put forth as absolute and binding; his note to Tamora's line, "Remember, boys, I poured forth tears in vain / To save your brother from the sacrifice" (2.2.163–4), that "In the Warner production, Estelle Kohler's normally powerful voice quivered here [at

'Remember, boys'], as Tamora recollected her dead son" (2.2.163n) makes explicit just one of a host of ways that this line could be delivered, but the note nevertheless opens up both the line and Tamora's delivery of it as sites of interpretation. Lastly, the notes afford Bate the space to allow Lavinia's body/language to signify from the margins; reading Bate's edited playtext and his notes, one encounters a Lavinia who screams, bleeds, sighs, and whose silences reverberate throughout much of the play. This attention to Lavinia helps to ensure that readers contend with her typographically mute, bodily presence and the challenges it raises in terms of memory, violence, and suffering.

Bate's handling of Lavinia thus befits her position within the play as a whole, a position that, from a broader perspective, serves as a useful analogy for considering the meaningful deployment of performance commentary. The vile treatment of Lavinia at the hands of Chiron and Demetrius exists in the world of the play as an unseen, past event that no one can begin to understand without some sort of guidance. Lavinia's family struggles to remember and re-member her, to imaginatively reconstitute her story and by extension, her body. The Andronici largely seek in vain for a narrative: "Lavinia, what accursed hand / Hath made thee handless in thy father's sight?" (3.1.67–8), asks Titus; "What means my niece Lavinia by these signs?" (4.1.8) echoes Marcus. As Bate recognizes in his introduction, the problem for Titus, despite his "confident" claims of prowess as a "semiotician," is that "he finds that gesture is more ambiguous than spoken language. Only when a text is inscribed upon the ground can interpretation be confirmed" (34). Bate here is hearkening to 4.1, where Lavinia is finally able to communicate her memories in a manner that makes use of a printed text and an autonomous, subjective act of writing. The mutilated and mute Lavinia first wrestles a copy of Ovid's *Metamorphoses* away from her nephew and manages to fumble to the page(s) recounting the rape of Philomel, the "tragic tale" (4.1.47) that mirrors her own. Philomel's story is at the core of what Lavinia is trying to share, and while it determines the range of potential interpretations of what happened to her, it is not definitive. Questions still remain: "Lavinia, wert thou thus surprised, sweet girl, / Ravished and wronged as Philomela was, / Forced in the ruthless, vast and gloomy woods?" (4.1.51–3); "Give signs, sweet girl... / What Roman lord it was durst do the deed" (4.1.61–2). Philomel's story requires a gloss. It is only after Lavinia has followed her uncle's example of writing in the "sandy plot" (4.1.69) by guiding a staff with his feet and mouth that the crucial details of her ordeal—the *names* of her attackers—are revealed to her family. Marcus encourages his niece to "print thy sorrows plain, / That we may know the traitors and the truth" (4.1.75–6), and the brevity of Lavinia's narrative is inversely related to its effectiveness: "*Stuprum—Chiron—Demetrius*" (4.1.78). Rape—Chiron—Demetrius.

It would be perverse to call Lavinia's writing "performance commentary," but what I would suggest is that the play dramatizes the impulses behind editorial citations of performance: the desire to return to the forever-absent past event, and the textual forms that do, and do not, make such a return possible. The imprints of Lavinia's writing in the sand—the physical manifestations of remembering—account for her violation in an utterly incomplete way. The story she shares hides much more than it reveals, but, set against the tale of Philomel, what little she does reveal is enough for her readers to make sufficient meaning out of. Performance commentary, in linking text and past event, in shaping potentialities by way of narrativized memories or imaginings, carries with it a similar potential for revelation, giving voice to those moments and figures that, like Lavinia, cannot speak for themselves.

CHAPTER 5

The Critical Edition as Archive

In his influential New Bibliographical study, *On Editing Shakespeare* (1966), Fredson Bowers makes what now seems like an astonishing claim. His eyes firmly set on the future of editorial practice as he contemplates the feasibility of "a definitive text of Shakespeare," he writes, "Some day the accumulation [of facts] will reach the limits of human endeavour and the fact-finding be exhausted. Then, and only then, can the final capstone be placed on Shakespearian scholarship and a text achieved that in the most minute detail is as close as mortal man can come to the original truth" (101). The project that Bowers foresees involves establishing absolutely the bibliographical and typographical "facts" of early modern printing practice; the more nuanced one's understanding of printing-house practice, the theory goes, the more accurately one can reconstruct the manuscripts that were, at various stages of removal, behind the printed objects themselves. Though fully aware that the transmission of Shakespeare's plays into print involved the shaping influence of various intermediaries and agencies (particularly scribes and compositors), Bowers's vision of the future is one in which meanings and authorities are delimited by editors, the critical edition becoming a means to establish Shakespeare's intentions (the "original truth" to which he refers).

Bowers's optimistic forecast is fueled by a scientific positivism that has been recognized for some time as ill-suited to the production of critical editions; the hackles of textual theorists, as well as many editors, now instinctively bristle at the mention of the very terms, such as "definitive" and "original truth," that Bowers's prophecy is built upon. As I outlined in chapter 1, many current theorists of editorial practice, quite unlike Bowers and the New Bibliographers, stress the proliferation of uncertainty, the inaccessibility of intentions, the impossibility of approximating originary moments, and the instability of texts.[1] Graham Holderness provides a summary of the current theoretical climate:

> Shakespeare now exists in an environment of textual multiplicity. Virtually all the new approaches, whether critical, theoretical or bibliographical, agree on this. The text is multiple, iterable, subject to an inevitable law of change. It is never original, always copied. The grounds on which *a priori* assumptions could be made about the automatic superiority of one text over another have disappeared: so texts remain to us as plural, relative to one another, not severed into separation by some absolute judgement, but embedded in network [sic] of differences. The text gives us no direct access to any pure space of authorial intention, for someone has always got there before us. (249)

When advocates of this "New Textualism"[2] set their sights on the future of editorial practice as it relates to drama in general, and Shakespeare in particular, the outlook and goals are, understandably, radically different than those articulated by Bowers, but the rhetoric and the claims that are made are often ironically infused with a similar spirit of promise and revelation. "Some might fear that . . . a theory of the radical instability of the material and conceptual text would lead to intellectual anarchy and the collapse of the possibility of a reliable knowledge of texts," writes Jerome McGann, for example, "[b]ut in truth, only from such a theoretical position can one begin to imagine the possibility of reliable knowledge" (*Textual Condition* 185).

The fundamental philosophical differences between New Bibliographers and New Textualists are only exacerbated by the rise of completely new media for textual production and reception in the years separating the two movements. We have arrived at a future that Bowers could not have foreseen: digital facsimiles, digital editions, the Internet, and the potential of computerized hypertexts have radically altered the ways that editing is both conceived and carried out. Indeed, the rise of poststructuralist theories informing New Textualism has gone hand in hand with the digitization of texts. The destabilizing potential inhering in the digital edition[3]—manipulable screens, hyperlinks, seemingly countless texts intersecting one another—offers a promise of liberation, of freedom from the restrictive confines of the codex and its constituent parts: pages, print, and limited representational capabilities. The theoretically infinite referentiality of the digital edition is inevitably juxtaposed with printed texts that are figured as stifling in their boundedness. McGann, for example, argues that "problems inhere in the codex form itself, which constrains the user of the critical edition to manipulate different systems of abbreviation, and to read texts that have (typically) transformed the original documents in radical ways"; any transformations of original documents by digitization do not, according to McGann, limit interpretation but enrich it: "In an electronic edition...both of these hindrances can be removed. Precisely because an electronic edition is not itself a book, it is able to establish itself in a theoretical position that supervenes the (textual and bookish) materials it wishes to study" ("Rationale of Hypertext" 37). David Scott Kastan writes that, unlike the book, "the electronic text offers a fantasy of freedom: there is no need to make choices; there are no consequences to accept" (*Book* 130); John Jowett makes the distinction in more pointed terms, suggesting that in the medium of the electronic text, "the discipline and constraint of the printed page immediately disappear [because] the hierarchy of material is not rigidly set; it is generated according to need." Given that the digital edition embraces "the malleability of the on-screen view," writes Jowett, "the possibilities are endless" (*Shakespeare* 164).

The vision of the future that permeates most theorizations of editorial practice has thus absorbed the possibilities offered by new technologies, resulting in rhetoric of a different kind of definitiveness: the definitively *indefinite* digital text that affords users the ability not to locate meaning, but to make meaning, and remake it, again and again. In this final chapter, I will reflect on Shakespeare's printed incarnations through a consideration of the hypertextual promise of digital editions. The representational and storage capabilities of digital editions have, without question, led to a widespread reassessment of the strengths and limitations of Shakespeare in print. Editors have been forced to rethink concepts like "authorship," "work," and "version," and to confront the challenges of attempting to approximate intentions and originary moments of textual production. Sonia Massai, for example, writes that "The notions of Text, Author, and Canon are culturally- and medium-specific," and she contends that "the electronic medium has made these categories obsolete" ("Scholarly Editing" 105). But while the refinement of editorial thinking brought about by digitization and hypertext has ultimately been beneficial, the claims that are made for digital editions are (as the above sampling of quotations suggest) too often made by way of unhelpful and oversimplified pronouncements that polarize printed and digitized texts. Digital texts, though relatively fluid and unstable things, nevertheless remain tied to a logic of print

culture at this stage of their evolution—notions of linearity and mediation continue to inform digital texts, even as their seemingly limitless
referential capabilities mean that electronic editions are often not reading editions at all, but rather archives of data that require the shaping
influence of a user.

Kastan's "fantasy of freedom" and Jowett's "endless possibilities" signal a tendency to wrap discussions of digital texts in terms of promise
and potential. To examine the most substantial and methodologically
rigorous digital editions of Shakespeare produced to date—such as those
found in *Internet Shakespeare Editions* and *The Shakespeare Collection*—
allows for a clearer picture of the possibilities of digital texts, but also
reasserts some of their oft-elided limitations. One claim often made
on behalf of the digital edition is that, in its openness, fluidity, and
mutability, it is more representative of performance potentialities than
a printed text could ever be; this point also needs to be reconsidered
since it tends to misrepresent the ability of readers of printed editions
to navigate textual spaces and bring various forms of information to
bear on their engagements with primary materials. *Performancescape*, a
term that I have used to this point in relation to printed texts, is a concept tied to a reader's freedom to move around the page (and between
pages), and while the imaginings of performance facilitated by digital
editions can be much more detailed than those offered by printed editions (especially through video or sound clips that exceed the capabilities of print), the representational potency of digital media should not
obscure an awareness of the different, meaningful ways that the reader
of a critical edition can engage with performance histories and possibilities. The way that printed editions necessarily shape performance
through acts of memory, imagination, and various forms of textual code
poses, relative to a digital edition, formal and interpretive restrictions;
however, printed editions' fractured, mediated representations of performance, are, paradoxically, a source of interpretive strength in that
they can offer readers of Shakespeare's plays glimpses of performance
that mirror the incomplete, partial ways that performance survives in
any form. The dream of comprehensiveness and neutrality that lingers
behind digital editions is in some ways fundamentally untrue to the
means by which performance is remembered and represented, since, as
Stanley Wells reminds us, "Performance is not an objective phenomenon" ("Foreword" xx). It is the subjective influence of editorial practice
and its concomitant delimitations that ensure the relevance of printed
editions in a digital age that thrives on access to ever-expanding horizons of information.

The Promise of the Digital Edition

As discussed in chapter 2, the rise of printing technology and the standardization of certain typographical codes helped to establish particular understandings of the relation between reading and performance, as well as enable certain claims to be made about reading experiences relative to theatrical ones. Print is a medium of conservation and endurance (Kastan, *Book* 7), and these characteristics become especially resonant in the case of printed plays because performed modes of realization are distinguished by their impermanence and ephemerality. Printed plays endure spatially and temporally in ways that performances simply cannot, and in previous chapters we have seen various examples of playwrights and publishers seizing on print's ability to "fix" (in the fullest sense of the word) a play: from claims that printed playtexts represent the play "as it was acted," to playwrights like Webster and Jonson embracing print as a more stable means of communicating work that was understood to have failed on stage. The fixedness of print has obvious implications for readers as well: save for annotation that a reader may inscribe, reading a printed play does not physically transform the text itself; as I have argued, this textual stability is a key factor in facilitating *performancescapes*: a reader's progress through a playtext can essentially be "paused," tangential moves can be made away from the playtext and information about performance gathered from numerous places within the critical edition, all while the playtext itself remains inert and unchanged.

With the ongoing, exponential growth of digital technologies, the relationship between reading and performance is in the midst of a fundamental restructuring. From the perspective of textual production, digitization has become conventional and normative: I am writing this chapter "on" a computer screen that changes with every keystroke; the text of this chapter is anything but stable—I am constantly cutting and pasting, deleting, saving newer versions that replace older ones. Moreover, I do not have enough familiarity with the inner workings of digital technology to know at all times "where" this chapter is located: until it is printed, my text lacks a physical form.[4] To have composed this chapter by hand or on a typewriter seems unfathomable. Creating texts digitally (even for books and articles that are intended for print markets) brings with it an understanding that digital texts are fluid and impermanent, an understanding that can be extended to include textual production in general: "What is perhaps most unnerving about electronic texts," writes Kastan, "is not merely that they are virtual but that they are no more virtual than any other text we read" (*Book* 116).

Reading digital texts (by the projected light of the screen rather than the light reflected off the page), though not yet as normative as *writing* digital texts, similarly complicates our understanding of one's relationship to that text. Scrolling through a computer screen rather than flipping pages constitutes a much different form of textual engagement. I do not mean this in a somatic sense that fetishizes the physicality of print; for some, surely part of the appeal of digital texts is that they offer "an escape from the felt tyranny of the book" (Kastan, *Book* 112), but the sense of a digital text's unboundedness and fluidity also stimulates larger ontological considerations—where does one locate a text's meanings if one cannot locate the text itself?[5] The hypertextual environments of digital texts accentuate a reader's role in making meaning, in ordering and connecting texts—perhaps even interlacing different media—and this navigational and interpretive freedom has significant implications for both editorial practice in general, and the relationship between reading and performance in particular. Worthen explains:

> ...hotlinking has the effect of making the text seem more dynamic: there is something you can do here (click), some place you can go, a trip through the text that might lead you away for good. In this sense the hotlinked word or phrase not only points to an explanatory discourse to be found elsewhere (the footnote or marginal gloss of printed textbooks), it also marks an intersection between the discourse of the text and that other discourse, a discourse potentially (though it is in most cases *only* potentially) without end. Hotlinked annotation is not a footnote, a piece of information subordinate to and dependent on its originating text; it marks the text's participation in an interactive economy of hyperlinked relations. (*Force* 209–10)

Thus the digital edition possesses the multi-pronged potential to render editorial annotation less prescriptive and binding (or at least make it feel less so), to present a text's various "intersections" in a nonhierarchical way, and, perhaps most importantly, to empower the reader to move within and between texts with great freedom.

Certain words and phrases in Worthen's formulation—"dynamic," "something you can do," "interactive"—are indicative of a discernible tendency in discussions of the digital editing of dramatic texts to emphasize digitization's affinities with performance—a move that further ossifies the opposition of digital and printed texts. The parallel between digitization and performance can be drawn subtly, as in Peter

Donaldson's claim that "[new] technology has the potential to extend greatly participation in the creative dialogue Shakespeare's plays have provoked since their first performance" (183). Kastan offers a more provocative assessment: "hypertext models a different conception of the play altogether, arguably one truer to its nature in that the hypertextual edition acknowledges in its very structure that the play is fundamentally something less stable and coherent than the printed edition necessarily represents it as being" (*Book* 131). Worthen himself moves beyond the conceptions of text and performance that digital texts encourage, suggesting that the participatory element renders reading digitized texts a kind of performative act: "[the] sense of reading through the text, of moving from the text as container (to be reproduced by performance) to the text as a site of movement, of passage, of production, suggests that hyperreading may have the potential to legitimate other kinds of reading, reading practices that locate the text in a context of production, not interpretation—theatrical reading" (*Force* 212). He adds, "hypertext...perhaps approaches the performative by more openly situating the text on the permeable horizon of performance, where meanings arise from what we do to texts in order to make something from them" (*Force* 213).

As these quotations make clear, what we as readers can "do" to digital texts—the ways in which we can "move" through (and between) them, manipulate them, *change* them—far surpasses the possible orders of engagement with printed texts. While I would agree that hypertextual environments perform the valuable service of encouraging readers to make connections between texts, annotation, and other supplementary materials, and to recognize the "multiple and variable" (Kastan, *Book* 131) forms in which a play exists, the claim that the act of reading digital editions of playtexts somehow approximates performance is one that I would resist. As discussed in chapter 4, recognizing reading and performing as distinct means of dramatic production ensures that the significations and interpretive procedures unique to each activity remain sharply defined, and I believe such a distinction remains important, even in the case of the dynamic, participatory reading that digital texts foster.[6] Moreover, the conflation of hypertextual reading and performance seems to me to overstate a reader's freedom: in reality, one cannot navigate a hypertextual environment in *any* direction, since only those words or phrases that have been tagged by an editor are offered as links. While the number of passageways a reader may follow are likely greater than those that can be offered in print, these passageways remain limited in number and direction. What Johndan Johnson-Eilola remarks of online reading experiences is applicable here:

> Although we commonly insist that the hypertextual organization of the Web suggests reading a network rather than a linear text, the experience of reading the Web for most users remains that of following a line. The temporal experience of page to page to page anchors the reading experiences in history, even a fragmented and abbreviated one. As such, most Web use remains tied to the consumption of time. (102)

Thus, despite the fact that digitization offers an escape from the material limitations of the codex, an escape that encourages readerly production and exploration of meaning, reading a digital text is still constrained by time, space, and editorial influence.

Michael Best, coordinating editor of *Internet Shakespeare Editions* (*ISE*, founded in 1996), acknowledges the staggering referential capabilities of digital editions, but offers a pragmatic assessment of the deployment of hypertext: "Editors are . . . presented with a potentially far larger canvas for their work: annotations have in effect no theoretical limit, since storage on disk has become so inexpensive in modern computers. Practical limitations, however, are important; readers still expect editors to make choices and to limit annotation to what can be seen as genuinely useful" ("Shakespeare" 159). Put more succinctly, "a click must link to something worth reaching" ("Shakespeare" 159). Accordingly, the editorial guidelines on the *ISE* website prove to be alert and responsive to the ways in which digital editors, despite the open design of their texts, nevertheless shape the potential directions of reading. Under a heading entitled, "'Good' hypertext," editors are reminded that the links they provide should add value, and are strongly encouraged to remain cognizant of readers' time and (im)patience: "No one wants to wait for a document to arrive if it is a simple line reference or a two-line comment. For this reason, you should include in-text references as much as possible, branching to other documents only when they will be worth the wait"; "Your Internet reader is not sitting in a comfortable armchair before the fire. She or he will want to locate information quickly, speed-read it, then download or move on" (Best, "Guidelines"). Paradoxically, then, digital editions, whatever their referential capacity, might very well hone an editor's awareness of the importance of *selectivity*. Hypertext is theoretically boundless, but one's physical ability and willingness to read are not.

The other argument put forth to link digital texts to performance revolves around digital texts' resemblance to oral communication. In the early 1980s, Walter Ong referred to a "secondary orality" (136) brought about by electronic technologies, and this claim continues to find traction. Jay David Bolter connects digital discourse to orality by way of an extended analogy with oral poetry: "The Homeric poet wrote by putting together formulaic blocks, and the audience 'read' his performance in terms of those blocks. The electronic writer and reader, programmer and user, do the same today. Like oral poetry and storytelling, electronic writing is a highly associative writing, in which the pattern of associations among verbal elements is as much a part of the text as the elements themselves" (*Writing Space* 59). Bolter finds other characteristics of orality that share common ground with electronic writing and reading: "immediacy and flexibility," "an interplay between the structures that the author has created and [a reader's] own associative structures," author and reader/listener "sharing" the same space (59).

The emphasis on the communal and interactive elements of digital texts definitely has merit, though digital texts and electronic writing most closely approximate orality (and by extension, performance) in that these discourses are "bound to the present" (Worthen, *Force* 191) in a number of senses. Certainly, digital textual production is entrenched in the notion of replacement (one saved version of a document replaces the earlier one), and digital editions (especially online ones) can, in theory, be subject to constant editorial modification and refinement—an editor of an online edition can be continually adding annotation or changing decisions as the passage of time brings new information to light.[7] It must also be said, however, that digital or online resources are confined to the present in the sense that they are vulnerable to sudden, and often unpredictable, inaccessibility. Hyperlinks get broken, websites become unavailable, funding for projects is exhausted, technology necessary to encode or "read" digital resources becomes obsolete. Recent essays by Christie Carson and Best have mapped the rather sizeable graveyard of digital editions of Shakespeare: among the most notable sites on this map are *The Arden Shakespeare CD-ROM* (1997), the Voyager *Macbeth* (based on A. R. Braunmuller's Cambridge text), *The Cambridge King Lear CD-ROM: Text and Performance Archive*, and *ArdenOnline*, the now defunct online version of the Arden texts. Projects such as these represent significant steps in the ongoing evolution of digitized Shakespeares, but all of them failed to make much of a sustained impact as teaching or research tools. Moreover, as Brett Hirsch observes, "The cost of preserving, maintaining, and updating electronic editions in order to stave off technological obsolescence far exceeds the costs of publishing a print edition which, once it has been published, requires no further action (short of preserving it in a library) to ensure it remains usable" ("Kingdom" 578). The perpetual present-ness of creating, engaging, and sustaining digital texts helps to explain the persistent futurity that imbues the critical commentary surround-ing digital Shakespeares: the revolutions that might one day arrive remain more profound than the changes that have occurred to date; indeed, Hirsch's essay, a persuasive call for the powers of digital editions to be employed for expanding the canon of early modern drama for researchers and students alike, qualifies the "practical and theoretical opportunities and benefits... offered by the electronic medium" with the concession that "many" of these opportunities and benefits are "yet unrealized" (569–570). Part of the challenge of composing this chapter is that a comprehensive, digital collection of Shakespeare's works that is supported by an editorial rationale, and includes links to systematic and thorough collations, annotations, and commentaries simply does not (yet) exist. *ISE* comes the closest to meeting these criteria, though at the time of this writing, it has realized only a fraction of its remarkable potential to supply modernized, critical editions of the plays that are designed from start to finish as digitized objects. In its description of its modern editions, *ISE* invites users to "Read and explore... the plays and poems with full annotation and explanations, as well as an introduction and illustrations from performance" (Best, "Illuminated Text"); as of March 2014, editions of *As You Like It, Julius Caesar, Henry V, Twelfth Night, 1 Henry IV,* and *The Winter's Tale* are categorized as "Complete Editions." These peer-reviewed, modernized versions include compre-hensive annotations that, while often attentive to matters of staging and performance, do not as yet link to *ISE*'s substantial collection of performance-related materials. Writing in 2007, Best himself admits that "the potential of a Shakespearean text wholly designed for the elec-tronic medium is not yet fully realized" ("Shakespeare" 145).

It is thus crucial to distinguish between the theoretical *possibility* of digital editions, and what these editions can *actually* offer readers. As Kastan observes, "The book's reassuring offer of closure and author-ity gives way to the electronic text's exhilarating promise of possibility and an immunity from all restraint. It is, however, worth pausing to disrupt this neat binary by noting that its claim is only conceptually true" (*Book* 130). That an absolutely transparent and neutral collected edition of Shakespeare can only ever be a perpetually deferred, theo-retical concept means that it is necessary to assess a reader's relation-ship to such digital texts in more realistic, measured terms. On this matter Best makes an important concession: "it is likely that for the foreseeable future an electronic Shakespeare edition will be treated more as an archive for searching than as a way of reading the plays from beginning to end" ("Shakespeare" 154–5). This definition—the digital edition as archive—is a pervasive one, and though it is true to digital editions' vast storage and organizational capabilities, as Best makes clear, it also speaks to their limitations as *reading* texts. Best's concession is brought into relief by the fact that in order to disseminate editions for reading and studying, *ISE* has partnered with Broadview Press to produce printed versions of modernized *ISE* texts. The ISE website notes that the *ISE* / Broadview texts were meant to appear as early as 2006, but the first two editions, *As You Like It* and *Julius Caesar*, were published in 2012. These printed editions are described as making readers aware of "[t]he availability of additional materials on the *ISE* site," but beyond this feature, their promised characteristics sound indistinguishable from those of critical editions printed by most major publishers: "each *ISE* / Broadview edition will include a wide range of background materials—providing information on the staging of each play, as well as on its historical and intellectual context—in addition to the text itself, introduction, chronology, and bibliography" (Best, "Collaboration"). To point out the irony of *ISE* texts making their way into print is in no way meant to slight the work of *ISE*'s capable editors or disparage the aims of the *ISE* project and its sustained commitment to groundbreaking scholarship. It is striking, however, that a project aimed at empowering readers to engage with fluid texts and contextual materials in the digital realm clearly does not understand its mission as being incompatible with, or compromised by, the production of editions stabilized by print. I would suggest that this transition to the relative permanence and stability of print is, at this stage in the development of digital editions of Shakespeare, a necessary one; it is the very fixedness of the printed version of *ISE* editions that will communicate to readers the validity and relevance of editorial mediation and decision making. Reading a play from beginning to end is predicated on engaging with a text that is delimited, not limitless, and the *ISE* / Broadview texts signal an awareness that combining vast archival resources and theoretically boundless readerly freedom do not necessarily yield reading editions that can sustain critical inquiry and dialogue.

To recognize digital editions as archives further distances and distinguishes digital texts from "the formal limits of all hard copy's informational and critical powers" (McGann, "Rationale of Hypertext" 22). Rather than use the notion of the archive to negate comparisons between digitized and printed modes of textual reception, however, I would like to incorporate some of the current thinking on archives into a consideration of readers in both media. That is, it is useful to understand digital *and* printed editions as possessing archival characteristics. To do so reasserts the readerly ability that has been at the heart of this book: the capacity to navigate textual spaces—printed or digital—and bring various forms of information to bear on engagements with primary materials. As the preceding discussion has made clear, digital texts remind us that *all* texts are in some sense virtual and fluid things, but this point can be rotated slightly: if digital texts and hypertexts enhance and accentuate readers' navigational freedom, one must remember that this freedom is something that *all* texts—even printed ones—necessarily provide.

Digital and Textual Archives: Reading and Participating

At first glance, editorial impulses—the removal of ambiguity, the presentation of interpreted texts in new form(s)—and archival impulses—the retention and accumulation of "raw" information, the preservation of original form(s)—seem to be at odds. These ostensibly contradictory impulses inform Massai's comparison of digital and critical editions:

> [A] change brought about by the electronic medium is that the end result of an editor's labours is not a critical *edition* but a critical *archive*. A critical edition is structured hierarchically and privileges the modern text over other textual alternatives, which are cryptically and partially summarized in the textual apparatus. The critical archive provides accurate and searchable digital versions of the editions from which those textual alternatives derive. Besides, a critical edition gives an account of the theatrical/cinematic and critical reception of a play-text whereas a critical archive provides the very materials—scripts, reviews, press releases, photographs, interviews, extracts from published sources—which the critical edition interprets on behalf of the reader. ("Scholarly Editing" 103)

The force of Massai's argument rests on "archive" being understood in a specific way. Although she concedes that the electronic archive "provides predetermined searches," Massai aims to create a stark contrast with a critical edition's "clear hierarchy of meanings and interpretations." Unlike the hierarchized printed edition, "the structure of the archive is open-ended and the virtually endless combinations of pathways which the user can follow utterly arbitrary. The user is thus encouraged to abandon linear reading in favor of dynamic interaction with texts and intertextual analysis." Massai's distinction hinges on the fact that "the critical edition interprets on behalf of the reader" ("Scholarly Editing" 103), while the electronic archive does not. Peter Donaldson describes the *Shakespeare Electronic Archive* in a similar vein (this project is only accessible at MIT and the Folger Library, though an abbreviated sample of the undertaking, *Hamlet on the Ramparts*, is freely available online[8]). Donaldson contrasts "an electronic archive, eventually networked and available throughout the world, in which documents of all kinds—films, sound recordings, texts, digital facsimiles—would be linked in electronic form to one another and to the lines of text to which they refer or which they enact" (173) with the ostensibly rigid interpretations and "impression of finality" of standard critical editions: "Introductions, apparatus criticus, marginal, median and final notes, textual appendices—all these simultaneously acknowledge and minimize, by their 'specialist' format, the untidiness and uncertainty of the textual record. The impression left on readers and students is that the text has been established firmly, and that such variant readings as there may be can be safely ignored" (178–9).

Both Massai and Donaldson assign archival characteristics to the electronic edition in order to distinguish it—absolutely—from the heavily mediated, limited referential capabilities of printed editions. In their effort to establish a strict opposition between printed and electronic media, they suggest that the electronic archive offers an unmediated, unfiltered trove of data that the capable user can peruse at will, engaging any number of textual or performative instantiations of the work; readers of printed editions, however, are restricted to editorially imposed interpretations, with alternative viewpoints available in hierarchized, "cryptically and partially summarized" (Massai, "Scholarly Editing" 103) forms. Helen Freshwater writes that a large part of the "allure of the archive" (731) is its "essential doubleness as physical collection or space and as a concept or idea" (751), and Massai and Donaldson, in embracing the hypothetical lack of spatial restrictions facing electronic archives—their theoretical capability to include or link to every piece of information that might matter—suggest that users will eventually confront whatever "thing" they might be searching for: Massai refers to the critical archive supplying "the very materials" that standard editions can only "give an account of," while Donaldson claims "the *documentary hypertext* presents images of the evidence itself" rather than the "distillation of the evidence" found in printed editions (186). What they claim, in other words, is that the indeterminacy supplied by the capaciousness of electronic editions liberates the reader from standard editorial procedures that foreclose ambiguity and shape information in potentially misleading or misrepresentative ways.

What Massai and Donaldson are relying upon, however, is arguably a misrepresentative formulation about how archives come to be, and how users engage with them. The neutrality and comprehensiveness that so distinguish their descriptions of electronic archives from printed editions inevitably distort current, widely held understandings of the archive (as both a theoretical and physical construct).[9] After Derrida's influential work (1995), the inherent paradoxes of the archive have become well-rehearsed: far from being an objective repository, the archive is now primarily understood as a mediated construct that "preserves and reserves, protects and patrols, regulates and represses" (Voss and Werner i); in other words, "Every archive has undergone a process of selection, during which recorded information may have been excluded and discarded as well as preserved" (Freshwater 739). On this matter, Paul Voss and Marta Werner employ a cogent metaphor: "the archive's dream of perfect order is disturbed by the nightmare of its random, heterogeneous, and often unruly contents" (ii). It is the (often messy, unwieldy) constructedness of the archive that Massai and Donaldson elide in their respective formulations, and a closer look at the kinds of archived materials available at Donaldson's *Hamlet on the Ramparts* website helps to clarify my point.

Hamlet on the Ramparts, as its title suggests, focuses exclusively on 1.4 and 1.5 of the play. Its "Reading Room" allows users to read parallel texts of various editions, including critically edited "base" texts (the Folger edition, by Barbara Mowat and Paul Werstine; the Arden 2 edition, by Harold Jenkins) and digital facsimiles of the early textual witnesses (Q1, Q2, and F).[10] Users can toggle between texts with great ease and juxtapose each and every possible combination of editions; the rapidity with which users can realign portions of text facilitates stark and revealing reminders of the play's disparate printed forms. What the "Reading Room" makes possible, then, is not so much a *reading* of two scenes from *Hamlet* (Kastan remarks that the "exhausting copiousness" of electronic resources like Donaldson's "make the play...virtually unreadable" (*Book* 129)), but an opportunity for users to compare and contrast textual forms that are likely otherwise unavailable to them—users of the "Reading Room" engage with an archive, not an edition. Donaldson's claim that "electronic forms" make it possible to "read in new ways that combine the coherence, context, and sequence of what we now know as reading with an immediate awareness of alternative possibilities" (183) finesses key issues. In order to enable the consideration of alternative readings and textual forms, *Hamlet on the Ramparts* willingly *sacrifices* context and sequence (only decontextualized fragments of the various editions are available), and even coherence as well (parallel texts, for all that they can reveal, do not make for easy reading). My intention here is not to quibble with where one might draw the line between a reading edition and an archive; rather, what I mean to point out is that the resources provided by sites like *Hamlet on the Ramparts* have inevitably travelled through numerous interpretive and editorial filters, and these forms of mediation are occluded by critical narratives that stress a user's access to ostensibly limitless amounts of information. Donaldson may suggest that, unlike printed editions, electronic texts do not convey an "impression of finality" that "minimize[s] . . . the untidiness and uncertainty of the textual record" (178), but once again, such a claim is only true in purely theoretical terms. After all, *Hamlet on the Ramparts* reproduces only a single facsimile version for each of Q1 and F (from the Huntington and Folger libraries, respectively), and two versions of Q2 (one from the Huntington, one from the Folger); one could argue this selectivity minimizes disparities produced by early modern printing practice—no two copies of F are exactly alike, but users of the website might very well come away with the impression that F exists in a final, fixed state. In actuality though, it is the site's selectivity that makes it valuable and useful: few users are likely to be interested in poring over the minutiae that might distinguish one version of F from another; in providing a facsimile of a portion of a single version, the website refines the amount of information involved in a user's interpretive procedures.

The digital facsimiles that electronic archives like *Hamlet on the Ramparts* can provide must nevertheless be assessed in pragmatic terms. In his writings, Donaldson repeatedly suggests that digital facsimiles are a means of representing "a world beyond the computer screen, or beyond the 'text'" (191). He implies that these facsimiles provide "real" access to the very things they are meant to represent: "[the] electronic text can seem to evoke a real world, bringing a part of that world to the screen, or, to use an equally common metaphor, permit travel to a distant location—in this case the Folger Library, [or] the British Library" (191); "the external boundaries of the documentary hypertext" are described by Donaldson as "permeable," and "at their outer limit [they] lead back to real objects, and to the specific locations, in the 'real world' in which Shakespeare materials are preserved, interpreted, and used" (195). Donaldson's assessment of the "reality" of facsimiles, their genuine approximation of the "real thing," is both helpful and misleading. As a scholarly resource, facsimiles are extremely valuable, allowing large numbers of users to work closely with primary materials otherwise located in select spaces and available to very few. Certainly, much of my own analysis of pre-twentieth-century editions of Shakespeare and other early modern playwrights would not have been possible without digital facsimiles. What is imperative to remember, however, is that even a high-quality digital facsimile performs "its own act of idealization" (Kastan, *After Theory* 68). The camera—digital or photographic—is anything but a neutral observer, and the production of a facsimile is an interpretive act.[11] The facsimiles available to users of *Hamlet on the Ramparts* do, in some sense, "lead back to real objects," though only in a tangential way; that is, one is provided with reproductions of "real objects" that are both remarkably detailed and inevitably partial. The fidelity and partiality of facsimiles become especially apparent when one considers the site's reproduction of the F text; like the reproductions of the Q1 and Q2 texts, the F facsimile is altered in size and shape so that it better aligns with any edition that a user might choose to juxtapose against it. Significantly, the F text is also digitally trimmed: what the site reproduces is not the relevant *page* of F, but the excised portion of the appropriate *column* of text. The "real object" in question, while relatively more present to visitors of the site than it might be to readers of a critical edition, nevertheless looks nothing like this. Users of the site do not encounter the F text, but a reconstructed, *mediated* version of it.

When it comes to representations of performance, Donaldson suggests that users of digital archives are provided with unique opportunities for interpretation: "a single performance can be regarded as a text, and its textual or text-like properties are greatly enhanced when performance is recorded or recast in a durable medium such as film or tape, so that it can be replayed, re-experienced, and closely read in ways that are analogous to the close reading of a poetic or literary text" (182). The repeatability and stability of film are, in other words, features that facilitate the "reading" of performance. Donaldson's suggestion that a performance can be read like a text (a claim that is central to much contemporary performance criticism[12]), is visually and structurally reinforced by the design of *Hamlet on the Ramparts*'s "Reading Room." Users are able to view clips of three different productions of the play that roughly correspond to the segment of playtext that has been selected. The clips align performance alongside the text, with users encouraged to experience the transformative powers that performance practices exert.

One body of clips is taken from the recording of Richard Burton's 1964 performance at the Lunt Fontanne Theater in New York City (directed by John Gielgud); the other two samplings are from silent versions from the early twentieth century: Svend Gade's *Hamlet: The Drama of Vengeance* (1920), and Sir Johnston Forbes-Robertson's abbreviated film (1913). The juxtaposition of film and text is a striking example of the archival and representational powers of the digital edition: though the clips are slow in loading and small in size, they realize a portion of the digital edition's theoretical promise, what McGann describes as "[moving] beyond the semantic content of the primary textual materials" ("Rationale of Hypertext" 21). One must concede, however, that the mixture of available film clips is curious, even strange. The Gade film is best thought of as an adaptation rather than a production of *Hamlet*: with Asta Nielson in the lead role, it suggests that Hamlet is actually a young woman raised as a man; perhaps most strikingly, given the website's strict focus on 1.4 and 1.5 of the play, *Hamlet: The Drama of Vengeance* involves no scenes on the ramparts of Elsinore. While taking fewer liberties in his version, Forbes-Robertson's adaptation relies heavily on an audience's pre-existing familiarity with the play—it clocks in at around 22 minutes in length. The clips of Burton involve the most sustained, "traditional" engagements with the playtext, but given that the Burton film was filmed over two nights with 15 cameras, users are viewing a single performance that, in a very real way, never actually took place.[13]

Surely the largest determining factor in what *Hamlet on the Ramparts* can make available is copyright restrictions that preclude the inclusion of both a wider range of material and the use of recordings of more recent productions or feature-length films. The website, then, epitomizes the multi-media possibilities and limitations of digital editions: three rare and unique interpretations of the play (one a century old) are archived and freely accessible, but cumulatively, they are a decontextualized, disjointed assemblage that connect to the central playtext in complicated ways that go largely unexplained. Ultimately, *Hamlet on the Ramparts* reminds us that the gap between the hypothetical boundlessness of digital editions and what they can realistically (and legally) execute is not insignificant.

The ostensible advantage of viewing digitized performances is that one need not engage with the absent event via the rememberings of others (in the form of play reviews, performance histories, diaries, etc.) nor does one have to grapple with the failings of memory. Recorded performances are relatively stable points of reference. Given Dennis

Kennedy's observation that "the book is memory materialized, solidified, made historical and referable, while performance always escapes it, leaving behind its remembered shadow" (330), then digitally archived clips of performance exist as something in between these two poles: less tangible than either the book of the play or the performed event (which nevertheless inevitably "decays before our eyes, and thus in the moment of its accomplishment escapes into memory" (Kennedy 329)), but more substantial than the mutable shades of recollection. Similar to digital facsimiles, digital recordings do not allow access to the "real object"—in this case, the performance itself—but they can be deployed within digital editions as vivid and evocative markers of performance potentialities. I have positioned *performancescape* as a term that links the *scape* of the page to the virtual *scape* of the imagined scene; in the case of digital editions, "virtual" takes on the added meaning of computer-generated, and in terms of enabling readers to conceptualize performance, the capabilities of computers to display recordings of actual performances certainly surpasses anything that a printed text can do. On this matter, Best draws a fitting analogy to print culture: "One of the strengths of the new electronic criticism is that it can integrate a discussion of film performance in a way that is as much an improvement on anything a print description can offer as a quotation from the text is more informative than a paraphrase of it." The end result is that the reader gains "the full experience of a graphic or video sequence [and] becomes more fully a participator in the critical process" (Best, "Text of Performance" 276, 279).

A user's *participation* is central to the design and execution of Best's *Internet Shakespeare Editions* and the site's engagements with performance. Described by Best as an "attempt to provide a comprehensive archive and edition of the plays" ("Shakespeare" 157), the *ISE* has the potential to substantively integrate textual and performative modes of realization. To this end, Best foresees fully edited *ISE* texts making use of three distinct "levels" of annotation: the first level would provide simple glossaries or explanatory phrases; the second level is described as a "full annotation" similar to that found in major critical editions, and "would link to illustrative, and often contrasting, performances of specific moments in the play" ("Shakespeare" 159, 160); the third level "is reserved for full discussions of an important point, of the kind that might become an appendix in a print edition" ("Shakespeare" 159–60). A reader of a modernized *ISE* text would thus have the ability to delve levels of annotation that satisfy his or her particular needs; moreover, any tangential move into the annotation could be linked to further layers of information. The traditional performance commentary found in a printed edition is analogous to a second level annotation, but the *ISE* annotation might be supplemented with hyperlinks to photographs, director's notes, playbills, video clips, or sound recordings. The extensive range of material that a reader might encounter is one thing, but the main difference in the organization of *ISE* annotation is how annotation itself is conceived and deployed: rather than the vertical or horizontal glosses found in a printed text that ask the reader to negotiate either a single page or perhaps look elsewhere within the edition, annotation in an *ISE* text is meant to be an extensible network that a reader is to explore freely. With a click, editorial commentary could appear beside the text, and this commentary could theoretically offer pathways through which to consider not just more comprehensive and complicated annotation, but also relevant material from performance history, as well as parallel passages elsewhere in the text or in other plays. As mentioned above, however, to date only a small number of plays are supported by editorial commentary, and the play's annotations do not yet realize *ISE*'s goal of allowing readers to follow links to relevant materials from performance history. The effectiveness of imprints of performance conceived specifically for an electronic edition cannot yet be assessed on the *ISE* site.

What *is* more readily observable is the *ISE*'s performance database, the archive portion of Best's vision of the *ISE* as "a comprehensive archive and edition of the plays" ("Shakespeare" 157). The "Shakespeare in Performance" area of the website is described as

> a searchable database of performance materials from over 1000 film and stage productions related to Shakespeare's works. Whether you are an actor, director, student, scholar or Shakespeare enthusiast, this database provides an exciting and innovative resource of items and artifacts related to stage production from start to finish. View online such items as director's notes, images of stage and costume design, performance stills, posters, information about a particular company or festival and the actors involved in Shakespeare performance, cast and crew listings. (Best, "Shakespeare in Performance: Home")

As the static nature of the items in the archive suggest, "The usual problems of copyright limit the kinds of artifacts that can be stored in the database" (Best, "Shakespeare" 160); in other words, filmed versions of performance remain difficult to obtain legally. That being said, the database is remarkably diverse and promises to continue growing (there is an open-ended invitation on the website for theater companies to contribute archival material for digitization). Best writes that "A particularly productive use of the larger space an electronic edition provides would be to link passages of the play to moments of performance, on stage or film" (Best, "Shakespeare" 160), and one can envision an *ISE* editor making great use of the "Shakespeare in Performance" database, inviting readers to consider the various stages of theatrical production, from promptbook preparation, to set design and costuming, to rehearsal, to advertising campaigns, to performance. The difficulty is that Best's "would be" signals yet again a significant gap between promise and practice. In terms of its current structure, text and performance are strongly differentiated—even distinct—on the *ISE* website: the "Library" (which houses facsimiles, transcriptions, and modernized versions) does not (yet) have any sort of systematic connection to the "Theatre" portion of the site (which houses the performance database). Over 1,000 production stills are currently available for searching, organized by date, play title and theater company; since these stills are usually not keyed to specific moments of play action or lines in the text, their significance or connection to the playtext might be unclear to certain users of the database. Thus, while it is certainly true that the *ISE* engages with the plays using "*a form native to the medium of the Internet*" (Best, "About the Internet Shakespeare Editions"), the hypertextual networks created by the website render explorations of textual and performance histories largely discontinuous activities.

Text and performance remain similarly differentiated in *The Shakespeare Collection*, another major online archive that is centered on digital editions of the plays. With full access to the Arden Complete Works, as well as the publishing resources of Cengage Learning (formerly Thomson-Gale), *The Shakespeare Collection* offers "comprehensive, cross-searchable coverage of Shakespeare's work, critical reception, textual history, performance history and cultural and historical context."[14] A search engine filters any stream of sought after data into seven major pools: "Texts—Arden Editions," "Texts—Historical," "Primary Sources," "Magazines and Journals," "Book Articles," "References," and "Multimedia"; additionally, certain resources, such as the Arden texts, transcriptions of primary source material, and journal articles, are themselves fully searchable. Clearly, the site is meant to range more widely than something like the *ISE*, which devotes the bulk of its energies to publishing critically edited texts and rigorously scrutinized transcriptions of original textual witnesses. *The Shakespeare Collection* is a research tool, with the Arden editions (a mixture of Arden 2 and Arden 3 versions is currently available) forming just one of the site's arteries of information. These digitized versions of the Arden texts offer a vivid picture of what the electronic text can offer: users can jump to any scene, toggle between text and commentary, peruse illustrations, and even exclusively search an edition's introduction, notes, and/or appendices for keywords.

Much like the *ISE*, *The Shakespeare Collection* is designed with the participatory possibilities of digitization in mind. At any time, users are given the opportunity "to compare on screen two different texts, or two different versions of the same work. The user locates and marks the texts he or she wishes to compare, opens the first text and clicks 'compare texts' to bring up the list of selected titles for comparison" ("Fact Sheet"). "Texts" here are broadly construed: the term includes the collection's "Multimedia" archive, which consists primarily of nontextual material like production stills, photographs, paintings, illustrations, and scans of promptbooks; according to the site's description, "These images facilitate the study of changes in production, costume and style as well as recording particular performances or providing historical context. A matching can be made of prompt books and photographs or illustrations for a particular production" ("Brochure" 7). Users are thus encouraged to set their own unique search parameters and create convergences of disparate materials, with juxtapositions of different forms and orders of information, even of nontextual material connected to performance practice, posited as a revealing method of analysis and interpretation. This trend toward juxtaposition means that a user's navigation of the collection is often linked to the codex—making use of *The Shakespeare Collection*'s comparison feature, in other words, is frequently like reading a book (or examining two books side by side). The collection's bookishness becomes apparent when one explores its digital facsimiles of early quartos and folios, which are often scans that approximate the book in question rather than just a single leaf. Putting historical and modernized playtexts side by side results in navigation screens that resemble facing pages. That the site is organized around transforming amorphous searches into rather stable one-to-one juxtapositions is likely why Best, thinking specifically of the archive's reliance on the Arden texts, laments that, "as an electronic edition of the plays themselves," *The Shakespeare Collection* "remain[s] stubbornly wedded to print" ("Shakespeare" 158).

Best's point is that the digitized versions of the Arden editions are essentially translated from print into an electronic medium rather than specifically designed *for* an electronic medium (as *ISE* editions are). Given their doubled existence in both printed and digitized realms, the

Arden texts archived in *The Shakespeare Collection* provide an oppor-tunity to consider two very different reading experiences of the same edited text. Consider Claire McEachern's Arden 3 version of *Much Ado About Nothing* (2006).[15] The digital version does its best to mimic the major organizational features of the printed edition: an "eTable of Contents" closely mirrors that of the printed version, and illustrations in the introduction appear in roughly the same size and position as they do in the Arden 3 book (though one scrolls down through differ-ent sections of the introduction as they appear on the screen). All of McEachern's collations and commentaries are reproduced in full, as is her appendix containing a casting chart. In short, save for the printed edition's index, every major piece of information in the original Arden 3 publication can be found *somewhere* in the digitized version. *Locating* information in the digital edition, however, takes some getting used to. The edited playtext and commentary notes must exist in separate win-dows, and while a user can manually adjust the size of these windows to place them side-by-side, it is the user's responsibility to continually keep the notes aligned with the lineation of the playtext. Proceeding through the play means scrolling through both playtext and notes; furthermore, unlike in the printed version, the notes are not keyed to specific line numbers, which can make it difficult to not only locate a gloss but to know which words, phrases, or passages in the playtext are annotated.

There is something decidedly awkward about navigating this digi-tal edition. For one thing, the introduction's footnotes are rendered invisible in their digitized state: not only must a user scroll to the bot-tom of the screen for each and every note that appears (the superscript numerals are not hyperlinked to their corresponding commentary) but the notes themselves at the bottom of the page are not supplied with a matching numeral—tracking down a footnote is an exercise in patience. Additionally, there is something inefficient about the number of clicks it takes to move from the commentary notes back to a relevant section of McEachern's introduction, an introduction that is unpaginated in the scrolling digital text, making cross-references within the edition extremely difficult to trace. Even cross-references in the notes to other points in the playtext are hard to follow: since the play is broken into individual scenes that can only be accessed from a drop-down menu at the top of each "page," following a reference in the notes to a specific line in a different scene entails exiting or closing the window of notes, (re-)opening the window of playtext, scrolling back up to the top of the currently open scene, selecting the referenced scene from the menu, and scrolling to the appropriate line in that scene; to return to one's previous position in the play, the same steps must be followed. One becomes accustomed to maneuvering within this system, but tangential moves away from the edited text can occur much more quickly and efficiently within a book.

If my criticisms of the digitized Arden texts sound pedantic or technophobic, they are not intended as such. Neil Gershenfeld, observing that since a book "boots instantly," "permits fast random access to any page," "is viewable from any angle, in bright or dim light," "can easily be annotated," and "requires no batteries or maintenance," argues that "if a book had been invented after the laptop it would be hailed as a great breakthrough." "It's not technophobic to prefer to read a book," writes Gershenfeld, "it's entirely sensible. The future of computing lies back in a book" (13–4). In terms of critically edited playtexts, the decision-making processes of editors, as well as the ordering and structuring of information necessitated by the physical restrictions of the book, all have value, and this value added by editorial labor is eroded when the Arden texts are digitized. McEachern herself recognizes that her decisions help to shape a reader's potential range of interpretations of the text, and that this editorial influence is most conspicuous when it comes to imagining performance practice. After explaining that she has "sought to modify and modernize the original text so as to make the play legible to the mind's eye" (132–3), McEachern writes,

> What is presented here is not the text of the original performance. It is not the text of any performance, and indeed it is intended to be open ended rather than restrictive (not to be confused with indecisive) in suggesting possibilities for stage action, despite the editorial temptation to block the play—a temptation made inevitable by the fact that this reader, like any other, builds in the course of her experience of the play expectations about how its characters might or might not behave. An edition truly scrupulous about these matters would perhaps provide multiple-choice SDs; however, there are enough notes on these pages as it is, the number of choices is unwieldy if not infinite, and my assumption is that other readers will have their own opinions about how characters might or might not behave, and will undoubtedly exercise them. (133)

McEachern nicely distills many of the contentious issues that swirl around any attempt to mediate page and stage: that the edited text can engage performance history without ever encapsulating it or accurately recounting it; that an editor's biases will affect the decision-making process; that editorial decisiveness when it comes to open moments of stage action does not necessarily result in interpretive restrictions being placed on the reader; that emphasizing the seemingly infinite options that might be available at moments of ambiguity might not make for the best reading experience. Above all, McEachern's methodology acknowledges the reader's central position in the meaning-making process: as selective and distorted as her edition's approximations of performance might be, "other readers will have their own opinions about how characters might or might not behave, and will undoubtedly exercise them."

McEachern's edition—in both its printed and digitized state—helps us to see that although it is digital editions that are often figured in archival terms (a definition that positions the printed edition on the other end of the spectrum, bound by the referential limitations of the book), it is useful to place digitized *and* printed editions on a kind of archival continuum. To understand both digital and print editions as archives reasserts the readerly freedom to engage with, and assess, mediated material. In Worthen's words, "the reader always controls the process of reading" (*Force* 185)—this principle is greatly emphasized in discussions of the revelatory powers of digital texts, but it is equally true of their differently mediated printed counterparts. Two examples of *performancescapes* from McEachern's edition serve as useful reminders of the way in which editors can target a reader's ability to access relevant information that is separate from the edited playtext proper. The first example is McEachern's commentary note to the opening of 2.3, the first of the two gulling scenes. As she does throughout her edition, McEachern gives her readers imaginative options as to how stage action might be realized; in this case, she writes,

> The location is Leonato's orchard. The staging needs to provide for Benedick's concealment from the gullers (though he must be visible to the audience); its elaborateness will depend on the nature of the production (on the Elizabethan stage, presumably the actor playing Benedick concealed himself downstage behind the pillars). Modern production choices have included shrubbery, trees, lattice, garden furniture, etc., as well as arbours, both imaginary and actual. Property arbours did exist in Elizabethan staging practice (one is featured on the title page of Kyd's *Spanish Tragedy*...). (2.3n)

The end of the note refers readers back to McEachern's introduction, where the title page of *The Spanish Tragedy* is reproduced, along with a more detailed discussion of the gulling scenes in *Much Ado*'s stage history—a discussion that makes use of four photographs and engravings from various eras in the play's theatrical life. With reference to these illustrations, McEachern remarks that "the chief criteria of the humour of these scenes, particularly that involving Benedick, depend on their listeners being visible to the audience, but thinking themselves invisible to their gullers. However, the scene can be often far funnier, and more dynamic, the less it is particularized by actual props" (113). The second example comes from 4.1, the church scene in which Claudio repudiates Hero. McEachern's notes in this scene repeatedly attend to the potential reactions of Leonato: Beatrice's "Help, Uncle!" (4.1.113) after Hero swoons "can indicate Leonato's stage distance from Hero" (113n); the "Strike" in Leonato's "Thought I thy spirits were stronger than thy shames, / Myself would on the rearward of reproaches / Strike at thy life" (4.1.125–7) "can serve as a cue for Leonato's action" (127n); appeals to mercy or reason later in the scene are "lost on Leonato" (149n), or directed to "Leonato alone" (180n); a longer note cites a study by John D. Cox that traces attempts from the eighteenth to the twentieth centuries "'to dignify and idealise Leonato in this scene'" (120–43n). As in the first example, McEachern's commentary recalls her introduction, where three illustrations demonstrate an increasing prominence given to Leonato's responses. In the frontispiece to Rowe's 1709 edition of the play, Leonato is indistinguishable in the crowd around the swooning Hero; in a 1790 engraving, Leonato is foregrounded and visibly affected; a 1791 engraving depicts a Leonato who "is central and virtually Lear-like in his distraught domination over the fallen form of his daughter" (88).

There can be no argument that McEachern's introductory remarks and commentary notes are a product of her own interests and biases, and that her attention to things like the use of props in the gulling scenes and Leonato's mannerisms in 4.1 frames considerations of the play in performance in unique ways (a glance at Sheldon Zitner's Oxford edition of *Much Ado*, for instance, reveals no such interest in describing how the humour of the gulling scenes might relate to their staging, nor does Zitner emphasize the varying levels of attention that can be paid to Leonato's displays in the church). What McEachern is doing is what all editors attempting to mediate performance do for their readers: dig into performance histories and extract fragments of information that they believe to be useful and compelling in the context of a textual encounter with the play. Margaret Jane Kidnie describes this process as a "creation of a textualized archive of archives, a self-perpetuating meta-archive" ("Citing Shakespeare" 122). Such discriminate samplings of performance practice or imaginings of performance possibilities can only partially recuperate the relevant details, but this editorial shaping of performance practice is a valuable form of decision making. As Wells explains, "all the verbal and visual records [of past] performances have passed through the transfiguring power of the imaginations and intellects" of various individuals, and the "very subjectivity" of these transfigurations "is in itself a strength as well as a weakness":

> We should gain no impression of the impact of the performances that gave rise to them if they did not at the same time tell us, or convey to us through the eloquence of their prose, or the power of their composition, something of the emotional and intellectual impact that they had upon their creators and which is the fundamental source of the value we place upon theatre. ("Foreword" xix)

The "emotional and intellectual impact" of performance that Wells figures as central to the power of the theatrical event is muted in electronic editions that allow performance records to "float" separate from the edited playtext. The digital version of McEachern's edition in *The Shakespeare Collection* contains all of the same information about *Much Ado*'s performance history, but the information is more readily accessible in the printed edition, where a reader's eyes flick between playtext and commentary on a single page, or pages are located quickly by way of cross-reference; in the digitized version, the introductory descriptions of the play in performance and the illustrations so crucial to McEachern's arguments are always a number of clicks or windows away. The *book* of the Arden 3 *Much Ado About Nothing*, in other words, expresses and organizes everything that its electronic counterpart does, only it does so more efficiently.

The less rigidly structured digitized text is, of course, part of the interpretive appeal of an electronic edition, but this openness is not without its consequences. John Lavagnino observes that what proponents of systems powered by hypertext often imagine is "that they would be transparent: they would not interpose an editor between the sources and the reader." Yet, such a position is flawed, argues Lavagnino, in that it

> implies that these sources themselves are always transparent, are never concealing something that scholarship can help us perceive. This idea, that we require no form of help with original documents, is not really very different from the idea that literary criticism is unnecessary because our untutored reactions to literary works are more authentic, and those reactions are likely to be repressed or distorted if we hear any discussion of what the texts mean. To refrain from editing is an easy way to alleviate our nagging professional worries about being wrong; but it also means

that we lose the opportunity to be right about anything, and to give other readers the benefit of our perceptions. (114)

Lavagnino is one of the general editors of the *Collected Works of Thomas Middleton* (Oxford), a major editorial undertaking that was published in 2007 after a long developmental history.[16] A brief consideration of the Oxford Middleton is worthwhile, since, as the quotation from Lavagnino (one of its chief contributors) indicates, its methodology reaffirms the importance of the kinds of selective, subjective processes that are brought into question by the potential scope and referentiality of digitization. Anticipating its appearance, David Greetham suggested that the Oxford Middleton significantly reshapes the early modern dramatic canon: "One of the main reasons Gary Taylor [the other General Editor] embarked on his multi-volume edition of Middleton (after having co-edited the one-volume Oxford Shakespeare) was to effect an act of cultural displacement: to turn what had been regarded as chaff, and thus disposable, into wheat" (9).

"Cultural displacement"—or at the very least, something like "enhanced cultural awareness"—is certainly a large part of the motivating force behind the Middleton project. The Oxford Middleton places great emphasis on editorial expertise and mediation. In fact, Taylor argues that what makes the edition significant is that it is the product of heterogeneous editorial principles. He describes the "self-consciously 'federal edition'" in the following terms:

> different EDITORIAL PRACTICES are adopted for different works; and the critical introductions adopt different critical perspectives [...]. This diversity is deliberate. It derives from a belief that authors and their readers are better served by a "federal" than a "unified" edition. By calling attention to the variety of ways in which the works of an author may be interpreted and edited, a "federal" edition celebrates the play of difference and acknowledges the foreclosure of possibilities entailed in every act of choice. ("How To Use This Book" 19)

Taylor's primary argument is that Middleton's generic and thematic diversity is best served by a correspondingly diverse range of editorial methodologies. For my purposes, the secondary claim being made is of equal importance: Taylor locates the collection's currency in its "self-conscious" awareness of the inevitable shaping influence of editorial mediation. The collection employs a number of different editorial strategies that yield dissimilar combinations of texts and paratexts—the commentary to *A Game at Chesse: An Early Form* "is dedicated to the play's historical and political referents"; the edition of *Old Law* "mixes textual apparatus with annotation and photography with type"; "the notes to *Your Five Gallants* pay particular attention to theatrical problems, options, and opportunities" ("How To Use This Book" 18). The precise strategies themselves are not the issue here: what is significant is that the Oxford Middleton's attempt at cultural displacement was initiated in print, in the belief that a reader's meaningful engagement with Middleton's work is enhanced by clear, accessible mediation. The project is founded on the notion that readers will profit from encountering material that has been pulled from the archives and deliberately shaped—that is, interpreted—by editorial hands. In 2012, The Oxford Middleton was digitally published in Oxford Scholarly Editions Online, a database that is aimed at "transform[ing] humanities scholarship, making texts more accessible, searchable, and interconnected than ever before" ("About"). Middleton's digital afterlife thus reverses that of Shakespeare's as it is found on the *ISE*: where the latter codes texts for the electronic medium and has since forayed into print into order to better connect with readers, the former is a carefully designed printed object that has since been digitized to facilitate a host of encounters. In both cases, books of plays remain engines of interpretation, driven by editorial decision making.

The Oxford Middleton, as many editorial projects tend to do, looks both backward and forward: "This edition does not claim to be definitive; we do not expect, or even hope, that it will last for ever" (Taylor, "Lives and Afterlives" 58). I began this chapter with an analogous, if also diametrically opposed, rhetorical flourish from Bowers, who was looking to the future of editing Shakespeare, and saw a vision of a definitive text approximating "original truth." Bowers's future is the present editorial scene that I have surveyed, and it is one that he could not have imagined (as evidenced by the gap between his "original truth" and the Middleton editors' professed disinterest in definitiveness). To risk speculating on the future of editorial practice myself, I think it is safe to predict that digital editions will continue to proliferate and undergo further refinement, with film clips (and clips of staged performances) becoming more prevalent and well integrated. From their facilitation of access to primary materials (or even relevant secondary sources), to the rapid, broad searches they make possible, there can be no doubt that digital editions will continue to be integral to Shakespeare studies because they enrich our ability to study early modern drama. But when it comes to *reading* drama, and imagining it within a continuous performance landscape, the referential and archival powers of digitization do not make electronic editions innately superior or preferable to the more highly mediated structures of print. For the foreseeable future, printed editions will remain relevant—and with good reason. To edit entails making choices, and although decisions stabilized by print might foreclose other interpretive possibilities, they also confer value and authority. The ordered and sustained imprints of editorial activity in the book of the play are what ensure the printed text's relevance in an increasingly digitized age, since choosing to trace these marked pathways is a continuous, participatory act that can lead to a fully engaged, affective, reading experience.

Epilogue: Prospero's Bands

In thinking of endings, I am drawn to the final page of the Folio text of *The Tempest* (see Figure E.1). The conclusion of *The Tempest*, particularly Prospero's epilogue, is perhaps the most overanalyzed and overrated moment in the canon; given the play's position in Shakespeare's career, its conclusion has taken on mythological proportions, with many reading it as the culminating statement of the playwright's life in, and farewell to, the theater.[1] Such a reading not only distorts the biographical record (Shakespeare continued to write for the theater after he completed *The Tempest*, collaborating with John Fletcher on *Henry VIII* and *The Two Noble Kinsmen*[2]) but it also places its emphasis exclusively on performed modes of dramatic realization. As discussed in the Prologue to this book, in terms of the printing history of Shakespeare's collected works, *The Tempest* represents not an ending, but a beginning, since it is the first play that appears in the Folio. The play occupies a singular position in that its placement at the beginning of the Folio initiates the experience of reading a collection of Shakespearean drama that is constructed according to a larger, specific editorial program: to "gather his workes, and giue them [to] you." With these factors in mind, and thinking of the earliest text of the play as a kind of threshold between performed and printed conceptualizations of drama, I return to some of my central concerns: what is it like to read this last page of *The Tempest* rather than seeing it performed? Or better, what is it like to read this moment and visualize it performed? How does the epilogue signify if it is not spoken by an actor but is instead conjured into existence by the imaginative powers of a reader?

As Figure E.1 makes clear, readers of the Folio version of the play would have confronted something much different than readers of a modernized critical edition. The Folio page is neatly divided into three distinct segments of text (four if one includes the "FINIS" near the

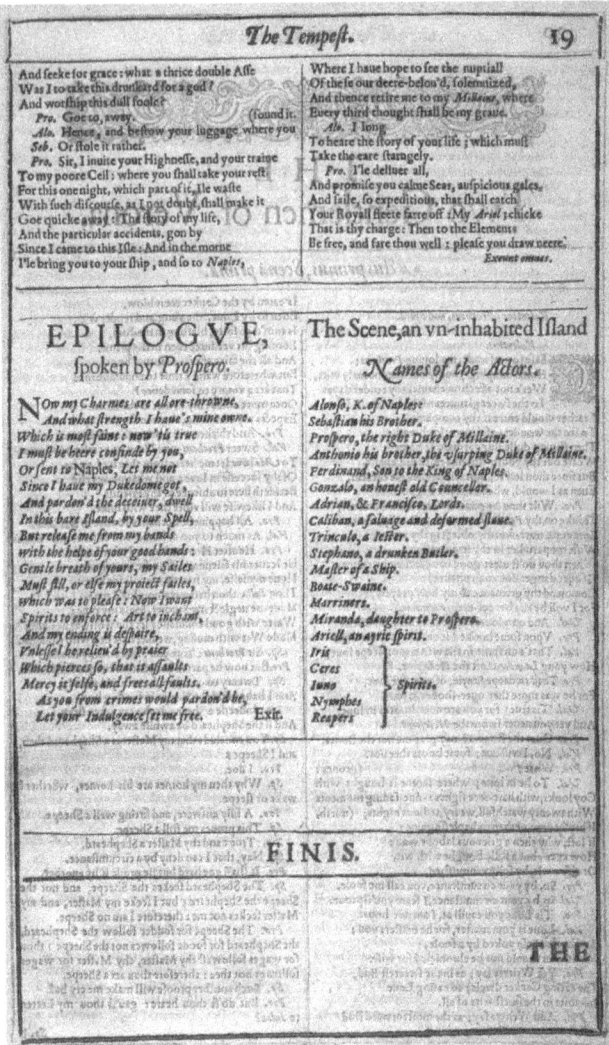

Figure E.1 The final page of *The Tempest* (F, 1623). By permission of The Horace Howard Furness Memorial Library, Rare Book and Manuscript Library, University of Pennsylvania.

bottom). The upper segment is the conclusion of the action of the play-text proper, complete with an *"Exeunt omnes."* The lower left-hand segment contains Prospero's epilogue (in italics), and a final direction for his "Exit." These two segments are linked perhaps by way of Prospero's "please you draw neere," the final line before the epilogue, which might be delivered to the other figures on stage, but might instead signal Prospero's turn toward the audience as he begins his appeal to "*be relieu'd by praier.*" The final partitioned segment, "The Scene, an vn-inhabited Island" and the list of the "*Names of the Actors,*" constitutes a powerful textual rebuttal to Prospero's prayer for freedom. The Folio text, that is, essentially resets itself—we end with a reminder of where the action took place, and of the characters motivating that action: almost as soon as Prospero finishes his petition to be free from "*this bare Island*" in the epilogue, the play's setting is reinforced for readers; similarly, Prospero remarks that "*I haue my Dukedome got, / And pardon'd the deceiuer,*" yet just to the right of these lines is the description of "*Anthonio his brother, the vsurping Duke of Millaine.*" Within the bounds of the Folio, Prospero's escape to political power is over before it begins. Let me be clear: my intention is not to put this forth as a legitimate reading to the end of the play; it is difficult to imagine anyone reading the F page quite this literally and understanding the "*Names of the Actors*" as somehow undermining or qualifying everything that has come before. But this is precisely the point: reading a play involves processing various kinds of textual information located in discrete or disparate locations; that readers are almost certainly able to resist such a literal interpretation of the raw data of the F page is indicative of the level of participation that inheres in the act of reading drama.

Beyond the interpenetrations of the tripartite textual layout, the page itself registers a range of information related to the material properties of the Folio text and early modern textual production that cannot be fully communicated in a critical edition. Different-sized type and fonts are used, and portions of both the title and initial lines of text of *The Two Gentlemen of Verona* can be seen bleeding through from the verso side of the sheet (the compositor's anticipation of this play is recorded in the catchword "THE" at the foot of the page). The page also appears to record certain features of its underlying manuscript: Ralph Crane has been identified as having prepared the manuscript copy used in the printing house, and some of his scribal habits are on display. Prospero's reference to "our deere-belou'd" reveals Crane's fondness for both hyphenated words and elision. It is also likely that the list of the "*Names of the Actors*" and its brief descriptions of the major players—Gonzalo is "*an honest old Councellor,*" Caliban is "*a saluage and deformed slaue,*" Ariel is "*an ayrie spirit*"—are the contribution of Crane, not of Shakespeare. Similar lists appear at the end of other Folio texts for which Crane is thought to have prepared copy (*The Two Gentlemen of Verona,* the Folio text of *The Merry Wives of Windsor*, *Measure for Measure*, *Othello*, and *The Winter's Tale*).³ Whether Crane's list is the product of his interpretation of what he witnessed in a performance of the play or his response to descriptions in Shakespeare's manuscript (Vaughan and Vaughan 127), the *"Names of the Actors"* represents a point at which textual production and imaginative participation in the performance of the play intermingle and energize one another. Comparable points of intersection shared by page and stage are also evidenced in many of *The Tempest's* stage directions; certain phrases in the directions—*"A tempestuous noise of Thunder and Lightning heard"* (TLN 2), *"with gentle actions of salutations"* (TLN 1537), *"to a strange hollow and confused noyse, they heauily vanish"* (TLN 1807–8), *"a franticke ge-/sture"* (TLN 2009–10)—lead John Jowett to argue that Crane, "apparently influenced by his experience of the play on stage...emphasiz[ed] visual aspects of the play as seen in the theatre and record[ed] them in a descriptive, complimentary, literary manner, in terms which aid the reader's appreciation of the play but which are unlikely to have been used by the dramatist instructing the players" (*Companion* 612).⁴

Much of the information encoded on the final Folio page of the play will be lost or significantly altered by the editorial and publishing processes that produce a modern edition. Typefaces, spelling, punctuation, and paper quality will all be regularized; the unique structure of the page itself will disappear, as Prospero's epilogue will likely be justified so that it appears in line with the playtext above it, and the *"Names of the Actors"* is shifted to the beginning of the play to serve as a list of *dramatis personae*. The re-coding options that are available to a modern editor, however, give something back to readers, even as they take away. Discussions in introductions or appendices can describe early modern manuscript production and Crane's scribal fingerprints, and these discussions can be linked to the playtext by way of cross-references in commentary notes; facsimile pages of the Folio text can be reproduced (the Arden 3 editors supply a reproduction of the final page of the play in their examination of Crane's contribution of "important information that appears to reflect his own judgment" (127)). Above all, editors can remain faithful to the program that Crane, an early reader and mediator of the playtext, appears to have instituted: produce a version of the text that facilitates a reader's ability to imaginatively approximate the play in performance. A commentary note on the epilogue in the Arden 3 edition recalls George D. Wolfe's 1995 production for the New York Shakespeare Festival, where "Patrick Stewart gave up the microphone he had used throughout the outdoor performance and here addressed the audience without the aid of amplification. If Prospero has exited and returned, he may have doffed some of his ducal trappings and appear in a simple shirt or gown. Such theatrical choices can indicate Prospero's loss of power or the actor's loss of his role" (Epilogue 1n). A full-page photograph of a plainly adorned and "pensive" Stewart as Prospero can be found in the Arden 3 introduction (122). Stephen Orgel, editor of the Oxford edition of the play, notes of the epilogue that "[it] is unique in the Shakespeare canon in that its speaker declares himself not an actor in a play but a character in a fiction. The release he craves of the audience is the freedom to continue his history beyond the limits of the stage and the text" (319n).

Whether the epilogue is spoken by the actor in a play or the character in a fiction is open to debate. It seems to me that the power of the epilogue rests largely on these two figures shading into one another; indeed, Orgel's emphasis on Prospero seeking release from both the stage *and* the text is indicative of the character's dual existence in performance and print—in speaking the epilogue, Prospero straddles the boundary between the textuality of the world of the play and the performance of the play in the world.[5] Elsewhere in the play, we have seen what happens to players and their craft: the masque of nymphs and reapers in 4.1 were a part of nothing more than what Prospero calls a "baseless fabric" (4.1.151): "These our actors," he says to Ferdinand, "were all spirits, and / Are melted into air, into thin air" (148–50).[6] That the actors (in the masque, and by extension, *The Tempest*) are involved in an "insubstantial pageant" (4.1.155) means that their performances only survive and resonate by way of memorial reconstructions. Prospero's epilogue picks up on this theme, striking to the heart of the ephemerality of the magic of the theater, and appealing to the audience's memories of what has just passed:

> Now my charms are all o'erthrown,
> And what strength I have's mine own,
> Which is most faint. Now 'tis true
> I must be confined by you,
> Or sent to Naples. Let me not,
> Since I have my dukedom got,
> And pardoned the deceiver, dwell
> In this bare island by your spell... (5.1.319–26)

As has often been noted, despite the religious language of the epilogue—its references to *"prayer," "Mercy,"* pardoning, and

"*Indulgence*"—the speech centers on what might be thought of as "theatrical faith" (Bate and Rasmussen 4). Here, however, I want to resist thinking of "theatrical faith" as a belief system exclusive to audience members in a theater. As I have demonstrated throughout this study, the book of the play harbours the potential to not only encourage but reward a reader's faith in the printed text's ability to engage with the histories and potentialities of the play in performance. In my reading, Prospero's final speech—which looks backward to the play that has just finished, and forward in anticipation of the play's afterlife—encapsulates the tensions between page and stage that the printed text of the play can, and cannot, alleviate. In subtly transitioning between past, present, and future tenses, Prospero marks the gaps that no text of the play will be able to close completely. Recalling, recapturing, or anticipating performance practice is something that all printed plays attempt to do through various textual and paratextual codes, meaning that readers not only encounter the play in fundamentally different terms than do theater-goers, but also face the prospect of remembering the play in much different ways. Imagined performances will necessarily be impoverished things relative to the sensorial richness of an actual performance, but readers can always make use of the stability of the printed page to continually alter their vision of the play. One can, as the final Folio page seems to encourage, end, and then begin again; and, as in my triangulation of the Folio sheet, readers can make tangential moves in nonlinear directions; and, as evidenced by my citations of recent editorial commentary, readers can venture away from the playtext to gather information located elsewhere that has been introduced by mediating parties. Remembering performance through the book is the reader's interpretive burden as well as the reader's interpretive opportunity.

In the end, for readers of the play, Prospero's appeal is to a purely conceptual "*Indulgence*" to "*release me from my bands.*" Most editors of the play gloss "bands" as "bonds," which itself remains richly multivalent, suggesting a debt or obligation as well as physical restraints. Given my emphasis on the textuality of the epilogue, it is also tantalizing that by the eighteenth century, "band" was associated with the cords or straps used for binding the quires of a book (*OED n.¹ 2b*). On the page, readers confront a virtual character asking for release into a realm that exists somewhere beyond the theatrical event and the playtext upon which this event depends. To read the epilogue is to heed a call for an escape. An escape from the text to a new world of imagined possibilities and performances. A performance-escape. A *performancescape.* Prospero's call invokes a participatory system that bridges printed and performed modes of dramatic realization, and it is within this system that readers, stimulated by the potent imaginative and memorial potential of textual representation, come to Prospero's final words: *"set me free."*

Notes

Prologue: Prospero's Storm

1. Quotations from the Folio follow the through-line numbers of the Hinman facsimile (New York: W. W. Norton, 1968).
2. A less fantastic moment is depicted in the 1714 edition of Rowe's text: the discovery of Ferdinand and Miranda playing chess.
3. Taken from the journal's website, accessed January 10, 2014. http://www.tandfonline.com/toc/rshk20/current.
4. Patrice Pavis advocates for a similar understanding. Pavis argues that text and performance "adhere to different semiotic systems. *Mise en scène* is not the reduction or the transformation of text into performance, but rather their confrontation" (26).

1 Mediating Page and Stage

1. Taylor proposes in a commentary note that Richard's "pledge" (4.1.120) to Somerset "need not necessarily be a glove or gauntlet (though this is customary). A white rose would be effective theatre."
2. For the sake of simplifying tangled narratives of critical practice, I will be wielding the term "performance criticism"—which Barbara Hodgdon rightly identifies as "an eclectic mix of critical styles and practices" ("Introduction" 2)—rather broadly throughout this chapter. More detailed summaries of the diverse approaches that get subsumed under the heading of "performance criticism" can be found in Hodgdon's Introduction to *A Companion to Shakespeare and Performance* (Malden, MA, and Oxford: Blackwell, 2005), 1–9, and in James C. Bulman's Introduction to *Shakespeare, Theory, and Performance* (New York and London: Routledge, 1996), 1–11.
3. For a perceptive assessment of the rise, fall, and legacy of the New Bibliography, see Gabriel Egan, *The Struggle for Shakespeare's Text* (Cambridge: Cambridge UP, 2010), especially pages 190–230.
4. Robert Weimann describes "the current upheaval in Shakespeare criticism" as an "exhilarating rapprochement among textual scholarship, theatre history, and

performance studies" (xi). In *Shakespeare's Literary Authorship*, Patrick Cheney identifies "stage-to-page" criticism as "a new field" that crosses "the divide between theatre and bibliographical criticism" (5).

5. The formulation of playtexts as dramatic scripts is so engrained in critical consciousness that it is now disseminated as an irrefutable fact. Consider Stephen Orgel's claim that "Shakespeare never conceived, or even re-conceived, his plays as texts to be read. They were scripts, not books; the only readers were the performers, and the function of the script was to be realized on stage" (*Imagining* 1). Erne, who has challenged this orthodoxy, provides a useful reminder of the fundamental historical difficulty that proponents of Orgel's position must overcome: if plays were only written in order to be performed, "the very fact that a playtext has come down to us implies that a publisher counted on a considerable number of people thinking otherwise" (*Literary Dramatist* 131).

6. See *Shakespeare and the Authority of Performance*, especially pages 151–91.

7. Tellingly, the First Gentleman processes the Third Gentleman's report into a kind of imagined performance: "The dignity of this act was worth the audience of kings and princes, for by such was it acted" (5.2.79–81). Unless otherwise noted, Shakespeare quotations are from *The Riverside Shakespeare*, gen. ed. G. B. Evans, 2nd ed (Boston: Houghton Mifflin, 1997).

8. Knowles's "materialist semiotics" was first articulated at length in *Reading the Material Theatre* (Cambridge: Cambridge UP, 2004).

9. Worthen makes this point in the process of responding to Anthony Dawson's essay, "The Impasse over the Stage." In that essay, Dawson notes that construing and then critically reading a performance as if it were a text "is a perfectly legitimate, indeed an inescapable, strategy, since performance itself is obviously not stable, transparent or intrinsically knowable" (318).

10. Gerard Genette deploys different terminology. In his formulation, "*paratext* = *peritext* + *epitext*" (5), with *peritext* defined as a spatial category containing elements "situated in relation to the location of the text itself: around the text and either within the same volume or at a more respectful (or more prudent) distance" (4). *Epitext* refers to "distanced elements": "all those messages that, at least originally, are located outside the book, generally with the help of media (interviews, conversations) or under cover of private communications (letters, diaries, and others)" (5). As will become clear, my focus is on what Genette would refer to as *peritext*.

11. Gabriel Egan has questioned the validity of the specific examples used by Kidnie to demonstrate early modern instances of indeterminacy in stage directions. See *The Struggle for Shakespeare's Text*, 212–214.

12. The editors of the *RSC Complete Works* have attached arrows to marginal stage directions to indicate that "a piece of business... may occur at various different moments within a scene" (lx). They appear to have arrived at this strategy independent of Kidnie, as they make no mention of her in their explanatory "User's Guide." I find the impact on the reading experience to be minimal simply because the arrow symbol is deployed very sparingly across the edition.

13. My thanks to M. J. Kidnie for bringing to light the potential richness of this ambiguity.

14. Manfred Pfister makes a similar point: "One consequence of the collective reception of dramatic texts is that the individual receiver is unable to vary the tempo of the reception process, nor can he usually interrupt it at will or have sections repeated if he has failed to understand the text. The reader…on the other hand, can determine his own reading speed, abandon or take up the text when he wishes, or even simply leaf through it forwards or backwards as his whim takes him" (36).

15. As Neill notes in his collation, the *"asleep"* portion of the direction was first introduced by Rowe.

2 Text and Performance on the Early Modern Page

1. The compositors that produced Q2 *Titus Andronicus* (1600) for James Roberts's printing house, for example, appear conspicuously diligent. It is generally accepted that they were not working from a manuscript, but set their text from a copy of Q1 (1594); in making improvements to Q1's rather shoddy punctuation as well as smoothing over certain textual ambiguities, these compositors (likely two of them) seem to be intent on emending their copy-text. Most admirably, the compositor setting the end of the play appears to repair damage to the final leaves of his copy of Q1 by reworking what should have been the last line of the play and then making up four more. This ingenuity passed unnoticed until a copy of Q1 was discovered in 1904. See Joseph S. G. Bolton, "The Authentic Text of *Titus Andronicus*," *PMLA* 44 (1929): 765–88.

2. See Julie Stone Peters, *Theatre of the Book, 1480–1880* (Oxford: Oxford UP, 2000); Zachary Lesser, *Renaissance Drama and the Politics of Publication* (Cambridge: Cambridge UP, 2004); Heidi Brayman Hackel, *Reading Material in Early Modern England* (Cambridge: Cambridge UP, 2005); Douglas Brooks, *From Playhouse to Printing House* (Cambridge: Cambridge UP, 2000); Evelyn B. Tribble, *Margins and Marginality* (Charlottesville and London: UP of Virginia, 1993); William W. E. Slights, *Managing Readers* (Ann Arbour: U Michigan P, 2001); Sonia Massai, *Shakespeare and the Rise of the Editor* (Cambridge: Cambridge UP, 2007); Jeffrey Masten, *Textual Intercourse* (Cambridge: Cambridge UP, 1997); and Marta Straznicky, ed., *The Book of the Play* (Amherst and Boston: U Massachusetts P, 2006).

3. A contemporary poem, "To my good freandes mr John Hemings & Henry Condall," similarly stresses their roles as collectors. The poem figures the two actors as treasure hunters who have not constructed the Folio so much as they have unearthed a preexisting prize and facilitated its availability for the public: "Joyntly with vndaunted paynes . . yowe haue pleased the lyving, loved the deadd, / Raysede from the woambe of Earth a Ritcher myne / Than [Cortez]." See E. K. Chambers, *William Shakespeare: A Study of Facts and Problems*, vol. 2, (Oxford: Oxford UP, 1930), 234–35.

4. The identity of the preface's author is uncertain, but Lesser speculates that it was written by the publishers of the quarto, Richard Bonian and Henry Walley, since they had the most to gain from the sales that a successful advertising campaign would presumably result in. Further, as Lesser points out, the epistle was added (along with changes to the title page) during the printing process, and few would have had access to the book at this late stage of production.

5. While there is no definitive evidence either way, the epistle's claim that the play was never performed is a dubious one (especially since it utterly contradicts the original title page). What is widely understood as the original entry for Shakespeare's play in the Stationers' Register in 1603 notes that it had been acted by the Lord Chamberlain's Men; further, some believe that *Troilus and Cressida*'s armed Prologue is a riff on a similar figure from Jonson's *Poetaster*, first performed in 1601. *Where* the play might have been performed—The Globe? The Inns of Court? Privately?—remains unsolved. Lesser offers an explanation for the epistle's sudden appearance that is persuasive in its simplicity: the publishers (Bonian and Walley) "changed their minds about the play," and sought, by adding the epistle, to position the play within "a particular niche of the print marketplace" (*Renaissance Drama* 1, 2).

6. This binary appears in the Prologue to the play, which appears only in the Folio version of the text.

7. For an extended consideration of "bibliographic codes," see Jerome McGann, *The Textual Condition* (Princeton: Princeton UP, 1991). The notion of bibliographic coding also informs the work of D. F. McKenzie; see, for example, *Bibliography and the Sociology of Texts* (Cambridge: Cambridge UP, 1999).

8. Peters remarks that "letters on the page in the earliest printed plays (as in other kinds of books during the period) tend to follow large-scale visual patterns, responding to decorative sensibilities rather than serving ease of reading. Words are often broken randomly to fit visual-spatial designs" (17).

9. O1 appears to have been unauthorized. A second edition of the play (O2) was printed in 1570: "The Tragidie of Ferrex / and Porrex, / set forth without any addition or alte- / ration but altogether as the same was shewed / on stage before the Queenes Maiestie, / about nine yeares past, *vz*. The / xviij. day of Ianuarie. 1561. / by the gentlemen of the Inner Temple." The 1570 text differs significantly from O1 in terms of both paratextual materials and substantive readings. For useful discussions of the relationship between the two editions, see Henry James and Greg Walker, "The Politics of *Gorboduc*," *English Historical Review* 110.435 (1995): 109–21, and Brooks, *From Playhouse to Printing House*, 24–40.

10. Gary Taylor argues that certain forms of "identification tables" (a broad term that includes lists of *dramatis personae*) are aimed directly at readers and "impinge upon the reading of the play text." These textual forms "inevitably summarize or characterize the play, affecting our assumptions about its fictional persons, and unlike other paratext they are often consulted or

cross-referenced during reading, potentially interposing themselves at any point in the text" ("Order of Persons" 54).

11. Eric Rasmussen finds the dumb shows' use of the past tense unusual: "Seventy-one English Renaissance plays include dumb shows, the overwhelming majority of which are either in the present or future tense" (417). He goes on to build a short but convincing case that the dumb shows were not a part of the manuscripts used as copy for either of the first two printed editions of the play (1565 and 1570); he concludes that the dumb shows "are memorial reconstructions—not directions for a performance, and as such, quite naturally, in the past tense" (418).

12. See chapter 1, pages 7–10.

13. In his New Mermaids edition of the play, Anthony Dawson notes that "there is no clear evidence that the earliest performances were at the Rose, but since [Edward] Alleyn was performing there in the 1580s and since a few years later Henslowe's *Diary* indicates that both *Tamburlaine* plays were performed there, it is certainly not impossible" (xi n.5).

14. For stage and textual histories, see Dawson, *Tamburlaine*, xxviii-xliv. Part One could be performed on its own or in combination with Part Two (usually on successive days).

15. The O1 title page identifies Jones as the printer, but Greg believes the work to have been done by an unidentified party. See *A Bibliography of English Printed Drama*, vol I, 171, and vol III, 1520–21.

16. "Iestures" is often modernized to "gestures," but the original form seems to keep both "gesture" and "jesting" in play.

17. Bruce Smith's remarks on the title page to Q1 *King Lear* are applicable here: "The printed script offers itself as a mnemonic device for purchasers who may have actually seen and heard the play in performance...The words on the page become a way of returning, in memory, to that experience" (33).

18. For Webster's involvement in preparing his plays for print as well as making press corrections, see J. R. Brown, "The Printing of John Webster's Plays," 3 parts: *Studies in Bibliography* 6 (1954): 117–40; 8 (1956): 113–28; 15 (1962): 57–69.

19. Webster's contempt recalls lines spoken by Planet, a character from John Marston's *Jack Drum's Entertainment*, who comments that—quite unlike those in public venues—audiences at Paul's indoor theatre "shall not be cho-akte / With the stenche of Garlicke, nor be pasted / To the barmy Iacket of a Beer-brewer" (H3v). It also echoes the epistle to the second issue of Q1 *Troilus*; see above, pages 35–38.

20. Webster does not specify which part (Richard) Perkins played, writing only that "the worth of his action did Crowne both the beginning and end." The general assumption is that Perkins played Flamineo, but if Webster intended to be taken literally, it is Lodovico who begins and ends the action of the play. The Q1 (1623) and Q2 (1631) texts of *The Duchess of Malfi* also recognize performance in a unique way, including a listing for "*The Actors*

Names" that uses roman numerals to distinguish between two different sets of actors who played the parts of Ferdinand, the Cardinal, and Antonio. Given Webster's involvement in the printing of his plays, it is tempting to interpret this distinctive format as another means by which he is utilizing the stability of the text to bracket the multifariousness and iterative nature of performance.

21. Lesser also finds a correlation between plays printed continuously and certain paratextual markers: these plays are more likely to contain Latin on their title pages and/or "some indication of the author's elevated social status" (*Renaissance Drama* 67, and see also Lesser's table on pages 68–9).

22. For explorations of folio production, authorship, and printed drama as literature in regards to Shakespeare, see Lukas Erne, *Shakespeare as Literary Dramatist* (Cambridge: Cambridge UP, 2003); Margreta de Grazia, *Shakespeare Verbatim: The Reproduction of Authenticity and the 1790 Apparatus* (Oxford: Clarendon, 1991), 14–48; and David Scott Kastan, *Shakespeare After Theory* (New York and London: Routledge, 1999), 50–78. On Jonson's Folio, see Mark Bland, "William Stansby and the Production of *The Workes of Beniamin Jonson*, 1615–1616," *The Library* 20 (1998): 1–33; Brooks, *From Playhouse to Printing House,* 104–39; Jennifer Brady and W. H. Herendeen, eds. *Ben Jonson's 1616 Folio* (Newark: U of Delaware P, 1991); and Lowenstein, *Jonson and Possessive Authorship* (Cambridge: Cambridge UP, 2002), 133–210.

23. Jonson, it should be noted, was actively involved in the printing of his plays before their collection in 1616. Lowenstein argues that Jonson's longstanding concern for the published shape of his plays—as expressed in his experimentation with epistles, dedications, apparatuses, and typography—served as an extensive preparation for the production of the Folio (*Jonson,* 152–94).

24. Citing typographic markers such as "the extra provision of white space around the text," and Jonson's strict control over the punctuation of his Folio playtexts—an attempt "to escape from the limitations of the written or printed word and to emphasize its orality"—Mark Bland goes so far as to state that Jonson and his publisher/printer William Stansby "altered the spatial relationship of the text" so as to foster "the idea of the book as its own theatre" ("Stansby," 23, 19, 28).

25. Much ink has been spilled in attempting to surmise what exactly "diuerse stolne, and surreptitious copies" refers to; a sampling of the more noteworthy interpretations would have to include Alfred Pollard's, which is integral to his influential theory of "bad" quartos (64–80); Kastan's belief that the reference is to *all* earlier printings of Shakespeare's plays (*Book,* 72–8); and Erne's conjecture that Heminge and Condell's comments are specifically aimed at a group of ten quartos published and collected by Thomas Pavier in 1619 (*Literary Dramatist,* 255–8).

26. Richard Levin believes that Heminge and Condell are implying that there is a "fundamental similarity between the experiences of seeing and of reading a play" (557), but this seems to put too great a burden on the notion of the plays having "had their triall already." Heminge and Condell are acknowledging that a certain segment of their potential readership is comprised of regular

playgoers, but I do not think it necessarily follows that reading and seeing a play are being described as essentially similar activities.

27. Folio prices were fluid relative to their bound or unbound state, but they would not have ranged within the denominations that Heminge and Condell cite. Unbound copies are estimated to have sold for 15s., with bound copies costing up to £1 (in plain calf). See Anthony James West, *The Shakespeare First Folio: The History of the Book. Volume I: An Account of the First Folio Based on its Sales and Prices, 1623–2000* (Oxford: Oxford UP, 2001), 8–13.

28. Erne is on relatively firm ground in exhibiting that Shakespeare wrote overly long plays from the perspective of early modern playing times, and it also seems plausible that Shakespeare did, at times, write with readers in mind. The claim that Shakespeare wrote extra material so as to "raise the literary respectability of plays" is much more speculative. Worthen, though he recognizes the important ways that Erne's study recognizes the complicated connections between printed playtexts, authorship, and performance, exposes Erne's literary biases: "Is it at all plausible that as house playwright, Shakespeare might well have had the incentive and the freedom to write extra material not for literary posterity but to provide a wider range of options and opportunities for his company to think through the play's performance potentialities?" (*Print* 25–6).

29. Erne notes that a 1997 Stratford production of *Cymbeline* "played for nearly three hours, even though a full thousand lines were omitted" (137).

30. Warren attributes a share of the literary nature of the directions to the influence of Ralph Crane, the scribe who likely prepared the transcript serving as the basis for the Folio text; Crane's influence on the playtext is discussed by Warren on pages 67–74.

31. Fredson Bowers provides a concise summary of conjectured attributions; see *The Dramatic Works in the Beaumont and Fletcher Canon*, vol. 10 (Cambridge: Cambridge UP, 1966–96), 751–52. For discussions of how the Beaumont and Fletcher Folio complicates modern conceptions of authorship, see Brooks, *From Playhouse to Printing House*, 140–88, and Masten, *Textual Intercourse*, 16–20; 113–55.

32. I have retained the original spellings in this passage, but the folio's "*Landscrap*" is clearly a misreading of "Landscape."

33. McMillin's position is outlined in the introduction to *The First Quarto of Othello* (Cambridge: Cambridge UP, 2001). For the limitations of McMillin's theory, see Neill's edition of *Othello* (405–33), and Edward Pechter, "Crisis in Editing?," *Shakespeare Survey* 59 (2006): 20–38.

34. Moseley's epistle is also essential to Erne's discussion of playing times in the theater: "If the relatively short 'Beaumont and Fletcher' plays were significantly abridged, how likely is it that the same company performed the full text of Shakespeare's substantially longer plays?" (150).

35. R. C. Bald writes that "the implication that the body of the book is the work of one printing-house is . . . not to be relied upon. The plays were divided into eight rather uneven sections, and each was handed to a different printer, who signed his section with a separate alphabet" (qtd. in Brooks, *From Playhouse to Printing House*, 151).

3 Performance and the Editorial Tradition

1. For a more detailed list of the cuts, see Anthony Dawson, *Hamlet,* Shakespeare in Performance (Manchester and New York: Manchester UP, 1995), 23–4; Lukas Erne, *Shakespeare as Literary Dramatist* (Cambridge: Cambridge UP, 2003), 167; and Gary Taylor, *Reinventing Shakespeare: A Cultural History from the Restoration to the Present* (New York: Weidenfeld & Nicolson, 1989), 46–51.

2. The Arden 3 edition of the play, for instance, glosses—in the margins, of course—"native hue" as "natural colour" and "sicklied o'er with the pale cast of thought" as "unhealthily covered [with the] pallid tinge of contemplation" (Thompson and Taylor 287).

3. For a detailed look at Rowe's use of the 1676 quarto, see Barbara Mowat's "The Form of *Hamlet*'s Fortunes," *Renaissance Drama* 19 (1988): 97–126, especially pages 98–107.

4. Rowe was selected to edit Shakespeare by the Tonson publishing cartel, who also published the editions of Pope, Theobald, Warburton, Johnson, Steevens, and Capell. Encouraging their editors to use a received (Tonson) text would have been a means for the Tonsons to perpetuate copyright privileges. See Peter Seary, *Lewis Theobald and the Editing of Shakespeare* (Oxford: Clarendon, 1990), 133–5; and Murphy, *Shakespeare in Print: A History and Chronology of Shakespeare Publishing* (Cambridge: Cambridge UP, 2003), 57–100.

5. Rowe later remarks that "many of his Plays were surrepticiously and lamely Printed in his lifetime" (vol. 1, p. x).

6. Rowe's decision to use F4 as his copy-text is deeply troubling to modern editorial sensibilities; G. B. Evans, for instance, argues that "the result was a generally inferior text that seriously vitiated later editions for the next sixty years or more" (60). But see above, note 4.

7. See Barbara Mowat, "The Form of *Hamlet*'s Fortunes"; and Sonia Massai, "Working with the Texts: Differential Readings," *A Concise Companion to Shakespeare and the Text.* Ed. Andrew Murphy (Malden, MA, and Oxford: Blackwell, 2007), 190–2.

8. Rowe's text provides more information about the brothers than what is found in Edward Ravenscroft's influential 1687 adaptation of the play, which describes them both as "*Sons of the Deceas'd Emperour.*" Ravenscroft makes significant structural changes to the play, and transforms Aaron into a more vulnerable, noble figure; Rowe, working from F4, did not adopt these alterations. For a summary of Ravenscroft's adaptation, see Jonathan Bate's edition of *Titus Andronicus* (London: Thomson Learning-Arden Shakespeare, 2004), 49–55.

9. It is important to note that fictionalized localities and directions are not an invention of the eighteenth century. See Lukas Erne, *Shakespeare's Modern Collaborators* (London and New York: Continuum, 2008), 81–3, for examples of fictionalized directions in Shakespeare's original playtexts.

10. Stuart Sillars notes that publisher Jacob Tonson hired "artists at the beginning of their careers" and suggests the engravings were produced with considerable

haste: "the straightforward mathematics" of the time between Tonson securing the rights and the edition's publication "indicate a little more than two
weeks for each image" (33).

11. See the Prologue to this book, page xviii. Rowe's 1709 edition employed
designs by François Boitard and engravings by Elisha Kirkall; the 1714 edition, which reproduced many of the 1709 engravings, was handled by Louis
du Guernier. See Sillars, *The Illustrated Shakespeare, 1709–1875* (Cambridge:
Cambridge UP, 2008), 33–72, for more on the backgrounds and techniques
of these artists.

12. Betterton is in fact singled out by Rowe for his "fine Performance" of Hamlet,
and the actor is acknowledged as providing numerous details for Rowe's
"Account of the Life" of Shakespeare. In his *Pictorial Shakspere* (1838), Charles
Knight reproduces the illustration from Rowe, remarking that "we see Hamlet
pointing to the large pictures on the arras. Our readers will smile at the costume, and will observe that the stage trick of kicking down the chair upon the
entrance of the ghost is more than a century old" (qtd. in Sillars 8).

13. Murphy quotes the *Weekly Journal* (November 18, 1721), in which Pope
appeals to the general public for quarto editions of "the Tempest, Mackbeth,
Julius Caesar, Timon of Athens, King John, and Henry the 8th." Of course,
no such quartos are known to exist: all of these plays were first published in F
(1623). What *did* Pope have access to? "It appears from his 'Table of the Several
Editions of *Shakespear's* Plays, made use of and compared in this Impression'
[following the Index in volume VI], that Pope had access to at least one Quarto
edition of every play published in Shakespeare's own lifetime, with the excep-
tion of *Much Ado*, as well as to copies of the first and second Folios" (Walsh
130).

14. My thanks to Fiona Ritchie for bringing this point to my attention.

15. Since Pope's edition does not use line numbering, parenthetical references are
to page numbers.

16. One editor of *Macbeth* notes that "none of the surviving [miracle plays] has a
designated porter on the mouth of Hell, but various plays dealing with Christ's
activities after his death offer two or three devils on the gate" (Brooke 79).

17. See Robert Weimann, *Author's Pen and Actor's Voice: Playing and Writing in
Shakespeare's Theatre* (Cambridge: Cambridge UP, 2000), 201–7.

18. Many critics suggest that the Porter's description of the "equivocator" is an
allusion to the Jesuit Father Garnet, who claimed equivocation as a religious
right when under examination for his involvement in the Gunpowder Plot
of 1605. Steven Mullaney's "Lying Like Truth: Riddle, Representation and
Treason in Renaissance England," *English Literary History* 47.1 (1980): 32–47,
deftly weaves the play through the contemporary political atmosphere.

19. The full title of Theobald's piece is even more explicit (and damning):
*Shakespeare Restored: Or, A Specimen of the Many Errors, as well Committed, as
Unamended, by Mr Pope in his Late Edition of this Poet.*

20. Pope exacts his revenge by immortalizing Theobald as the disciple of the god-
dess Dulness in *The Dunciad* (1728). Theobald gets the last laugh, however,

when it comes to editorial practice: Seary points out that Pope's second edition of the plays (also published in 1728) incorporated—more often than not, *silently*—some 106 corrections that Theobald had proposed (97).

21. Theobald's claim that he read "above 800 old *English* plays" (vol. 1, p. lxviii) is likely hyperbolic, but Walsh observes that *"The Catalogue of the Library of Lewis Theobald, Deceas'd* (1744) contains some hundreds of such items, including a lot of 'One hundred ninety-five old English Plays in Quarto'...in addition to works by Marston, Massinger, Lyly, and Beaumont and Fletcher, as well as Theobald's copies of early texts of Shakespeare himself" (140–1). See also Seary, *Lewis Theobald,* 231–6.

22. Theobald is rhetorically crafty about this: where defending or restoring an F reading, he refers to it as the "old" or "first" Folio; where he is *emending* an F reading, F is often described as the "players' edition" (Jarvis 101).

23. I am compelled to point out that Neill's edition organizes a tremendous amount of information about the play in performance and about the performance of the monument scene in particular. His text led me to a commentary note attached to his stage direction mentioning the "controversial" matter of hauling Antony aloft. This same note directed me to an appendix in the back of the edition devoted to the stage business in question; this appendix included two photographs, one representing a more traditional staging (Shakespeare Memorial Theatre, 1951), and one a more stylized staging in which Antony is not lifted up but dragged across the stage (Royal Shakespeare Theatre, 1978). The tangential moves supported and encouraged by Neill's edition supplied me with a range of *performancescapes* that now inform my reading of the text.

24. See George Winchester Stone, Jr., "Garrick's Presentation of *Antony and Cleopatra," Review of English Studies* 13 (1937): 20–38. Stone writes that "the plan, as it proved, was [for Capell] to render the play actable by excision and rearrangement only, not by the addition of scenes or the creation of new speeches" (25).

25. Elam identifies four temporal levels in total, the other three being "plot time"—"the order in which events are shown or reported"; "chronological time"—"the actual temporal ordering of events" abstracted by a spectator; and "historical time"—"the precise counterfactual background to the dramatic representation" (117). All four temporal levels would be intuited differently by readers and spectators, but I would argue that the notion of "discourse time" is heightened for readers since it involves the most interpretive labor to reconstruct—a reader's awareness of matters of plot, chronology, and history are not as contingent upon imagining performance practice.

26. Which is not the same as saying that these directions are incomplete; I agree with Kidnie's argument that early modern stage directions "are not deficient in any absolute or transhistorical sense. They just seem deficient to us" ("Staging" 160). As Neill hypothesizes regarding the staging of the monument scene in his edition of the play, "we must conclude either that the technical solutions were so self-evident that Shakespeare did not bother to elaborate his stage

direction, or that he relied on the ingenuity of his colleagues to realize a scene he had conceived in largely symbolic terms" (365–6).

27. Capell's employment of this last symbol is suspect, if for no other reason than the fact that he "remarks no instances of irony in *Hamlet*" (Walsh 125). Vanessa Cunningham writes that "whether Garrick was consulted about including Capell's system of marks in the published text of *Antony and Cleopatra* is unknown, but he would surely have given credit to his collaborator for wishing to bring the experience of encountering the play in a library closer to that enjoyed in a theatre, however inadequately it was realised in practice" (103).

28. de Grazia's argument that Malone's edition instituted a practice that dictated subsequent Shakespeare scholarship's concern with individuality and authenticity has been challenged on a number of fronts: see Michael Bristol, *Big-time Shakespeare* (London and New York: Routledge, 1996), 79–87; Simon Jarvis, *Scholars and Gentlemen: Shakespearian Textual Criticism and Representations of Scholarly Labour, 1725–1765* (Oxford: Clarendon, 1995), 9–10; 187–8; Murphy, *Shakespeare in Print: A History and Chronology of Shakespeare Publishing* (Cambridge: Cambridge UP, 2003), 96–8; and Thomas Postlewait, "The Criteria for Evidence: Anecdotes in Shakespearean Biography, 1709–2000," *Theorizing Practice: Redefining Theatre History*. Eds. W. B. Worthen and Peter Holland (Basingstoke and New York: Palgrave, 2003), 61–4.

29. Some exceptions remained, such as Nahum Tate's adaptation of *King Lear* (first performed in 1681, complete with a surviving Lear and a betrothal for Edgar and Cordelia), which held the stage until the middle of the nineteenth century.

30. The editors themselves (William George Clark, John Glover, and William Aldis Wright) acknowledge that "Cambridge afforded facilities for the execution of the task such as few other places could boast of" (vol. 1, p. x).

31. Alan Farmer is useful here: "Although frequently misunderstood, Greg's essay ["The Rationale of Copy-Text"] called for increased editorial freedom in the decisions that editors make, in contrast to the previous theory of limited editorial interference, and critics who view it as a 'strict formula' consequently misunderstand its central import: different documents might be closer to the author's original text in different ways, and, as a result, editors should not feel especially beholden to the readings in any one text alone" (168).

32. For an influential assessment of many of the New Bibliography's major conjectures and textual categories, see Paul Werstine, "Narratives About Printed Shakespeare Texts: 'Foul Papers' and 'Bad' Quartos," *Shakespeare Quarterly* 41.1 (1990): 65–86. Giorgio Melchiori's "The Continuing Importance of New Bibliography" offers a different, though equally important, retrospective. For a thorough assessment of the rise, fall, and continuing legacy of the New Bibliography, see Gabriel Egan, *The Struggle for Shakespeare's Text* (Cambridge: Cambridge UP, 2010).

33. "Often referred to now as if it stood for a clearly defined programme at a particular moment in time, the New Bibliography would be more justly described

as a journey of discovery undertaken by a group of colleagues who could not know exactly where they were going" (Honigmann 77). The New Shakespeare series from Cambridge, for instance, under the direction of John Dover Wilson (aided by Arthur Quiller-Couch until 1925), was initially motivated by New Bibliographic principles, but as the project wore on between 1921 and 1966, Wilson "simply did not engage with the developing field" (Egan 249). For accounts of the New Shakespeare project, see Egan, *The Struggle for Shakespeare's Text*, 247–50, and Murphy, *Shakespeare in Print*, 229–236.

4 Performance Commentary: Writing in the Sand

1. Unless otherwise noted, citations of *Hamlet* in this chapter refer to Jenkins's edition.

2. While assigning *Titus* to Shakespeare no longer leaves quite the foul taste that it once did, stylistic and computational analyses suggest that it is not entirely his. There is a consensus that George Peele has a sizeable hand in the play; Peele appears to have written much, and perhaps all, of Act One, as well as 2.1 and 4.1. A detailed argument in support of Peele's contribution can be found in Brian Vickers, *Shakespeare as Co-Author* (Oxford: Oxford UP, 2002), 148–243. There are, of course, limitations to computational stylistics directed at co-authored plays, including the fact that current computer models necessarily work to divide segments of a play into discretely authored segments, producing data sets that are unable to account for things like imitation, revision, or multiple writers working together. In their recent book deploying computational stylistics in relation to questions of early modern authorship, Hugh Craig and Arthur Kinney point out that "we must assume single authorship of sections of the play to find an authorial signature. Testing, at our present stage of developing methods, must be based on an individual style displayed in work elsewhere; the alternative—writers collaborating or revising each other's work—would make attribution almost impossible" (91). Thus, Peele's hand can be detected in *Titus*, but the precise nature of his collaboration with Shakespeare remains unknown.

3. See chapter 2, pages 39–46.

4. Useful summaries can be found in Stanley Wells and Gary Taylor, *William Shakespeare: A Textual Companion* (Oxford: Oxford UP, 1987; New York and London: W. W. Norton, 1997), 396–402; Paul Werstine, "The Textual Mystery of *Hamlet*," *Shakespeare Quarterly* 39 (1988); Steven Urkowitz, "'Well-sayd olde Mole': Burying Three *Hamlets* in Modern Editions," *Shakespeare Study Today*, Ed. Georgianna Ziegler (New York: AMS, 1986); and Leah Marcus, *Unediting the Renaissance: Shakespeare, Marlowe, Milton* (London: Routledge, 1996), 132–76.

5. Theories abound: the hypothesis that an unauthorized reconstruction of a longer version of the play was produced for the printing house is now largely out of favor; this "bad quarto" theory of memorial reconstruction (first coined by

A. W. Pollard) has been replaced by the theory that Q1 represents a text that in some way reflects a script used by a company for touring the provinces, though Lukas Erne posits that "short" quartos like Q1 *Hamlet* might be representative of performances in London (see *Literary Dramatist* 192–219). There is also a camp that recognizes Shakespeare's direct involvement at some stage in the preparation of Q1: see Urkowitz, who explores the possibility of Q1 representing an early draft of the play, and Melchiori, "*Hamlet,*" who proposes that the underlying text behind Q1 might be an authorial *revision* for the stage.

6. Citations of "Thompson and Taylor²" refer to *Hamlet: The Texts of 1603 and 1623* in the bibliography. This edition, containing the Q1 and F texts is "designed to be supplementary to the Arden *Hamlet* volume containing the 1604–5 (Q2) version" (1). The centerpiece of the Arden 3 *Hamlet* is the edition of the Q2 text, which will be cited as "Thompson and Taylor".

7. Holderness's assessment gestures at the Ur-*Hamlet*. Jenkins provides an account of this lost play in the introduction to his edition of *Hamlet*: see 82–101.

8. Q1 *Hamlet* appears to call for the gravedigger to hand the skull over: "I prethee let me see it" (echoed by F's "Let me see"). In Q2 and F, the grave-digger's use of the demonstrative shifts from "this" to "that," which implies that he has handed the skull to Hamlet (though he and Hamlet could perhaps be gesturing or pointing instead):

> *Clo*[wn]: . . . This same Scull Sir, this same Scull sir, was *Yoricks* Scull, the Kings Iester.
> *Ham*: This?
> *Clo*[wn]: E'ene that. (F TLN 3368–71)

9. de Grazia reinforces the centrality of the space of the grave to the entire scene: "From beginning to end, the Graveyard scene centers on the grave. Upon entering, all characters gravitate there: the sexton appears with spade in hand and proceeds to dig the grave; Hamlet and Horatio linger there contemplating its exhumations; and the royal funeral procession clusters around it for the burial service. [. . .] Everything in 5.1 is focused on that little patch of recessed ground that at the Globe would have been indicated by the open trap, the 5' x 2' rectangle at the center rear of the stage floor" (*Hamlet* 129).

10. "Readers" (and their various needs) fast becomes a slippery term in this discussion, a point that I will address more fully later in this chapter.

11. Edwards claims that "this is assumed to refer to Hamlet, but the sad lover meaning to die sounds more like Romeo" (5.1.225 SDn).

12. To be fair, Marcus acknowledges the difficulty in fulfilling the theoretical promise of postmodern editing: "An edition that left everything open (if indeed that were possible) would be so formless as to be unusable in practice for all but the most sophisticated readers, its postmodernist art of 'perpetual negation' working against the need of most readers to have something tangible to grasp as an identifiable text of Shakespeare" (142). Interestingly, this

would suggest that the most open, "postmodern" text is something akin to the unedited, early modern one.

13. "[T]he job of the editor is a paradoxical one, wherein an excess of clarity can falsify but yet where too little intervention results in muddle" (Dawson, "What Do Editors Do?" 178).

14. Unless otherwise noted, references are to Jonathan Bate's Arden 3 edition, 2004.

15. On the play's authorship, see above, note 2. George Peele's contributions to *Titus* have no bearing on my arguments related to the play's performance commentary, although I would point out that some of the quotations that I cite in the remainder of this chapter are from a context prior to the general acceptance of Peele's involvement, and thus they make reference to Shakespeare as sole author of the play.

16. The essays in question are "Annotation and Performance in Shakespeare," *Essays in Criticism* 46 (1996): 289–301; "Actors, Editors, and the Annotation of Shakespearian Playscripts," *Shakespeare Survey* 55 (2002): 181–98; "'To Show our Simple Skill': Scripts and Performances in Shakespearian Comedy," *Shakespeare Survey* 56 (2003): 167–83; "'Are We Being Theatrical Yet?' Actors, Editors, and the Possibilities of Dialogue," *A Companion to Shakespeare and Performance*. Eds. Barbara Hodgdon and W. B. Worthen (Malden, MA, and Oxford: Blackwell, 2005), 399–414; and "'Wrought with things forgotten': Memory and Performance in Editing *Macbeth*," *Shakespeare, Memory and Performance*. Ed. Peter Holland (Cambridge: Cambridge UP, 2006), 87–116.

17. Warner's production serves as an especially rich resource for editors, since it presented the play in its entirety—"trust the script" was the production's mantra (Dessen 57). According to Dessen, Brook's production "cut about 650 lines" (51).

5 The Critical Edition as Archive

1. See pages 4–7.

2. This is a somewhat arbitrary term, as I am referring to a set of widely held theoretical tenets rather than an affiliated group of individuals. Leah Marcus refers to "new philology" (*Unediting* 22); Edward Pechter prefers "Newer Bibliography" ("Crisis in Editing?" 21).

3. I am using "digital" in a broad sense throughout this chapter. I mean for it to include editions encoded on discs (such as CD-ROM), as well as online editions that make use of web-browsers and hypertext. I find "digital" the most applicable term, since, as Worthen points out, "Digital technology is a technology of *transformation*: rather than copying text, image or sound to distinct stable media, it transforms them into a common electronic code. Because this code, regardless of what it encodes, is stored the same way, these different dataforms are susceptible to being combined, exchanged, realized in ways that depart significantly from the form of their initial recording" ("Fond Records" 296).

4. Jay David Bolter observes that "the most unusual feature" of electronic writing is that "electronic hard structures are not directly accessible either to the writer or to the reader. The bits of the text are simply not on a human scale. Electronic technology removes or abstracts the writer and reader from the text" (*Writing Space* 42).

5. The challenges and opportunities posed to readers of digital texts have been interrogated for decades now, and it greatly exceeds the scope of this chapter to attempt a summary of critical writing on this topic. This eloquent passage from Roger Chartier clarifies the oppositions that I am sketching in rough strokes:

> The electronic representation of texts completely changes the text's status; for the materiality of the book, it substitutes the immateriality of texts without a unique location; against the relations of contiguity established by print objects, it opposes the free composition of infinitely manipulable fragments; in place of the immediate apprehension of the whole work, made visible by the object that embodies it, it introduces a lengthy navigation in textual archipelagos that have neither shores nor borders. (*Forms and Meanings* 18)

6. See pages 119–20. Worthen, however, identifies a major shift in reading's relationship to performance. Reading printed plays, he argues, is an act of neither transformation nor embodiment ("Texts" 211), but when it comes to digital texts, he remarks, "The space of dramatic production is not a different space from the space of electronic media: it is the same space" (Worthen, *Force* 175).

7. The guidelines for *ISE* state that "Electronic texts are capable of continuing refinement and improvement; thus the text on the site will never be in a "fixed" or final state" (Best, "Guidelines").

8. <http://shea.mit.edu/ramparts/>.

9. George Myerson has categorized the various metaphors through which the electronic archive is conceived; Massai and Donaldson would fall under his category of the "Rigorous" defense, where "the archive is a new chemistry of thought, the intellectual equivalent of cold fusion. Now we can make things react with each other and produce infinitely more new compounds. The electronic archive is one sign of a new age of 'artificial intelligence', which will surpass the old eras of natural intelligence, as new substances differ from wood or iron" (95).

10. The site provides much more material than what is found in the "Reading Room," including links to critical essays, tutorials and teaching guides, and facsimiles of various adaptations and promptbooks.

11. Taylor notes that one must "choose which copies of which editions of which works to photograph; whether to reproduce a single extant copy, or to compose an 'ideal' copy using either formes or pages from several copies; whether to photograph corrected or uncorrected states of press-variant formes; which photographic process to use; what apparatus to provide" (*Textual Companion* 4).

12. See chapter 1, pages 7–10.

13. See Worthen, *"Hamlet* at Ground Zero," for a fascinating analysis of a 2007 production by the Wooster Group that staged *Hamlet* "in dialogue with the Burton film from beginning to end" (306). Worthen incorporates the Wooster Group's "restoration and remediation" (320) of the Burton film into his larger claim, "that a dichotomy between writing and performing, the recorded and the live, are inadequate to the critical assessment of performance today, if they ever were really adequate at all" (308).

14. <http://gale.cengage.co.uk/shakespeare/>.

15. According to the site's online brochure, *"The Shakespeare Collection* will be updated with new *Arden* editions twelve months after their publication" (3).

16. Ironically, Taylor attributes the substantial delay in the publication of the Oxford Middleton to issues of digitization: "As I write this [1998], I and the other editors of *The Collected Works* are waiting for John Lavagnino to finish the computer work that only he knows how to do" ("c:/" 48).

Epilogue: Prospero's Bands

1. In *Shakespeare and the Idea of Late Writing*, Gordon McMullan argues that the idea of a "late style" is itself a critical construction. McMullen's introduction quotes Anthony Dawson on *The Tempest*'s position in critical narratives: that the play "comes at the end of Shakespeare's career means that it will be read retrospectively, as climactic" (1).

2. The lost *Cardenio*, another collaboration with Fletcher, might also postdate *The Tempest*. Based on records of court payments to the King's Men, the *Textual Companion* dates the lost play to 1612–13. *The Tempest* was performed at court in November 1611.

3. Some believe that Crane also prepared copy for *The Comedy of Errors*, but the case for this seems less certain (see *Textual Companion* 266). For a detailed assessment of Crane's influence on stage directions, see Jowett, "New Created Creatures: Ralph Crane and the Stage Directions in *The Tempest*," *Shakespeare Survey* 36 (1983): 107–120.

4. Neill writes of the play's conspicuously literary directions that "there is general agreement that the stage directions consistently attempt to recreate the experience of actual performance" ("'Noises'" 37). See the Prologue to the present book, pages xvi–xviii.

5. Weimann describes epilogues as a "liminal space," "the ultimate frontier between the representation of a textually inscribed dramatic story and the occasion of its theatrical production and reception" (218).

6. References are to Orgel's Oxford edition.

Bibliography

Primary Texts

Barnes, Barnabe. *The Divils Charter.* London: G. E., 1607.

Beaumont, Francis, and John Fletcher. *Comedies and Tragedies.* London: Humphrey Robinson and Humphrey Moseley, 1647.

Dekker, Thomas. *The Magnificent Entertainment.* London: T. C., 1604.

——. *Satiro-Mastix, or the Untrussing of the Humorous Poet.* London: for Edward White, 1602.

Everyman. London: John Skot, 1528.

Fletcher, John. *The Faithful Shepheardesse.* London: for R. Bonian and H. Walley, (1610?).

——. *Philaster, or love lies a bleeding.* London: W. J., 1634.

Jonson, Ben. *Seianvs his fall.* London: G. Elld for T. Thorpe, 1605.

——. *The Workes of Benjamin Jonson.* London: W. Stansby, 1616.

Marlowe, Christopher. *Tamburlaine the Great.* London: Richard Jones, 1590.

Marston, John. *Iack Drums Entertainment.* London: for Richard Olive, 1601.

——. *Parasitaster, or The Fawne.* London: T. P. for W. C., 1606.

Massinger, Philip. *The Roman Actor.* London: for Robert Allot, 1629.

Norton, Thomas, and Thomas Sackville. *The Tragedie of Gorbodvc.* London: William Griffith, 1565.

Pope, Alexander. *The Dunciad, an Heroic Poem. In Three Books.* London: A. Dodd, 1728.

Shakespeare, William. *The Famous Historie of Troylus and Cresseida.* London: G. Eld for R. Bonian and H. Walley, 1609.

——. *The Historie of Troylus and Cresseida.* London: G. Eld for R. Bonian and H. Walley, 1609.

——. *The Most Lamentable Romaine Tragedie of Titus Andronicus.* London: John Danter, 1594.

——. *The Tragicall Historie of Hamlet, Prince of Denmarke.* London: for N. L. and Iohn Trundell, 1603.

——. *The Tragicall Historie of Hamlet, Prince of Denmarke.* London: I. R. for N. L., 1604.

Webster, John. *The Tragedy of the Dvtchesse of Malfy*. London: Nicholas Okes, 1623.

———. *The White Divel*. London: N. O., 1612.

Other Primary Texts—Editions of Shakespeare

Bate, Jonathan, ed. *Titus Andronicus*. Arden 3. 1995. London: Thomson Learning-Arden Shakespeare, 2004.

Bate, Jonathan, and Eric Rasmussen, eds. *The RSC Shakespeare. William Shakespeare: Complete Works*. New York: Modern Library, 2007.

Brooke, Nicholas, ed. *The Tragedy of Macbeth*. Oxford: World's Classics-Oxford UP, 1998.

Capell, Edward, ed. *Mr. William Shakespeare his Comedies, Histories, and Tragedies*. 10 vols. London: Dryden Leach for J. and R. Tonson, 1768.

———. *Notes and Various Readings to Shakespeare*. 3 vols. London: Henry Hughs, 1779–1783.

———. *Prolusions; or, Select Pieces of Antient Poetry*. London: 1760.

Clark, William George, John Glover, [and William Aldis Wright], eds. *The Works of William Shakespeare*. 9 vols. Cambridge and London: Macmillan and Co., 1863–66.

Cox, John D., and Eric Rasmussen, eds. *King Henry VI, Part 3*. Arden 3. London: Thomson Learning-Arden Shakespeare, 2001.

Davenant, William. *The Tragedy of Hamlet, Prince of Denmark. As it is now Acted at his Highness the Duke of York's Theatre. By William Shakespeare*. London: 1676.

Edwards, Philip, ed. *Hamlet, Prince of Denmark*. Updated edition. Cambridge: Cambridge UP, 2003.

Evans, G. Blakemore, gen. ed. *The Riverside Shakespeare*. 2nd ed. Boston: Houghton Mifflin, 1997.

Halio, J. L., ed. *The Merchant of Venice*. Oxford: Clarendon, 1993. Oxford: World's Classics-Oxford UP, 1998.

Hibbard, G. R., ed. *Hamlet*. Oxford: Clarendon, 1987. Oxford: World's Classics-Oxford UP, 1998.

Hinman, Charlton. *The Norton Facsimile: The First Folio of Shakespeare*. New York: W. W. Norton, 1968.

Holland, Peter, ed. *A Midsummer Night's Dream*. Oxford: Clarendon, 1994. Oxford: World's Classics-Oxford UP, 1998.

Holland, Peter, ed. Introduction. *The Works of Mr. William Shakespear. Edited by Nicholas Rowe*. 7 vols. London: Pickering & Chatto, 1999.

Hughes, Alan, ed. *Titus Andronicus*. Updated edition. Cambridge: Cambridge UP, 2006.

Jenkins, Harold, ed. *Hamlet*. London: Methuen, 1982. London: Thomson Learning-Arden Shakespeare, 2003.

Johnson, Samuel, ed. *The Plays of William Shakespeare.* 8 vols. London: J. and R. Tonson, et al., 1765.

Malone, Edmund, ed. *The Plays and Poems of William Shakespeare.* 10 vols. London: 1790.

Martin, Randall, ed. *Henry VI, Part Three.* Oxford: World's Classics-Oxford UP, 2001.

McEachern, Claire, ed. *Much Ado About Nothing.* Arden 3. London: Thomson Learning-Arden Shakespeare, 2006.

McMillin, Scott, ed. *The First Quarto of Othello.* Cambridge: Cambridge UP, 2001.

Neill, Michael, ed. *Anthony and Cleopatra.* Oxford: World's Classics-Oxford UP, 1994.

———. *Othello.* Oxford: World's Classics-Oxford UP, 2006.

Orgel, Stephen, ed. *The Tempest.* Oxford: Clarendon, 1987. Oxford: World's Classics-Oxford UP, 1998.

Pope, Alexander, ed. *The Works of Shakespear.* 6 vols. London, 1723–5.

Ravenscroft, Edward. *Titus Andronicus, or, The Rape of Lavinia.* London: 1687.

Rowe, Nicholas, ed. *The works of Mr. William Shakespear; in six volumes.* London: 1709.

Taylor, Gary, ed. *Henry V.* Oxford: Clarendon, 1982. Oxford: World's Classics-Oxford UP, 1998.

Taylor, Michael, ed. *Henry VI, Part One.* Oxford: World's Classics-Oxford UP, 2003.

The Shakespeare Collection. Brochure. Cengage Learning, 2008. <http://www.galeuk.com/shakespeare/pdfs/brochure.pdf>.

The Shakespeare Collection. Fact Sheet. Cengage Learning, 2008. <http://www.galeuk.com/shakespeare/pdfs/shakespeare_fact.pdf>.

Theobald, Lewis. *Shakespeare Restored: or, a Specimen of the Many Errors, As well Committed, as Unamended, by Mr. Pope in his Late Edition of this Poet.* London: 1726.

———. *The Works of Shakespeare.* 7 vols. London: 1733.

Thompson, Ann, and Neil Taylor, eds. *Hamlet.* Arden 3. London: Thomson Learning-Arden Shakespeare, 2006.

Thompson, Ann, and Neil Taylor, eds. *Hamlet: The Texts of 1603 and 1623.* Arden 3. London: Thomson Learning-Arden Shakespeare, 2006.

Vaughan, Virginia Mason, and Alden T. Vaughan, eds. *The Tempest.* Arden 3. London: Thomson Learning-Arden Shakespeare, 1999.

Waith, Eugene M. ed. *Titus Andronicus.* 1984. Oxford: World's Classics-Oxford UP, 1998.

Warren, Roger, ed. *Cymbeline.* Oxford: World's Classics-Oxford UP, 1998.

Wells, Stanley, and Gary Taylor, gen. eds. *William Shakespeare: The Complete Works.* 1986. Compact ed. Oxford: Clarendon, 1998.

Zitner, Sheldon P. ed. *Much Ado About Nothing.* Oxford: Clarendon, 1993. Oxford: World's Classics-Oxford UP, 1998.

Secondary Texts

"About." *Oxford Scholarly Editions Online*. University of Oxford, 2012. <http://www.oxfordscholarlyeditions.com/page2/about>

Berger, Harry, Jr. *Imaginary Audition: Shakespeare on Stage and Page*. Berkeley and Los Angeles: U of California P, 1989.

Bergeron, David M. *Textual Patronage in English Drama, 1570–1640*. Aldershot and Burlington, VT: Ashgate, 2006.

Best, Michael. "About the Internet Shakespeare Editions." University of Victoria, 2005. <http://internetshakespeare.uvic.ca/Foyer/about.html>.

———. "Collaboration with Broadview Press." University of Victoria, 2011. <http://internetshakespeare.uvic.ca/Foyer/broadview.html>

———."Guidelines: Introduction." *Internet Shakespeare Editions*, University of Victoria, 2005. <http://internetshakespeare.uvic.ca/Foyer/Guidelines/g-intro.html>.

———. "The Illuminated Text." *Internet Shakespeare Editions*, University of Victoria, 2005. <http://internetshakespeare.uvic.ca/Foyer/illuminated.html>.

———. "Shakespeare and the Electronic Text." *A Concise Companion to Shakespeare and the Text*. Ed. Andrew Murphy. Malden, MA, and Oxford: Blackwell, 2007. 145–61.

———. "Shakespeare in Performance: Home." *Internet Shakespeare Editions*, University of Victoria, 2005. <http://internetshakespeare.uvic.ca/Theater/sip/index.html>.

———. "The Text of Performance and the Performance of Text in the Electronic Edition." *Computers and the Humanities* 36 (2002): 269–82.

Bevington, David. "Working with the Text: Editing in Practice." *A Concise Companion to Shakespeare and the Text*. Ed. Andrew Murphy. Malden, MA, and Oxford: Blackwell, 2007. 165–84.

Bland, Mark. "The Appearance of the Text in Early Modern England." *TEXT: An Interdisciplinary Annual of Textual Studies* 11 (1998): 91–154.

———. "William Stansby and the Production of *The Workes of Beniamin Jonson*, 1615–1616." *The Library* 20 (1998): 1–33.

Blayney, Peter W. M. "The Publication of Playbooks." *A New History of Early English Drama*. Eds. John D. Cox and David Scott Kastan. New York: Columbia UP, 1997. 383–422.

Boase, T. S. R. "Illustrations of Shakespeare's Plays in the Seventeenth and Eighteenth Centuries." *Journal of the Warburg and Courtauld Institutes* 10 (1947): 83–103.

Bolter, Jay David. *Writing Space: The Computer, Hypertext, and the History of Writing*. Hillsdale, NJ: Lawrence Erlbaum Associates, 1991.

Bolton, Joseph S. G. "The Authentic Text of *Titus Andronicus*." *PMLA* 44 (1929): 765–88.

Bowers, Fredson, gen. ed. *The Dramatic Works in the Beaumont and Fletcher Canon*. 10 vols. Cambridge: Cambridge UP, 1966–96.

————. *On Editing Shakespeare*. Charlottesville: UP of Virginia, 1966.

————. "The New Textual Criticism of Shakespeare." 1959. *Shakespeare: An Anthology of Criticism and Theory, 1945–2000*. Ed. Russ McDonald. Malden, MA, and Oxford: Blackwell, 2004. 269–79.

Bradley, A. C. *Shakespearean Tragedy*. 1905. London: MacMillan & Co.; New York: St. Martin's, 1960.

Brady, Jennifer, and W. H. Herendeen, eds. *Ben Jonson's 1616 Folio*. Newark: U of Delaware P, 1991.

Braunmuller, A. R. "On Not Looking Back: Sight and Sound and Text." *From Performance to Print in Shakespeare's England*. Eds. Peter Holland and Stephen Orgel. Houndmills, Basingstoke, and New York: Palgrave, 2006. 135–151.

Bristol, Michael D. *Big-time Shakespeare*. London and New York: Routledge, 1996.

Brooks, Douglas. *From Playhouse to Printing House: Drama and Authorship in Early Modern England*. Cambridge: Cambridge UP, 2000.

Brown, John Russell. "Annotating Silence." *In Arden: Editing Shakespeare*. Eds. Ann Thompson and Gordon McMullan. London: Thomson Learning-Arden Shakespeare, 2003. 157–174.

————. "The Printing of John Webster's Plays," 3 parts. *Studies in Bibliography* 6 (1954): 117–40; 8 (1956): 113–28; 15 (1962): 57–69.

Bulman, James C. "Introduction: Shakespeare and Performance Theory." *Shakespeare, Theory, and Performance*. Ed. James C. Bulman. New York and London: Routledge, 1996. 1–12.

Carlson, Marvin. *The Haunted Stage: The Theatre as Memory Machine*. Ann Arbor: U of Michigan P, 2001.

Carson, Christie. "The Evolution of Online Editing: Where Will It End?" *Shakespeare Survey* 59 (2006): 168–81.

Cerasano, S. P. "The Chamberlain-King's Men." *A Companion to Shakespeare*. Ed. David Scott Kastan. Oxford: Blackwell, 1999. 328–45.

Chambers, E. K. *The Elizabethan Stage*. 4 vols. Oxford: Oxford UP, 1923.

————. *William Shakespeare: A Study of Facts and Problems*. 2 vols. Oxford: Oxford UP, 1930.

Chartier, Roger. *Forms and Meanings: Texts, Performances, and Audiences from Codex to Computer*. Philadelphia: U of Pennsylvania P, 1995.

Cheney, Patrick. *Shakespeare's Literary Authorship*. Cambridge: Cambridge UP, 2008.

Cordner, Michael. "Actors, Editors, and the Annotation of Shakespearian Playscripts." *Shakespeare Survey* 55 (2002): 181–98.

————. "Annotation and Performance in Shakespeare." *Essays in Criticism* 46 (1996): 289–301.

————. "'Are We Being Theatrical Yet?' Actors, Editors, and the Possibilities of Dialogue." *A Companion to Shakespeare and Performance*. Eds. Barbara Hodgdon and W. B. Worthen. Malden, MA, and Oxford: Blackwell, 2005. 399–414.

Cordner, Michael. "'To Show our Simple Skill': Scripts and Performances in Shakespearian Comedy." *Shakespeare Survey* 56 (2003): 167–83.

———. "'Wrought with things forgotten': Memory and Performance in Editing *Macbeth*." *Shakespeare, Memory and Performance*. Ed. Peter Holland. Cambridge: Cambridge UP, 2006. 87–116.

Cox, John D. "Open Stage, Open Page? Editing Stage Directions in Early Dramatic Texts." *Textual Performances: The Modern Reproduction of Shakespeare's Drama*. Eds. Lukas Erne and Margaret Jane Kidnie. Cambridge: Cambridge UP, 2004. 178–93.

Craig, Hugh, and Arthur F. Kinney. *Shakespeare, Computers, and the Mystery of Authorship*. Cambridge: Cambridge UP, 2009.

Cunningham, Vanessa. *Shakespeare and Garrick*. Cambridge: Cambridge UP, 2008.

Dawson, Anthony B. "Correct Impressions: Editing and Evidence in the Wake of Post-modernism." *In Arden: Editing Shakespeare*. Eds. Ann Thompson and Gordon McMullan. London: Thomson Learning-Arden Shakespeare, 2003. 31–47.

———. *Hamlet*. Shakespeare in Performance. Manchester and New York: Manchester UP, 1995.

———. "The Imaginary Text, or the Curse of the Folio." *A Companion to Shakespeare and Performance*. Eds. Barbara Hodgdon and W. B. Worthen. Malden, MA, and Oxford: Blackwell, 2005. 141–161.

———. "The Impasse over the Stage." *English Literary Renaissance* 21.3 (1991): 309–27.

———, ed. *Tamburlaine Parts One and Two*. London: A & C Black; New York: W. W. Norton, 1997.

———. "What Do Editors Do and Why Does It Matter?" *How To Do Things with Shakespeare*. Ed. Laurie Maguire. Malden, MA, and Oxford: Blackwell, 2008. 160–80.

Dawson, Anthony B., and Paul Yachnin. *The Culture of Playgoing in Shakepeare's England: A Collaborative Debate*. Cambridge: Cambridge UP, 2001.

de Grazia, Margreta. *Hamlet without Hamlet*. Cambridge: Cambridge UP, 2007.

———. *Shakespeare Verbatim: The Reproduction of Authenticity and the 1790 Apparatus*. Oxford: Clarendon, 1991.

de Grazia, Margreta, and Peter Stallybrass. "The Materiality of the Shakespearean Text." *Shakespeare Quarterly* 44.3 (1993): 255–84.

Derrida, Jacques. *Archive Fever: A Freudian Impression*. Trans. Eric Prenowitz. Chicago and London: Chicago UP, 1995.

Dessen, Alan C. *Titus Andronicus*. Shakespeare in Performance. Manchester and New York: Manchester UP, 1989.

Dobson, Michael. "The Design of the Oxford Shakespeare: An Ever Writer to a Never Reader?" *Analytical and Enumerative Bibliography* n.s. 4.1 (1990): 91–7.

———. *The Making of the National Poet: Shakespeare, Adaptation, and Authorship, 1660–1769*. Oxford: Clarendon, 1992.

———. "Writing About [Shakespearian] Performance." *Shakespeare Survey* 58 (2005): 160–8.

Donaldson, Peter. "Digital Archive as Expanded Text: Shakespeare and Electronic Textuality." *Electronic Text: Investigations in Method and Theory*. Ed. Kathryn Sutherland. Oxford, Clarendon: 1997. 173–97.

Dugas, Don-John. *Marketing the Bard: Shakespeare in Performance and Print, 1660–1740*. Columbia and London: U of Missouri P, 2006.

Egan, Gabriel. *The Struggle for Shakespeare's Text: Twentieth-Century Editorial Theory and Practice*. Cambridge: Cambridge UP, 2010.

Elam, Keir. *The Semiotics of Theatre and Drama*. London and New York: Methuen, 1980.

———. "The Wars of the Texts." *Shakespeare Studies* 24 (1996): 81–92.

Erne, Lukas. *Shakespeare as Literary Dramatist*. Cambridge: Cambridge UP, 2003.

———. "Shakespeare for Readers." *Alternative Shakespeares 3*. Ed. Diana Henderson. London and New York: Routledge, 2008. 78–94.

———. *Shakespeare's Modern Collaborators*. London and New York: Continuum, 2008.

Farmer, Alan B. "Shakespeare and the New Textualism." *The Shakespeare International Yearbook 2*. Eds. W.R. Elton and John M. Mucciolo. Burlington, VT: Ashgate, 2002. 158–79.

Farmer, Alan B., and Zachary Lesser, "Vile Arts: The Marketing of English Printed Drama, 1512–1660." *Research Opportunities in Renaissance Drama* 39 (2000): 77–165.

Foakes, R. A. "Performance Theory and Textual Theory: A Retort Courteous." *Shakespeare* 2.1 (2006): 47–58.

Franklin, Colin. *Shakespeare Domesticated: The Eighteenth-Century Editions*. Aldershot: Scolar, 1991.

Freshwater, Helen. "The Allure of the Archive." *Poetics Today* 24.4 (2003): 729–58.

Genette, Gerard. *Paratexts: Thresholds of Interpretation*. Trans. Jane E. Lewin. Cambridge: Cambridge UP, 1997.

Gershenfeld, Neil. *When Things Start to Think*. New York: Henry Holt, 1999.

Greetham, David. "'Who's in, who's out': The Cultural Poetics of Archival Exclusion." *Studies in the Literary Imagination* 32 (1999): 1–28.

Greg, W. W. *A Bibliography of English Printed Drama to the Restoration*. 4 vols., 1939–59. London: Bibliographical Society, 1970.

———. *The Editorial Problem in Shakespeare: A Survey of the Foundations of the Text*. 3rd ed. Oxford: Clarendon, 1954.

———. "The Rationale of Copy-Text." 1950. *Bibliography and Textual Criticism: English and American Literature, 1700 to the Present*. Eds. O. M. Brack, Jr. and Warner Barnes. Chicago and London: U of Chicago P, 1969. 41–58.

Grigely, Joseph. *Textualterity: Art, Theory, and Textual Criticism*. Ann Arbour: U of Michigan P, 1995.

Gunby, David, David Carnegie, and Anthony Hammond, eds. General Textual Introduction. *The Works of John Webster*. Vol I. Cambridge: Cambridge UP, 1995. 34–54.

Hackel, Heidi Brayman. "The 'Great Variety' of Readers and Early Modern Reading Practices." *A Companion to Shakespeare*. Ed. David Scott Kastan. Oxford: Blackwell, 1999. 139–57.

———. *Reading Material in Early Modern England: Print, Gender, and Literacy*. Cambridge: Cambridge UP, 2005.

Hirsch, Brett D. "The Kingdom Has Been Digitized: Electronic Editions of Renaissance Drama and the Long Shadows of Shakespeare and Print." *Literature Compass* 8.9 (2011): 568–591.

Hodgdon, Barbara. *The End Crowns All: Closure and Contradiction in Shakespeare's History*. Princeton: Princeton UP, 1991.

———. "Introduction: A Kind of History." *A Companion to Shakespeare and Performance*. Eds. Barbara Hodgdon and W. B. Worthen. Malden, MA, and Oxford: Blackwell, 2005. 1–9.

———. "New Collaborations With Old Plays: The (Textual) Politics of Performance Commentary." *Textual Performances: The Modern Reproduction of Shakespeare's Drama*. Eds. Lukas Erne and Margaret Jane Kidnie. Cambridge: Cambridge UP, 2004. 210–23.

———. *The Shakespeare Trade: Performances and Appropriations*. Philadelphia: U of Pennsylvania P, 1998.

Holderness, Graham. *Textual Shakespeare: Writing and the Word*. Hertfordshire: U of Hertfordshire P, 2003.

Holland, Peter. "Modernizing Shakespeare: Nicholas Rowe and *The Tempest*." *Shakespeare Quarterly* 51.1 (2000): 24–32.

Honigmann, Ernst. "The New Bibliography and its Critics." *Textual Performances: The Modern Reproduction of Shakespeare's Drama*. Eds. Lukas Erne and Margaret Jane Kidnie. Cambridge: Cambridge UP, 2004. 77–93.

Ingarden, Roman. *The Literary Work of Art: An Investigation on the Borderlines of Ontology, Logic, and Theory of Literature, With an Appendix on the Functions of Language in the Theatre*. Trans. George G. Grabowicz. Evanston, IL: Northwestern UP, 1973.

Jackson, Alfred. "Rowe's Edition of Shakespeare." *Library* 10 (1930): 455–73.

James, Henry, and Greg Walker. "The Politics of *Gorboduc*." *English Historical Review* 110.435 (1995): 109–21.

Jarvis, Simon. *Scholars and Gentlemen: Shakespearian Textual Criticism and Representations of Scholarly Labour, 1725–1765*. Oxford: Clarendon, 1995.

Johnson-Eilola, Johndan. *Datacloud: Toward a New Theory of Online Work*. Cresskill, N.J.: Hampton, 2005.

Jowett, John. "'Fall before This Booke': The 1605 Quarto of *Sejanus*." *Text* 4 (1988): 279–95.

———. "New Created Creatures: Ralph Crane and the Stage Directions in *The Tempest*." *Shakespeare Survey* 36 (1983): 107–120.

———. *Shakespeare and Text*. Oxford: Oxford UP, 2007.

Kastan, David Scott. *Shakespeare After Theory*. New York and London: Routledge, 1999.

———. *Shakespeare and the Book*. Cambridge: Cambridge UP, 2001.

Kennedy, Dennis. "Memory, Performance and the Idea of the Museum." *Shakespeare, Memory and Performance*. Ed. Peter Holland. Cambridge: Cambridge UP, 2006. 329–45.

Kidnie, Margaret Jane. "Citing Shakespeare." *Shakespeare, Memory and Performance*. Ed. Peter Holland. Cambridge: Cambridge UP, 2006. 117–32.

———. "The Staging of Shakespeare's Drama in Print Editions." *Textual Performances: The Modern Reproduction of Shakespeare's Drama*. Eds. Lukas Erne and Margaret Jane Kidnie. Cambridge: Cambridge UP, 2004. 158–77.

———. "Text, Performance, and the Editors: Staging Shakespeare's Drama." *Shakespeare Quarterly* 51 (2000): 456–73.

———. "Where is *Hamlet*? Text, Performance, and Adaptation." *A Companion to Shakespeare and Performance*. Eds. Barbara Hodgdon and W. B. Worthen. Malden, MA, and Oxford: Blackwell, 2005. 101–120.

King, Edmund G. C. "Fragmenting Authorship in the Eighteenth-Century Shakespeare Edition." *Shakespeare* 6.1 (2010): 1–19.

Kivy, Peter. *The Performance of Reading: An Essay in the Philosophy of Literature*. Malden, MA, and Oxford: Blackwell, 2006.

Knight, G. Wilson. *Wheel of Fire: Interpretations of Shakespearian Tragedy*. 1930. Oxford: Oxford UP, 1965.

Knowles, Ric. "Encoding/Decoding Shakespeare: *Richard III* at the 2002 Stratford Festival." *A Companion to Shakespeare and Performance*. Eds. Barbara Hodgdon and W. B. Worthen. Malden, MA, and Oxford: Blackwell, 2005. 297–317.

———. *Reading the Material Theatre*. Cambridge: Cambridge UP, 2004.

Lavagnino, John. "Reading, Scholarship, and Hypertext Editions." *TEXT* 8 (1995): 109–24.

Lesser, Zachary. *Renaissance Drama and the Politics of Publication: Readings in the English Book Trade*. Cambridge: Cambridge UP, 2004.

———. "Typographic Nostalgia: Play-Reading, Popularity, and the Meanings of Black Letter." *The Book of the Play: Playwrights, Stationers, and Readers in Early Modern England*. Ed. Marta Straznicky. Amherst and Boston: U of Massachusetts P, 2006. 99–126.

Levin, Richard. "Performance-Critics vs Close Readers in the Study of English Renaissance Drama." *Modern Language Review* 81.3 (1986): 545–59.

Lowenstein, Joseph. *Jonson and Possessive Authorship*. Cambridge: Cambridge UP, 2002.

———. "Printing and 'The Multitudinous Presse': The Contentious Texts of Jonson's Masques." *Ben Jonson's 1616 Folio*. Eds. Jennifer Brady and W. H. Herendeen. Newark: U of Delaware P; London and Toronto: Associated UP, 1991. 168–91.

Marcus, Leah. "Editing Shakespeare in a Postmodern Age." *A Concise Companion to Shakespeare in Print*. Ed. Andrew Murphy. Malden, MA, and Oxford: Blackwell, 2007. 128–44.

———. *Unediting the Renaissance: Shakespeare, Marlowe, Milton*. London: Routledge, 1996.

Massai, Sonia. "Editorial Pledges in Early Modern Dramatic Paratexts." *Renaissance Paratexts*. Eds. Helen Smith and Louise Wilson. Cambridge: Cambridge UP, 2011. 91–106.

———."Scholarly Editing and the Shift from Print to Electronic Cultures." *Textual Performances: The Modern Reproduction of Shakespeare's Drama*. Eds. Lukas Erne and Margaret Jane Kidnie. Cambridge: Cambridge UP, 2004. 94–108.

———. *Shakespeare and the Rise of the Editor*. Cambridge: Cambridge UP, 2007.

———. "Working with the Texts: Differential Readings." *A Concise Companion to Shakespeare and the Text*. Ed. Andrew Murphy. Malden, MA and Oxford: Blackwell, 2007. 185–203.

Masten, Jeffrey. *Textual Intercourse: Collaboration, Authorship, and Sexualities in the Renaissance*. Cambridge: Cambridge UP, 1997.

McGann, Jerome J. *A Critique of Modern Textual Criticism*. Chicago: U of Chicago P, 1983.

———. "The Rationale of Hypertext." *Electronic Text: Investigations in Method and Theory*. Ed. Kathryn Sutherland. Oxford: Clarendon, 1997. 19–46.

———. *The Textual Condition*. Princeton: Princeton UP, 1991.

McGuire, Philip C. *Speechless Dialect: Shakespeare's Open Silences*. Berkeley, Los Angeles, and London: U of California P, 1985.

McKenzie, D. F. *Bibliography and Sociology of Texts*. Cambridge: Cambridge UP, 1999.

McKerrow, R. B. *Prolegomena for the Oxford Shakespeare*. Oxford: Clarendon, 1939.

McMullen, Gordon. *Shakespeare and the Idea of Late Writing: Authorship in the Proximity of Death*. Cambridge: Cambridge UP, 2008.

Meisel, Martin. *How Plays Work: Reading and Performance*. Oxford: Oxford UP, 2007.

Melchiori, Giorgio. "*Hamlet*: The Acting Version and the Wiser Sort." *The 'Hamlet' First Published (Q1, 1603)*. Ed. Thomas Clayton. Newark: U of Delaware P; London: Associated UP, 1992. 195–210.

———. "The Continuing Importance of New Bibliography." *In Arden: Editing Shakespeare*. Eds. Ann Thompson and Gordon McMullan. London: Thomson Learning-Arden Shakespeare, 2003. 2003. 17–30.

Melnikoff, Kirk. "Jones's Pen and Marlowe's Socks: Richard Jones, Print Culture, and the Beginnings of English Dramatic Literature." *Studies in Philology* 102.2 (2005): 184–209.

Mowat, Barbara. "The Form of *Hamlet*'s Fortunes." *Renaissance Drama* n.s. 19 (1988): 97–126.

———. "Nicholas Rowe and the Twentieth-Century Shakespeare Text." *Shakespeare and Cultural Traditions: The Selected Proceedings of the International Shakespeare Association World Congress, Tokyo, 1991*. Eds. Tetsuo Kishi, Roger Pringle, and Stanley Wells. Newark: U of Delaware P; London and Toronto: Associated UP, 1994. 314–22.

Mullaney, Steven. "Lying Like Truth: Riddle, Representation and Treason in Renaissance England." *English Literary History* 47.1 (1980): 32–47.

Murphy, Andrew. "The Birth of the Editor." *A Concise Companion to Shakespeare in Print*. Ed. Andrew Murphy. Malden, MA, and Oxford: Blackwell, 2007. 93–108.

———. "Introduction: What Happens in *Hamlet*?" *A Concise Companion to Shakespeare in Print*. Ed. Andrew Murphy. Malden, MA, and Oxford: Blackwell, 2007. 1–14.

———. *Shakespeare in Print: A History and Chronology of Shakespeare Publishing.* Cambridge: Cambridge UP, 2003.

Myerson, George. "The Electronic Archive." *History of the Human Sciences* 11.4 (1998): 85–101.

Neill, Michael. "'Noises / Sounds, and sweet airs': The Burden of Shakespeare's *Tempest*." *Shakespeare Quarterly* 59.1 (2008): 36–59.

Ong, Walter J. *Orality and Literacy: The Technologizing of the Word.* London and New York: Methuen, 1982.

Orgel, Stephen. *The Authentic Shakespeare, and Other Problems of the Early Modern Stage.* New York and London: Routledge, 2002.

———. *Imagining Shakespeare: A History of Texts and Visions.* Houndmills, Basingstoke, and New York: Palgrave, 2003.

Parker, Patricia. "Murder in Guyana." *Shakespeare Studies* 28 (2000): 169–74.

Paul, Gavin. "A Brief History of the Edited Shakespearean Text." *Literature Compass* 3.2 (2006): 182–94.

Pavis, Patrice. *Theatre at the Crossroads of Culture.* Trans. Loren Kruger. London: Routledge, 1992.

Pechter, Edward. "Crisis in Editing?" *Shakespeare Survey* 59 (2006): 20–38.

Peters, Julie Stone. *Theatre of the Book, 1480–1880: Print, Text, and Performance in Europe.* Oxford: Oxford UP, 2000.

Pfister, Manfred. *The Theory and Analysis of Drama.* Trans. John Halliday. Cambridge: Cambridge UP, 1988.

Pollard, Alfred W. *Shakespeare Folios and Quartos: A Study of the Bibliography of Shakespeare's Plays, 1594–1685.* London: Methuen, 1909.

Postlewait, Thomas. "The Criteria for Evidence: Anecdotes in Shakespearean Biography, 1709–2000." *Theorizing Practice: Redefining Theatre History.* Eds. W. B. Worthen and Peter Holland. Houndmills, Basingstoke, and New York: Palgrave, 2003. 47–70.

Rasmussen, Eric. "The Implications of Past Tense Verbs in Early Elizabethan Dumb Shows." *English Studies* 67.5 (1986): 417–19.

Schalkwyk, David. "Shakespeare's Ghosts." *Shakespeare* 1.1–2 (2005): 219–40.

Schoenbaum, S[amuel]. *Shakespeare's Lives.* New ed. Oxford and New York: Oxford UP, 1993.

Seary, Peter. *Lewis Theobald and the Editing of Shakespeare.* Oxford: Clarendon, 1990.

Shillingsburg, Peter L. *Scholarly Editing in the Computer Age: Theory and Practice.* 3rd ed. Ann Arbour: U of Michigan P, 1996.

Sillars, Stuart. *The Illustrated Shakespeare, 1709–1875.* Cambridge: Cambridge UP, 2008.

Slights, William W. E. *Managing Readers: Printed Marginalia in English Renaissance Books.* Ann Arbour: U of Michigan P, 2001.

Smith, Bruce R. "Speaking What We Feel About *King Lear.*" *Shakespeare, Memory and Performance.* Ed. Peter Holland. Cambridge: Cambridge UP, 2006. 23–42.

Spevack, Marvin. "The End of Editing Shakespeare." *Connotations* 6.1 (1996/97): 78–85.

Stone, George Winchester, Jr. "Garrick's Presentation of *Antony and Cleopatra.*" *Review of English Studies* 13 (1937): 20–38.

Straznicky, Marta, ed. *The Book of the Play: Playwrights, Stationers, and Readers in Early Modern England.* Amherst and Boston: U of Massachusetts P. 2006.

Styan, J. L. *The Shakespeare Revolution: Criticism and Performance in the Twentieth Century.* Cambridge: Cambridge UP, 1977.

Tanselle, G. Thomas. *A Rationale of Textual Criticism.* Philadelphia: U of Pennsylvania P, 1989.

Taylor, Gary. "c:\wp\file.txt 05:41 10–07–98." *The Renaissance Text: Theory, Editing, Textuality.* Ed. Andrew Murphy. Manchester and New York: Manchester UP, 1998. 44–54.

———. "How To Use This Book." *Thomas Middleton: The Collected Works.* Gen. eds. Gary Taylor and John Lavagnino. Oxford: Clarendon, 2007. 17–22.

———. "Thomas Middleton: Lives and Afterlives." *Thomas Middleton: The Collected Works.* Gen. eds. Gary Taylor and John Lavagnino. Oxford: Clarendon, 2007. 25–58.

———. *Moment by Moment by Shakespeare.* London: Macmillan, 1985.

———. "The Order of Persons." *Thomas Middleton and Early Modern Textual Culture. A Companion to the Collected Works.* Gen. eds. Gary Taylor and John Lavagnino. Oxford: Clarendon, 2007. 31–79.

———. "The Renaissance and the End of Editing." *Palimpsest: Editorial Theory in the Humanities.* Eds. George Bornstein and Ralph G. Williams. Ann Arbour: U of Michigan P, 1993. 121–149.

———. *Reinventing Shakespeare: A Cultural History from the Restoration to the Present.* New York: Weidenfeld & Nicolson, 1989.

Tribble, Evelyn B. *Margins and Marginality: The Printed Page in Early Modern England.* Charlottesville and London: UP of Virginia, 1993.

Tronch-Pérez, Jesús. *A Synoptic Hamlet.* Valéncia: Sederi, Universitat de Valéncia, 2002.

Turner, Henry S. *The English Renaissance Stage: Geometry, Poetics, and the Practical Spatial Arts 1580–1630.* Oxford: Oxford UP, 2006.

Urkowitz, Steven. "'Well-sayd olde Mole': Burying Three *Hamlets* in Modern Editions." *Shakespeare Study Today.* Ed. Georgianna Ziegler. New York: AMS, 1986. 37–70.

Vickers, Brian. *Shakespeare as Co-Author: A Historical Study of Five Collaborative Plays.* Oxford: Oxford UP, 2002.

Voss, Paul J., and Marta L. Werner. "Toward a Poetics of the Archive: Introduction." *Studies in the Literary Imagination* 32.1 (1999): i–viii.

Walker, Greg. *The Politics of Performance in Early Renaissance Drama.* Cambridge: Cambridge UP, 1998.

Walsh, Marcus. *Shakespeare, Milton, and Eighteenth-Century Literary Editing: The Beginnings of Interpretive Scholarship.* Cambridge: Cambridge UP, 1997.

Weimann, Robert. *Author's Pen and Actor's Voice: Playing and Writing in Shakespeare's Theatre.* Cambridge: Cambridge UP, 2000.

Weimann, Robert, and Douglas Bruster. *Shakespeare and the Power of Performance: Stage and Page in the Elizabethan Theatre.* Cambridge: Cambridge UP, 2008.

Wells, Stanley. Foreword. *Shakespeare, Memory and Performance.* Ed. Peter Holland. Cambridge: Cambridge UP, 2006. xvii–xx.

———. *Re-Editing Shakespeare for the Modern Reader.* Oxford: Clarendon, 1984.

Wells, Stanley, and Gary Taylor, "The Oxford Shakespeare Re-Viewed by the General Editors." *Analytical and Enumerative Bibliography* n.s. 4.1 (1990): 6–20.

Wells, Stanley, Gary Taylor, with John Jowett, and William Montgomery. *William Shakespeare: A Textual Companion.* Oxford: Oxford UP, 1987. New York and London: W. W. Norton, 1997.

Werstine, Paul. "Narratives About Printed Shakespeare Texts: 'Foul Papers' and 'Bad' Quartos." *Shakespeare Quarterly* 41.1 (1990): 65–86.

———. "The Textual Mystery of *Hamlet*." *Shakespeare Quarterly* 39 (1988): 1–26.

West, Anthony James. *The Shakespeare First Folio: The History of the Book. Volume I: An Account of the First Folio Based on its Sales and Prices, 1623–2000.* Oxford: Oxford UP, 2001.

Worthen, W. B. "Fond Records: Remembering Theatre in the Digital Age." *Shakespeare, Memory and Performance.* Ed. Peter Holland. Cambridge: Cambridge UP, 2006. 281–304.

———. "*Hamlet* at Ground Zero: The Wooster Group and the Archive of Performance." *Shakespeare Quarterly* 59.3 (2008): 303–322.

———. "Intoxicating Rhythms: Or, Shakespeare, Literary Drama, and Performance (Studies)." *Shakespeare Quarterly* 62.3 (2011): 309–339.

———. *Print and the Poetics of Modern Drama.* Cambridge: Cambridge UP, 2005.

———. *Shakespeare and the Authority of Performance.* Cambridge: Cambridge UP, 1997.

———. *Shakespeare and the Force of Modern Performance.* Cambridge: Cambridge UP, 2003.

———. "Texts, Tools, and Technologies of Performance: A Quip Modest, in Response to R. A. Foakes." *Shakespeare* 2.2 (2006): 208–19.

Index

CPI Antony Rowe
Chippenham, UK
2018-06-11 22:58